Rising above It All

Rising above
It All

The Art and Science
of Organizational Transformation

JOHN L. LEE

 iUniverse

Rising above It All
The Art and Science of Organizational Transformation

For additional information contact John L. Lee at 8634 Acorn Lane, Sandy, Utah 84093

iUniverse books may be ordered through booksellers or by contacting:

iUniverse
1663 Liberty Drive
Bloomington, IN 47403
www.iuniverse.com
1-800-Authors (1-800-288-4677)

ISBN: 978-1-4759-3065-8 (sc)
ISBN: 978-1-4759-3066-5 (hc)
ISBN: 978-1-4759-3067-2 (e)

Library of Congress Control Number: 2012911309

Print information available on the last page.

iUniverse rev. date: 11/17/2017

This book is dedicated to the following:

My parents,
Jim and Edna Lee,
whose sacrifices for their children literally wore them out.
I will never be able to repay you.
Thanks!

My lovely wife, whom I deeply love,
Rita

My children, who are the pride of my life,
Craig
Chad
Brian
Jason

My grandchildren,
for whom I wrote this book

CONTENTS

INTRODUCTION   IX

1.   INTRODUCTION TO TRANSFORMATION   1

2.   THE DEMING STORY   87

3.   PERSONAL TRANSFORMATION   108

4.   CULTURAL TRANSFORMATION   126

5.   RULES OF PHASE III BEHAVIOR   177

6.   TOOLS TRANSFORMATION   202

7.   SYSTEMATIC PROBLEM-SOLVING   254

8.   PROBABILITY STATISTICS   287

9.   CONTROLLING PROCESSES   305

10.   CLOSING THOUGHTS   345

INDEX   363

Introduction

This book was written to teach you how to keep your business alive. The average life expectancy for Fortune 500–type companies is between forty and fifty years. There are many arguments for why organizations die at such a young age. This book looks at the problem from the perspective of a quality consultant.

I have spent my whole career learning how to make an organization's primary competitive advantage one of product or service quality. I have documented my findings in hundreds of hours of online training programs, which include such topics as Six Sigma, quality engineering, reliability engineering, quality auditing, Lean, and Theory of Constraints. I am one of eleven people who hold fourteen of the eighteen ASQ (American Society for Quality) certifications. I have implemented and taught these principles to approximately 150 corporations over the last two decades. I currently serve as president of Alpha Training and Consulting, which is a full-service quality consulting firm.

I am a sought-after lecturer and an adjunct faculty member for eight different universities and colleges. I received my mechanical engineering degree from BYU and my post-graduate degree in business administration from the University of Phoenix.

Rising above It All argues that the reason companies have such short life spans is because they do not understand how to effectively transform themselves. The book defines organizational transformation as "evolving to higher levels of sustained performance." I have found that most companies are capable of evolving to a given level of performance, which I refer to as the 95 percent level. One of the problems in transformation is that the skill level needed to reach the 95 percent performance level is not the same skill set that is needed to rise above the 95 percent level of performance. Most organizations do not understand this phenomenon, and as a result companies will eventually go extinct as customer expectations rise above the 95 percent performance levels.

Rising above It All breaks organizational transformation into three subtransformations:

- Personal Transformation
- Cultural Transformation
- Tools Transformation

I argue that most companies skip the personal and cultural transformation and jump right into the tools transformation, which is the reason companies die at such a young age. The fundamental problem is that an organization must have a culture that supports modern-day analytical tools or the tools will not effectively work within the borders of the organization. I define what a functional culture looks like and the leadership skills necessary to achieve it. *Rising above It All* defines leadership as the ability to change culture and introduces a model of human behavior that will help the reader understand how to become a leader who has enough influence to evolve organizational culture, which is key to long-term organizational survival.

This is not a rehash of old ideas introduced under a redesigned book cover. This information is meant to be informative, new, revolutionary, and at times, perhaps, controversial. This information came from my experiences of living life. Although it is being published as a business book, you will find that it is that and much more.

The writing of this book was not a natural act for me, and I could not have completed such an act without the patient help of my chief editor and friend Dorothy Openshaw. The reason I took on this challenge is really quite simple—I just want to make a difference. When I started lecturing on the way I viewed life and business, I realized that it inspired people. Many people told me that my simple lecture changed their lives. They asked me to write a book, and so I did. In short, the target audience for this book is you. I hope it inspires you to create more effective organizations so we can improve upon the human condition. I truly believe that we are in the dark ages of our human potential. I hope to teach you how to rise above these dark ages into a new and more enlightened understanding of what we call life. Only you, the reader, can judge my success or lack thereof.

The book starts out with a definition of organizational transformation. It then develops a mathematical argument for why transformation is necessary. If you don't like math, this may be the more challenging element of the work. I tried to make it as understandable as my capability allows, so for some I may have oversimplified the explanation. Whatever may be the case, please exercise patience as you come to understand the fundamental argument for organizational transformation. This will not be the most inspiring part of the work but must be well developed and understood by the reader if the end result is to experience any lasting value. After objectively understanding the necessity for transformation, the book will explain the complexities of organizational transformation through defining the three fundamental elements of transformation mentioned earlier: personal transformation, cultural transformation, and tools transformation.

Ultimately, my hope is that you, the reader, will be inspired by your newfound knowledge and go out and make the world a better place for the people and organizations that you serve.

CHAPTER ONE

INTRODUCTION TO TRANSFORMATION

Transformation Defined

We will begin our discussion with a definition of organizational transformation. Organizational transformation is evolving to a higher level of sustained performance. Next we will discuss the question "Why is organizational transformation necessary?" I have included some artwork to help us answer this question (see Figure 1). The objective of this exercise is to fill the bucket full of water. To do this, I have set up some plumbing so I can start and stop the flow of water into the bucket and reach the objective of filling the bucket full of water. Before continuing our discussion, let's first stop and talk about probability statistics.

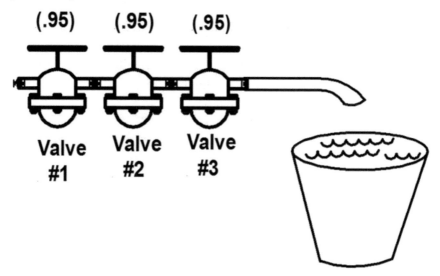

Figure 1

In probability statistics there are two general problem statements: the "and" statement and the "or" statement. What will Figure 1 be? Will this be an "or" statement problem—Valve #1 must work *or* Valve #2 must work *or* Valve #3 must work to fill up the bucket? Or is it an "and" statement—Valve #1 must work *and* Valve #2 must work *and* Valve #3 must work to fill the bucket full of water? The answer to this question is that it's an "and" statement— to fill the bucket, Valve #1 *and* Valve #2 *and* Valve #3 must work. Once Valve #1 *and* Valve #2 *and* Valve #3 work properly, I can successfully fill the bucket with water.

Fortunately, the "and" statement is relatively easy to calculate. In the "and" statement analysis, all we need to do is simply multiply the probabilities together. This is assuming independence between events. By independence I mean that whether Valve #2 fails or does not fail, it will not impact the failure rate of Valve #3 or Valve #1. So if one valve fails it will not impact the probabilities of the other valves' performance. This is what we refer to as independence. In this example we are assuming independence, and once we assume independence, we can simply multiply the probabilities together to give us the overall probability of success (filling the bucket full of water).

"And"/"Or" Statements?

You'll notice that I have labeled the reliability of each of the valves. Valve #1 is .95 (95 percent), Valve #2 is .95, and Valve #3 is .95. This may seem like a relatively good probability, but when you multiply them all together, notice what happens.

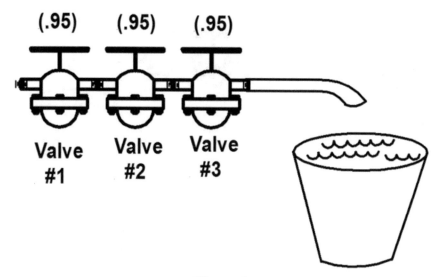

Figure 2

Three "And" Statements

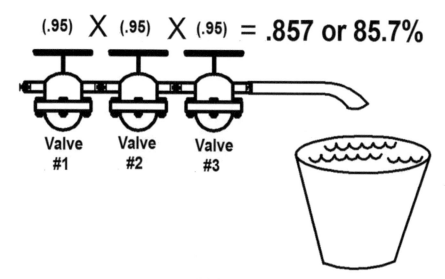

Figure 3

Under the assumptions given, the probability of Valve #1 working *and* Valve #2 working *and* Valve #3 working is 85.7 percent. The important thing to remember here is that as we add more "and" statements, our probability of success goes down.

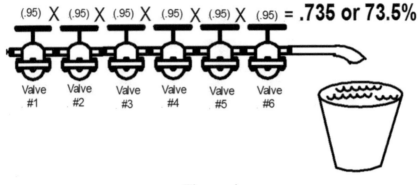

Figure 4

Notice in Figure 4 that we added three additional valves. In the last example we had three valves, and now we have six valves, meaning that we have six "and" statements. Notice that the probability of success, or reliability, of each of the valves remains the same at .95. But now we multiply the .95 by itself six times and we end up with a result of .735, or 73.5 percent. So the probability of Valve #1 *and* Valve #2 *and* Valve #3 *and* Valve #4 *and* Valve #5 *and* Valve #6 working is 73.5 percent. Again, notice that as we add more "and" statements our probability of success goes down.

Six "And" Statements

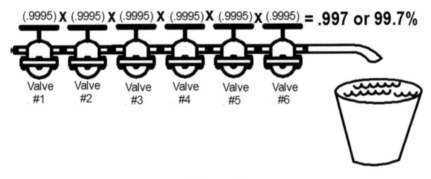

Figure 5

Looking at Figure 5, you will notice that we have decided to buy some more reliable valves. So instead of 95 percent reliability, we have .9995, or 99.95 percent. We have improved the probability of our "and" statements here, and when we multiply .9995 by itself six times we end up with 99.7 percent. Notice that the "and" statement formula is really a rather simple formula. There are two numbers involved—first the number of valves necessary, or the number of "and" statements, and second the reliability of each "and" statement.

We can improve the reliability in two ways. We can either improve our reliability of success on specific "and" statements or we can reduce the number of "and" statements. Those are the only two options.

Ten Thousand "And" Statements

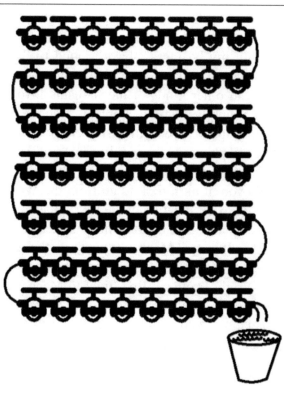

Figure 6

Figure 6 shows symbolically that we have ten thousand "and" statements, so we're assuming ten thousand "and" statements or ten thousand valves. Notice that I don't really have enough room to put ten thousand valves, so it's just symbolic. But the point is this: as time goes along, we keep adding "and" statements to the consumer's life.

Just a couple of generations ago, your grandparents or great-grandparents lived in the "horse and buggy days," and there weren't a lot of "and" statements compared to today. They didn't have televisions; they didn't have automobiles; they didn't have computers or cell phones. That's why we call it the "horse and buggy days"—they had a horse and a buggy. All right, they probably also had a house. However, the house probably didn't have electricity, at least early on in their lives. They probably didn't have running water either. So there were relatively few "and" statements, which made for a rather simplistic life that most likely had its advantages and disadvantages.

Since then, over the last couple of generations, we have added many "and" statements into our lives. Today I have three televisions in my house; with my business I have around twelve computers. I have radios, printers, electricity, and running water in a house that has valves and other kinds of mechanisms involved to make everything work properly. I have a couple of water heaters, a couple of heaters, and a couple of ovens; the list goes on and on. I think we have four or five cell phones in the family. The "and" statements have gone exponential and have done so very quickly.

How long do you think it took to go from the Wright Brothers' first powered flight to the creation of the SR71 Blackbird? The SR71 Blackbird is an airplane used by the United States Air Force that is said to be capable of flying at Mach 3 (three times the speed of sound, or approximately 2,304 mph). So again, how long do you think it took to go from the Wright Brothers' first flight to Mach 3 in the SR71? Would you believe it was only sixty-one years? Which one of the two do you think had more "and" statements? Obviously the SR71 or the Mach 3 airplane had many more "and" statements than the Wright Brothers' plane did. The velocity of change is really mind-blowing if you think about it.

This brings us to the problem in society of how we manage these "and" statements to the point that all our machinery and processes will still function in a way that's acceptable.

Let's refer back to the last figure and do some math. Let's assume that we have a machine with ten thousand "and" statements. I'm certain the automobile has at least ten thousand "and" statements, and probably more. I have a friend who went to look at a car the other day and upon returning said, "John, you wouldn't believe it—it has seven computers!" And I thought, *Wow, that's a lot of "and" statements.* Of course, he was excited at all the functionality. I wasn't quite so excited about it, because I know the "and" statements and therefore have an idea of the probability of success.

Let's do an example problem. Let's say that all the "and" statements had a probability of success of 95 percent, or .95. So if you take .95 and multiply it by itself ten thousand times, guess what you get? Zero—for all practical purposes anyway. Actually there are 222 zeros after the decimal point, followed by the number 172. Would you like to buy a car whose probability of not violating its specification limits or its "and" statements is a decimal with 222 zeros and a number behind it? I wouldn't think so. Consumers will not buy that type of product or service, at least not after the word of poor quality gets out.

Now let's play around with that "and" statement a little bit. Let's say that instead of 95 percent we get our "and" statement, or probability of success, up to 99.73 percent. Wow! That's very close to 100 percent. That means only a .27 percent chance of not being successful, or 2.7 times in a thousand. That sounds pretty good to me. I suspect that it does to you also. However, if we take that .9973 and multiply it by itself ten thousand times, guess what we get? For all practical purposes, it's zero again. Actually, this time there are eleven zeros past the decimal point and then the number 181. This is a terrible probability of success. Consumers will not tolerate this kind of performance in the products and services they purchase.

Now let's say we get very serious with our "and" statements and we run them up to 99.9996 percent. Sounds much better; boy, we're getting very close to 100 percent now. But let's multiply that number by itself ten thousand times. So .9999964 multiplied by itself ten thousand times gives us 96.5 percent, or .965. This is much better than the past examples. In fact, it shouldn't come as a surprise that at the time of this writing, the .9999964 is the standard in the automotive industry. Organizations that create "and" statements that go into an automobile must build those "and" statements to a minimum success probability of 99.99964 percent. So, again, if you multiply the .999996 by itself ten thousand times you will get a reliability of 96.5 percent. Now get this: if you take one of those nines out of the probability of success, which would make it .999964 (four nines after the decimal point instead of five), and you multiply .999964 by itself ten thousand times, the overall probability of success drops from 96.5 percent to 69.7 percent, and that is just from dropping one of the nines. It comes down to this: you must learn to manage your "and" statements or your "and" statements will manage you. Or even worse yet, your incapable "and" statements will manage your customers' lives. This being the case, the customer will move to someone that can manage their "and" statements.

What I hope you see here is that there's a big difference between 99.73 percent and 99.9996 percent, although they're both very close to 100 percent when we look at them individually. When we multiply them by themselves ten thousand times, there is a big difference. There is even a big difference if you change your probability of success from 99.99964 percent to 99.9964 percent (drop one nine).

Now is probably a good time to ask you a question. What do you think will happen in the future? Will "and" statements keep increasing? Or do you think they'll decrease? If you said that you feel the "and" statements will increase in the future, then I'm with you. I agree with that, and as a result, that 99.9996 percent may not be good enough in the future. Chances are we'll have to keep increasing that probability of success. By the way, 99.9996 percent is another way of saying six sigma, which we'll talk about later.

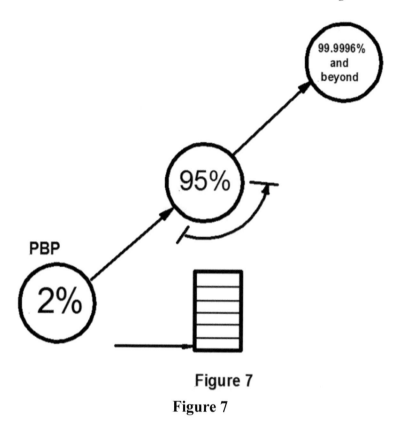

Figure 7

Figure 7

In Figure 7 we have a rather simple but very important model. This is a model for transformation. It describes the history of transformation, why transformation is necessary, and how we can go about having a successful transformation. Now notice the round symbol with the 2 percent in it and the arrow rising up to the 95 percent, and then there's that semicircle just below the 95 percent symbol. That semicircle represents the act of transformation ("evolving to a higher level of sustained performance"). Notice that down below the 95 percent symbol, there is also, symbolically, a brick wall with an arrow at the bottom. The model suggests that if you can get over the wall (transform), then you can potentially increase your "and" statement probability of success up to 99.9996 percent and beyond.

We're going to tear this model down and go over each piece separately, and when we put it all back together you'll understand a lot more about transformation, why it's necessary, and what we have to do to make it happen.

Figure 8

In setting up our argument for transformation ("evolving to a higher level of sustained performance"), let's go over some important events in history. In the mid-1700s the Industrial Revolution was in its embryonic stage—and beware, the "and" statements are about to take flight. The Industrial Revolution is what took us from the horse and buggy days to where we are today with all these "and" statements. Don't get me wrong—all these "and" statements tend to improve the human condition. Because of these additional "and" statements we are able to cure diseases that were not curable in the past, we are able to control our environment with such systems as air-conditioning, we are able to take pictures of distant planets, we are capable of communicating to worldwide audiences in just seconds, we are able to solve problems in seconds compared to what once took months or years, and we can literally travel around the world in a matter of days. Generations of the past could not even imagine what we are capable of accomplishing in one lifetime. In short, we can stuff more life into a lifetime than anyone in history was even capable of imagining—all because of these wonderful "and" statements.

In the end these "and" statements have created opportunity. The good news is that these "and" statements will continue to grow even more exponentially into the future, and future generations will be given opportunities that we today cannot even imagine. Therefore, we had better get very good at managing "and" statements if we expect to have a place in the future of building products and providing services in this environment of ever-increasing "and" statements. You must always remember that as "and" statements increase, the consumer will become less patient with dysfunctional "and" statements, thus making organizational transformation a necessity and not just a nicety. In summary, "and" statements and customer expectations will continue to increase exponentially into the future.

Now let's study the history of the expanding "and" statements. The dramatic expansion of the "and" statement started in the mid-1700s when there was a lot of excitement going on in the intellectual world. This period of time was the pre-Industrial Revolution, and scientific societies started showing up throughout Europe. One of these societies was named the Lunar Society. The Lunar Society operated out of the Soho house located in Birmingham, England. This is very much a historical building of great significance. At the Lunar Society, scientists and philosophers would gather together in the nighttime and run scientific experiments. They wouldn't run them every night: they'd only run their experiments when there was a full moon, because back then they didn't have street lights—talk about fewer "and" statements—so they would run these experiments only when there was a full moon so the members of the society could safely walk home at night.

One of the members of this Lunar Society—in fact one of the leaders—was named Matthew Boulton. He was a key member of the Lunar Society. Matthew loved to build artistic things out of metal. He built swords and trinkets that people could hang up on their walls, and that's what he did for a living.

Matthew Boulton

There were many members of the Lunar Society. Some of the more famous ones included James Watt, the man who came up with a more efficient steam engine, which would ultimately power the Industrial Revolution and in turn would ultimately power the number of "and" statements found in society.

James Watt

Josiah Wedgwood

Steam Engine

(Free software Foundation, Inc.)

Sample of Wedgwood Pottery

Other famous members included Benjamin Franklin, who showed up for several of the experiments, as did Thomas Jefferson.

Josiah Wedgwood was also a member of the Lunar Society and is given credit for creating specialized labor in the pottery industry and essentially using it to usher in the Industrial Revolution. What do I mean by specialized labor? First, you have to understand that Josiah Wedgwood had a disease when he was a young man or a young boy, most likely smallpox, which injured his leg. In the meantime—I don't know if it was through his family or a friend—but he got involved in the pottery industry. Josiah had a difficult time turning the potter's wheel with only one healthy leg, so he sat around and brainstormed on how he could make the industry better, make it more profitable, and make better pottery for the customers, and he did that. He started by specializing his own labor and later expanded the idea throughout the factory. One person would be on the potter's wheel and build the pottery. Someone else would become a specialist at baking these pots, and then someone else would paint them. A fourth person would decorate them. He leveraged people's talents to make the best pottery. He also experimented a lot and developed some of the glossiest finishes in the pottery industry. He would sell his pottery to the kings and queens of England, and then, of course, everyone wanted it and he became a rather wealthy gentleman.

Not only did Josiah Wedgwood come up with specialized labor in the pottery industry, he was also a staunch abolitionist in Europe and was famous for having created the symbol for European abolitionists that said, *"AM I NOT A MAN AND A BROTHER?"* He

made these symbols in a coin-type shape and handed them out to everyone in an effort to help them question the issue of slavery.

Josiah Wedgwood was famous on many fronts, but perhaps he was most famous because of his grandson, Charles Darwin. Another thing that was rather interesting about Josiah Wedgwood was that he really took quality seriously. He'd walk around with his cane and if he saw a plate that didn't meet his standards, he would smash the plate with his cane and yell out to the factory workers: "This is not good enough for Josiah Wedgwood." I enjoy reenacting this seen whenever the opportunity is provided.

Charles Darwin

A further point of interest is that Josiah Wedgwood's factory is still running today and still makes Wedgwood pottery.

Another important individual in the mid-1700s was Honoré LeBlanc. Mr. LeBlanc was a very famous gunsmith in France and was the first individual to fabricate gun parts to allowable tolerances.

This most likely began when customers would bring in their guns to LeBlanc and say, "Hey, I broke the trigger on my gun. Could you build me another one just like it?"

And he'd say, "Well, where's the broken part?" and the customer would answer, "Well, I broke it and it's gone." Since he didn't have any standard or print to work off of, he'd hammer out another part and put it on the gun; maybe it worked as well as the other one and maybe it didn't, and usually the customers were disappointed because they had become accustomed to the way the gun worked before the part broke. Anyway, it bothered Honoré Le Blanc that this problem existed, so he thought, *Hey, what if I created standard parts so that I could have replaceable parts?* It was his dream that he'd have guns that he could interchange parts with, so he tried to convince his fellow Frenchmen of the possibilities of this new and radical idea.

As it turns out, Honoré LeBlanc's fellow Frenchmen were not overly impressed with this new idea. They saw it as a threat to their employment and social status. As a result, Le Blanc instead sold the idea to an American gentleman. This man was Thomas Jefferson, the American ambassador to France at the time. Thomas Jefferson was extremely impressed with the idea of interchangeable parts. He realized that such a system would allow the United States to build up its gun industry and make it less dependent on European armories.

Thomas Jefferson

George Washington

Thomas Jefferson's friend and ally in the cause of interchangeable parts was George Washington. George, it turns out, had had some bad experiences with European suppliers of guns during the Revolutionary War. For example, at one point Congress purchased a relatively large number of weapons from France, and France gave them an excellent deal as they considered themselves allies to the American cause (they desired to embarrass the British). But when the guns arrived on the battlefield, very few of them were capable of functioning, which hindered the odds for a successful revolution.

In summary, Washington and Jefferson were not overly impressed with their dependence on foreign suppliers for American soldiers. This revolutionary system of interchangeable parts would also allow the Americans to build up a gun industry in the northern part of the United States. This was important because there was always a fear that eventually the United States would break out in civil war over the issue of slavery, and this new idea would allow them to build up the weapon industry in the northern states relatively quickly. In short, both Thomas Jefferson and George Washington were very impressed with the possibilities of this new radical idea of interchangeable parts. It was a revolutionary idea for the ultimate in revolutionaries.

Eli Whitney

Eli Whitney's Factory

Shortly after George Washington left the presidency, a contract was awarded for twelve thousand muskets to an individual named Eli Whitney. Eli was an interesting character. At age fourteen, during the Revolutionary War, he opened a nail factory in his father's shop.

From the very beginning Eli was very much an entrepreneur and very much an innovator—and, of course, ultimately he came up with the cotton gin, which made short-staple cotton a very profitable crop and had the unintended consequence of strengthening the economic foundation for slavery in the South. Eli Whitney played a significant role in American history.

Eli's original contract of twelve thousand muskets did not demand interchangeable parts, but later on the secretary of war handed Whitney a pamphlet from France on interchangeable parts for guns. This pamphlet was most likely from LeBlanc, so Eli Whitney took it, read it, became a real champion of interchangeable parts, and actually took credit for the idea himself.

Eli went to great lengths to help foster the implementation of this new idea of interchangeable parts, but as you may imagine, the implementation of "interchangeable parts" was not easy for Eli.

Eli Whitney's Cotton Gin

Ultimately he was supposed to deliver approximately fifteen thousand muskets by 1800. In the end, the muskets were not completely delivered until 1809. So initially it was not a great success. Eli Whitney does deserve credit, though, for going through the initial sacrifices necessary in establishing interchangeable parts in the United States and, ultimately, the rest of the world. Eventually, in 1820, Eli built an arms factory in New Haven, Connecticut, so evidently the American government didn't give up on him. Eli tenaciously continued working on the interchangeable parts idea and eventually experienced continuous process-improvement.

You may ask the question, how hard did Eli Whitney struggle? Well, it was *quite* a struggle. Eli's first manufacturing run consisted of seven hundred guns. Of those seven hundred, only fourteen of them could be assembled successfully; in other words, the process produced 2 percent good parts. That is why the first part of that transformation model included the 2 percent. The 2 percent represents a starting point, or a baseline, for the first attempt at mass production and what kind of "and" statement success (quality) it created. It was somewhat of a disaster, and Eli was nine years late on delivering the requirements of the contract (and you thought you were having a bad day!).

Many historians have convincing arguments that suggest Eli never did master the new art of mass production. The acronym "PBP" located above the 2 percent circle stands for "personify, blame, and punish." PBP is a methodology of solving problems. The advantage of this methodology is its simplicity. PBP works something like this: first, you have a problem; second, you personify the problem; third, you blame someone for the problem; and finally, you punish the people responsible for the problem, and then they get better. At least that is the assumption and the objective. PBP worked pretty well for Eli. It brought his organization up from 2 percent to approximately 95 percent, but Eli pretty much demanded that quality be generated from the people and not the system. Studies suggest that work systems max out around 95 percent when PBP methodologies are used; this is why, on our transformation model, it went from 2 percent to 95 percent, because that's all personify, blame, and punish is capable of on "and" statement success rates (about 95 percent). Left to human nature, it is the best that can be expected.

If you add procedures and fixtures to processes (referred to as a system), then systems can have a better impact on your "and" statement probabilities and you can get up to today's high "and" statement probability of 99.9996 percent. But again, Eli was just doing what was common for the day. He was doing personify, blame, and punish techniques, and those methods would only allow the system to evolve so far. So Whitney ended up running the factory with highly skilled tradesmen. He initially tried to run the factory with lower-skilled labor and use machines to create better parts, but he didn't have the culture to support the tools, so he had to go back to personify, blame, and punish for his lower-skilled workers. In the end, it just didn't work and he ended up with a factory of skilled tradesmen. Valid arguments suggest that Eli Whitney never did master this new art of mass production.

Eli Terry

Experts suggest that the first successful mass production run took place with Eli Terry in 1814 at Plymouth, Connecticut. The factory in Plymouth mass produced clocks made from wooden parts.

Another interesting fact is that several miles down the road from Eli Terry lived a man by the name of Simeon North. Simeon created the world's first milling machine. Using this new machine, he successfully mass-produced guns in the United States.

Let's review what we have learned and apply it to the transformation model. Look at the transformation model shown in Figure 9; you already know where the 2 percent comes from. Remember that this is Eli Whitney's first attempt at mass production, and PBP stands for "personify, blame, and punish." PBP is a problem-solving methodology; when we have a problem, we personify it, we blame it on someone, and then we punish him or her. The assumption is that as a result of PBP, we should get better over time.

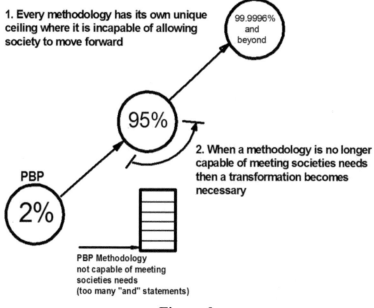

1. Every methodology has its own unique ceiling where it is incapable of allowing society to move forward

99.9996% and beyond

95%

PBP

2%

2. When a methodology is no longer capable of meeting societies needs then a transformation becomes necessary

PBP Methodology not capable of meeting societies needs (too many "and" statements)

Figure 9

But let's read that first point: every methodology has its own unique ceiling where it is incapable of allowing society to move forward. For example, studies have suggested that personify, blame, and punish methodology is only capable of an approximately 95 percent success rate on the individual "and" statement. This is a big improvement over the 2 percent, so no one is arguing that personify, blame, and punish did not have its consequential place in history, and if it were to take us beyond that 95 percent, then I would still be recognizing its merits today. But the simple fact of the matter is that it's not capable of sustained performance **above** the 95 percent mark. In the meantime, the "and" statements are growing exponentially. These ever expanding "and" statements quickly make 95 percent a dysfunctional standard for the demands of modern-day business. This is why transformation is necessary—because we have methodologies that reach their limits and those limits are not capable of dealing with all the "and" statements.

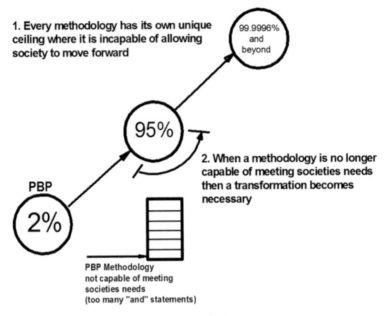

Figure 9-A

Let's read all the points on the illustration to make sure you understand them. I'm going to go over Point 1 again. Remember that every methodology has its own unique ceiling where it is incapable of allowing society to move forward. Point 2 says this: when a methodology is no longer capable of meeting society's needs, then a transformation becomes necessary. This is where you "hit the wall." We call it "hitting the wall" when your methodology is no longer capable of meeting society's needs.

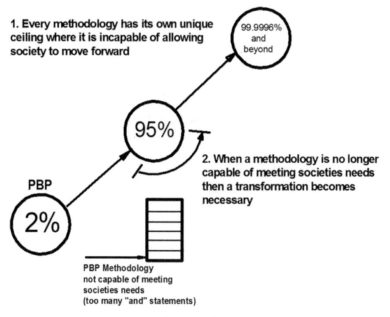

Figure 10

Now look at the symbolic wall. Notice there's an arrow hitting the bottom of the wall, which symbolizes the personify, blame, and punish methodology's inability to meet society's needs. Why? Because there are too many "and" statements. Back in a time when there were not as many "and" statements, 95 percent was an acceptable standard. But since the "and" statements are going exponential—we have ten thousand of them—then obviously 95 percent is not a good enough standard. Please remember that with ten thousand "and" statements, if we multiply .95 by itself ten thousand times, we end up with two hundred-some zeros after the decimal point and then a number, and that doesn't meet society's needs. The automotive industry cannot survive at a 95 percent standard because of the massive amounts of "and" statements in their product.

There may have been a day when PBP could have met society's needs (low "and" statements and low expectations), but those days are long gone, and everyone that was determined to exercise personify, blame, and punish in high "and" statement industries, such as automotive, are no longer in business. They went extinct— so that's a pretty strong message to remember, and it explains why transformation is necessary. In lower "and" statement industries PBP is still alive and well, at least until the "and" statements reach critical mass, which in most industries they eventually will.

In summary, transformation is necessary because our old methodologies are no longer capable of meeting society's needs (PBP), and so, to move forward, we have to change the way we think, we have to change our problem-solving models, and we have to use new tools.

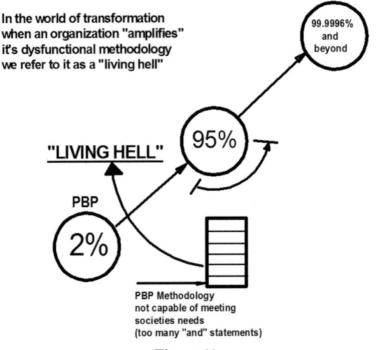

In the world of transformation when an organization "amplifies" it's dysfunctional methodology we refer to it as a "living hell"

99.9996% and beyond

95%

"LIVING HELL"

PBP

2%

PBP Methodology not capable of meeting societies needs (too many "and" statements)

Figure 11

When an organization hits the wall—in other words, when its old methodologies are no longer capable of meeting society's needs—its first impulse tends to be to amplify the old methodology. So it takes personify, blame, and punish and it amplifies it. This becomes very frustrating to everyone involved because everyone wants to succeed. In the past the organization has succeeded, so it becomes hell-bent on amplifying this old, dysfunctional methodology to solve the problem. So there we are: we amplify personify, blame, and punish. Everyone starts to personify, blame, and punish everyone else. It quickly becomes a very frustrating situation. You'll hear things like, "You know, we once had a generation of people who were capable of running this company," and the problems are blamed on the people, when in reality what has happened is that your old methodology is not capable of creating the "and" statement success rate necessary to meet society's demands.

We went from 2 percent to 95 percent, so you think that using personify, blame, and punish must work, and it is easy to extrapolate into the future and assume PBP will take your organization beyond a 95 percent "and" statement success rate. But I have evaluated hundreds of companies around the world, and I have yet to find a company that uses PBP methodologies that is capable of sustaining a success rate greater than 95 percent. I personally don't think it is possible for PBP to sustain this level of performance. It comes down to a pretty simple concept. An organization has two possible choices to make: the system is more important than the people or the people are more important than the system. If the organization decides that the system is more important than the people, then they will spend all their resources trying to fix the people. The natural by-product of this type of thinking is PBP. If an organization believes that the people are more important than the system, then they will constantly fix the system so it will more effectively support the needs of the people. In the end, if an organization feels that the people are there to serve the system and not the system to serve the people, they will make human nature the constraint, which is capable of approximately a 95 percent success rate. If an organization feels that the system is there to serve the needs of the people, then the system becomes the constraint. I don't believe that anyone has truly found the end capability of a system that supports the needs of the people. I can tell you from experience that if an organization believes the system is there to support the people and thus constantly improves the system, it is capable of many nines behind the decimal point. Such systems are readily capable of the .999996 number mentioned earlier. I have never seen a company achieve the .999996 number when they felt the people were subordinate to the system; in fact it is an oddity if they operate at over a 95 percent success rate. If you were to visit a highly competitive and high "and" statement industry, such as tier l suppliers to the auto industry, you would find an organization that found the system subservient to the people. Relatively speaking the automotive industry sees problems as system problem's and solves them as system problems in an effort to survive in a very competitive world. Teirl suppliers to the automotive industry see the system as the constraint or they have went extinct.

We must start looking at problems as system problems and not people problems. People can build systems that are capable of going beyond 95 percent, but systems are not capable of forcing people to perform much above 95 percent. Skilled craftsmen like Eli Whitney and his team perceived the people to be subordinate to the system, which in turn forced them into being skilled craftsmen who could approach the 95 percent potential. I do not mean to be disrespectful of Eli Whitney. It is more natural for the human mind to see the people as subordinate to the system rather than the system being subordinate to the people. We owe a lot of gratitude to Eli and his sacrifices as he is one of the key figures who allowed us to evolve to the point we are at today. We must learn from others' experiences if we are to move forward. If you are not in a highly competitive high "and" statement industry, then chances are your organization sees the people as subordinate to the system and PBP is the main methodology for solving process problems.

Remember that Eli Whitney went from 2 percent to 95 percent, so I'm not knocking personify, blame, and punish; I think it had a positive place in history. The only problem is that you have to recognize when the methodology is no longer capable of meeting society's needs so you can transform. Too many organizations amplify dysfunctional methodologies and end up going extinct. It's extremely important that you understand that this is a methodology problem, not a people problem.

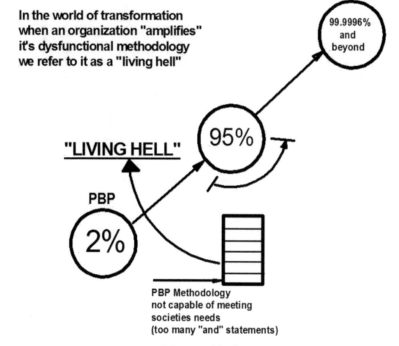

Figure 11-A

I'm going to reread that first point in the illustration where it says: In the world of transformation, when an organization "amplifies" its dysfunctional methodology, we refer to it as a "living hell." I understand that "living hell" doesn't sound like a very technical term, and perhaps I should come up with another word for it; however, I do believe that the phrase describes the frustration that goes on when an organization "hits the wall" and amplifies dysfunctional methodologies. So, for the time being, I'll stick with that phrase to describe that element of the transformation process.

1,000' / day
or "ELSE"

Figure 12

Now we will use a story to help us understand these concepts. Imagine yourself coming in to your office on a winter morning and seeing a man outside digging a trench into the frozen ground. He digs maybe three feet per day, but he works really hard at it, and his boss comes by and says, "You know, this isn't good enough. With three feet per day, sir, we can't keep you around if you can't do better than that. You have to dig one thousand feet per day or else." And the boss put a big banner across a couple of trees that reminds the digger of this goal. When you go home that night, you notice that the guy is working, and when you come back in the morning he is still digging the trench. He's working around the clock trying to do this—he has a mortgage he's trying to pay plus trying to support his kids and other expenses. So it's extremely important to him that he keeps this job, and he's giving it everything he has, but unfortunately it's just not enough. There's no way he's going to meet the goal of one thousand feet per day.

So the boss comes back and sees the progress. The man went from three feet per day to eight feet per day, but still he's way below the goal, so he gets a write-up that says, "We'll give you one more chance, but if you can't do it, you'll be finished tomorrow." You're feeling sorry for the guy, and then you're looking around and you notice that there's a backhoe back in the woods, so you go out and say, "Sir, I know this is none of my business, but wow, did you know there was a backhoe behind you?" The worker looks behind him and says, "Oh yeah, I saw that, but I have no idea how to use that tool." You're from a construction family, and so you jump in there and show him how to run the new tool. You show him the controls and you show him how to dig the trench, and this guy, it turns out, is a natural, and he just starts digging away. In fact, his skill level quickly exceeds yours, and before you know it, he's digging four thousand feet per day.

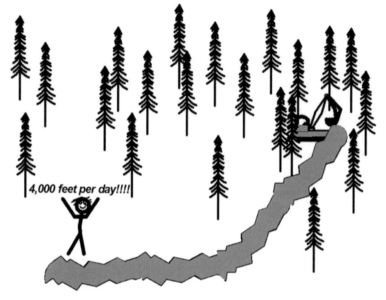

Figure 13

Imagine how relieved this gentleman is now that he can meet society's needs—and not only meet society's needs, but exceed those needs. And he's not working twenty-four hours a day; he gets it all done in an eight-hour shift. Imagine how frustrating it is watching people doing work and seeing the backhoe back in the woods and going over and saying, "Hey, you know, maybe you should use this backhoe" and seeing people not do it. They don't use the tools. We have many modern-day tools to make it better and easier to meet our society's requirements; we just have to learn how to use them and implement them. It's not all that easy—but it's also not that hard if you understand the rules. That's what this book is about: teaching you the rules necessary to have a successful transformation, which will allow your employees to effectively use modern-day analytical tools to serve the needs of society.

Back to our story. Now this guy is jumping for joy—he digs four thousand feet per day, and the boss comes by and is just totally amazed. So the digger impresses everyone and he's happy again.

Now, realize that a couple of things could happen here. The boss could come by and say, "Hey, wait a minute here—we don't use backhoes in this organization. In this organization we do it like our forbearers did—we use our backs; that really means something to us." And that's an example of where the culture would not support the tool.

Another outcome that could happen, and obviously will happen and should happen, is that the boss, instead of keeping the goal at one thousand feet per day, will say, "Hey, you're doing four thousand feet per day; that's great," and he'll change the goal to four thousand feet per day. I don't really have any problem with that as long as you have the tools to support the goal and the culture to support the tools. One thing that doesn't work is when you set a goal that the tools cannot support—that is when you hit the wall.

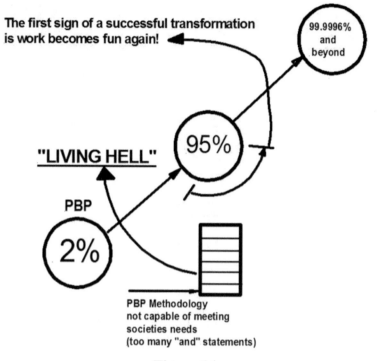

The first sign of a successful transformation is work becomes fun again!

99.9996% and beyond

95%

"LIVING HELL"

PBP

2%

PBP Methodology
not capable of meeting
societies needs
(too many "and" statements)

Figure 14

An important thing to keep in mind here is that the first sign you'll see of a successful transformation is that work becomes fun again. I once worked with a client, and we were teaching his employees how to use some new tools. We created some initial projects to implement these tools and solve various problems. The teams had great success at reaching the project objectives, which generated a lot of excitement among team members. I remember the sense of excitement as we went into the conference room where they presented their projects to the management team. I was pleasantly surprised when we came out of the meeting and there was a line of employees waiting to be involved in the next round of projects! From that experience and many others since I learned that the first sign that a transformation has gained important momentum is the employees find work to be fun again. In summary, the first sign of a successful transformation is that work becomes fun again!

Success is FUN!!

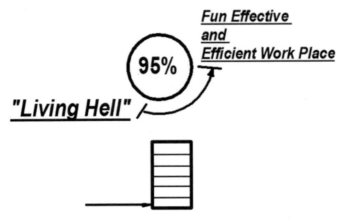

Figure 15

In this part of the transformation, we're going from a "living hell" to a fun, effective, and efficient workplace. This is one of the high points in the organizational transformation cycle. Of course after the first set of improvement projects are finished you should immediately have a second round of projects and a third round of projects, and you should never stop the continuous process-improvement cycle. I would suggest that you create a project-selection process before you begin your first set of projects so by the time the first set of projects are complete you will have the second-round projects identified and ready for submission to the improvement teams.

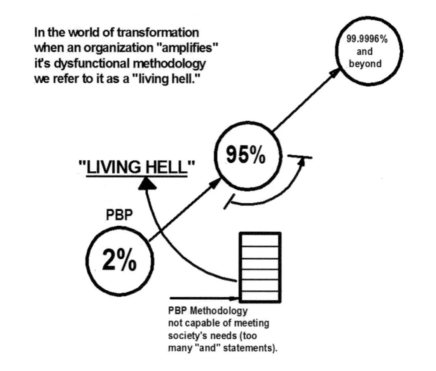

In the world of transformation when an organization "amplifies" it's dysfunctional methodology we refer to it as a "living hell."

99.9996% and beyond

"LIVING HELL"

95%

PBP

2%

PBP Methodology not capable of meeting society's needs (too many "and" statements).

Figure 16

Let's review Figure 16 using our newly gained knowledge. Remember the 2 percent? That's where Eli Whitney started in his mass-production experiment. Eli Whitney, some people argue, was never really successful at mass production. Back then, the methodology he used was personify, blame, and punish, and, as a result, his laborers turned into specialists. That isn't a bad thing. Don't get me wrong—extra skill is good—but they're counting purely on human nature to create good products. That's okay, except that it will only take you to about 95 percent. If you want to go **beyond** 95 percent, you have to use different tools and you have to build systems. Systems are capable of going beyond 95 percent, so it is important to look at problems as system problems, not personal problems. When you master the system perspective it will enable your organization to go over the proverbial wall and move forward to find new levels of performance that future markets will demand.

Continuing on with our summary, remember that when you hit the proverbial wall an organization will naturally amplify, personify, blame, and punish, and make everyone miserable, which we referred to as a "living hell," and drive your organization into extinction, or you can change the way you look at the world and start seeing problems as system problems. We referred to this earlier as subordinating the system to the people. You can even look at different countries throughout the world and notice that the countries that make the people subordinate to the system do not evolve as quickly as countries that make the system subordinate to the people. Most companies refuse to change; they're so committed to their past that they're unwilling to change for their future. But nature doesn't care. Nature is in charge, and if you don't follow the rules, you will be punished, and as an organization you will go extinct. What we're talking about here is the science of organizational survival.

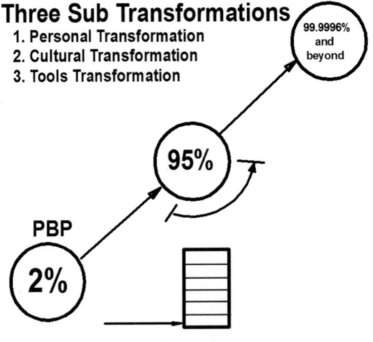

Figure 17

Thus far we have talked in general terms about transformation. In reality, transformation is difficult and nearly impossible for most organizations. The biggest reason for this difficulty is a lack of understanding of the rules of transformation. Once you understand the rules, organizational transformation becomes a manageable task, assuming you have the necessary leadership. Organizations with ineffective leadership are incapable of successfully transforming. Thus far we also have identified two important ingredients in a successful transformation: understanding the rules of transformation and effective leadership. Before you can understand the rules of organizational transformation, you must understand that there are three subtransformations that must take place to have a successful organizational transformation. These transformations include personal transformation, cultural transformation, and tools transformation. We'll go over these subtransformations in greater detail later.

The objective of the next set of illustrations is to show you conceptually how to change our barrier of 95 percent to 99.9996 percent, or whatever the standard needs to be in order to maintain the "and" statements at a competitive level. How do we go about doing that—what are the mechanics? I'm not going to write so much, right now, about the subtransformations, but from a statistical perspective how do we go from 95 percent up to more desired levels?

To answer this question we must first explain objectivity vs. subjectivity and the fundamentals of statistics. Once we understand these fundamental concepts, we can effectively describe the mechanics of improving "and" statement probabilities.

Objectivity vs. Subjectivity

Problem solving can effectively be placed under two general categories: objectivity and subjectivity.

Objectivity is often referred to as "black and white," suggesting that there is no grey area in objectivity. The main tool used for objective problem solving is mathematics. If you desired to learn the latest and greatest problem-solving techniques in objective problem solving, you would most likely select a major in mathematics, physics, engineering, or other related areas of study. When solving objective problems the solution is either correct or incorrect, and there is no room left for negotiation. For example, the fact that $1 + 1 = 2$ does not leave room for negotiation. The solution to the problem is either correct or it is incorrect. This is the nature of objective problem solving. Because of this phenomenon, objective problems are quick and decisive, assuming that someone with the proper training and expertise is solving the objective problem. Society's ability to solve objective problems in a timely manner was greatly increased with the advent of the modern-day computer accompanied with the appropriate software. The longest time constraint in objective problem solving is data collection. If data is readily available, then objective problem solving can effectively solve problems in minutes. As a society, we have become very efficient and effective at solving objective problems.

<u>**Objective Problem Solving**</u>
- **"Black and White"**
- **1 + 1 = 2**
- **Computerized equipment has automated objective problem solving.**

Figure 18

There is a rule associated with objective problem solving that is stated as "If you argue about a properly solved objective problem, you tend to lose credibility among your peers." For example, let's assume we are in a classroom of higher learning and I teach you that 2 + 1 = 3. Now imagine that someone begins to passionately argue with me that 2 + 1 does not equal 3 but that it equals 3.14! As you may imagine, the person arguing with me would lose credibility among his or her fellow students. It is highly unlikely that anyone would invite this student to their study groups.

Another unique property of objective problem solving is that when we solve higher-level objective problems we tend to create subjective problems. We will discuss this when we define subjective problem solving.

Another thing that's interesting about objective problem solving is that as organizations become more objective they also become more financially successful and create more opportunities for society.

Now we will discuss subjective problem solving. Subjective problem solving is unique in that to solve subjective problems, you must argue about them. This makes subjective problem solving and objective problem solving very different from one another. Remember that if we argue about a properly solved objective problem, we lose credibility. However, to solve subjective problems, we **have to argue** about them. Sometimes these arguments are constructive and sometimes they are destructive. As a society, we do not solve subjective problems as efficiently or effectively as we do objective problems.

Can you think of who, in our society, are practitioners of subjective problem solving? Who in society argues about problems to solve them?

Practitioners of subjective problem solving are lawyers, judges, politicians, etc. These people are trained to solve problems through constructive argument. Another unique thing about subjective problem solving is that an individual with adequate authority is necessary in solving higher-level subjective problems. Let's look at this statement.

As you know, lawyers argue to solve problems, but the lawyer could go on forever arguing if there wasn't such a thing as a judge or a jury, someone with adequate authority to solve subjective problems. For example, let's say that the lawyers present their arguments before the judge, and the judge listens to both arguments and ultimately makes a decision and says, "This is my decision." That's the end of the problem—it's solved (at least in theory). If the lawyers did not have the judge or jury, you can only imagine how dysfunctional the situation would become. So that is how we solve subjective problems. It's not necessarily the most efficient or effective way to solve problems, but if we can't measure something effectively (create data), then we can't solve the problem objectively. Because many things cannot be effectively measured, they are not candidates for objective problem solving and we must solve them subjectively. And of all the problems to solve, the most difficult ones, I would say, are the subjective problems. They tend to be the most expensive as well. Have you hired a lawyer lately and witnessed how much time it takes and how expensive it is? Higher-level subjective problems take more time to solve. The time it takes to solve subjective problems are more likely to be measured in years than minutes.

The relationship between objective and subjective problem solving suggests that when we successfully solve high-level objective problems we create subjective problem spinoff. In other words, when we solve objective problems we create other subjective problems. For example, the creation of the nuclear weapon was an exercise in objective problem solving (we sent scientists and engineers to

37

create the weapon, not lawyers and politicians). However, did the creation of the weapon create subjective problems, what I call "subjective problem spinoff"? Of course it did. After the bomb was created we had to solve such problems as who can use this power or when should we be allowed to use this power. When you solve a high-level objective problem you will create subjective problem spinoffs. As a result of this relationship we will never become so objective that we will be able to eliminate all subjectivity; in fact, the more objective problems we solve the more subjective problems we create. So if I were to ask the question, "Have we become more objective or subjective over time?" we would have to answer that we have become both. From the time of Isaac Newton onward we have definitely become more objective, but because of subjective problem spinoffs, we have also become more subjective. As you improve your expertise at organizational transformation you must understand that your organization must be functional at both objectivity and subjectivity if you are to be successful. Wherever possible you need to convert subjectivity into objectivity. There are several reasons for this, but one of them is quite simple—it is normally less expensive to solve high-level objective problems than high-level subjective problems. So whenever you convert subjectivity into objectivity you will become more economically efficient. Objectivity is also more capable of finding the optimal solution in comparison to subjectivity. Subjectivity is based upon someone's best judgment, which could be biased and often is. It is difficult to be without bias if you have any experience in life. Objectivity also creates power and subjectivity does not. Objectivity creates power for transformation and subjectivity does not. The ultimate goal is to get the right balance between objectivity and subjectivity. Ultimately objectivity creates power and subjectivity is supposed to harness power. One without the other can be devastating to organizations.

I have never witnessed an organization that is too objective, but I often see organizations that are too subjective. I believe the reason for this is that subjectivity is more natural for most organizations. For example, if I were to put a group of people on an island without any outside influences they would rather quickly come up with a methodology to solving subjective problems. Usually one of the members will stand out as a natural leader and the organization will make him or her the authority figure and they will bring arguments for and against different issues to the authority figure and respect the authority figure's opinion enough to put issues to rest. In the worst case the island community will break out in war to solve their subjective problems. But either way the subjective problems will ultimately be solved or the island community will go extinct. Objectivity, on the other hand, may not be witnessed on the island for thousands of years. People like Isaac Newton only come along every couple of centuries, and when they do, the subjective side of the community tends to see them as a threat and will put them in prison or put them to death—whichever seems to be the most convenient at the time. Remember Galileo? He has become known as the father of science. During his lifetime he was one of the only objective thinkers around, and he was put under house arrest for life. Objectivity must have a unique culture if it is to survive and thrive within an organization. In order to reach higher levels of organizational performance we must create an organizational culture that will embrace objectivity and not try to destroy it. In world history this has, at times, demanded a powerful force in the world of transformation, called war. War or revolution is not necessary if you have effective leadership (transformation from the top down). War results from lack of leadership or lack of a respected authority figure, and the authority figure must be respected from all parties in the conflict. If you cannot gain respect from all sides, then by definition you lack leadership. It may not be reasonable to meet the demands of leadership, but ultimately there will not be peace in any organization without effective leadership.

Occasionally throughout history there have been times when objectivity was respected. During these unusual times humanity evolved more quickly than at any other time in history. Examples of this include ancient Greece, the Roman Empire, and the Renaissance. From my perspective, history shows massive amounts of time where objectivity was not tolerated, and when subjectivity destroys objectivity social evolution stops. The Dark Ages in Europe are an example of this, and the fall of the Roman Empire ended the acceptance of objectivity and pure subjectivity took over for literally centuries. The period became known as the Dark Ages for good reason. When subjectivity rules the masses and destroys objectivity, all progress stops. When subjectivity takes over it no longer matters what you know but only who you know. Public education fell with the Roman Empire. When a man by the name of Charlemagne, the father of France, came along (he started his reign in 768 AD), he wanted to restore the glory of the Roman Empire. He began by making education available to all classes of his subjects in what was called the "Chain of Royal Schools." At this time very few people in Europe knew how to read, and Charlemagne decided to be an example to his community by bringing in a monk to teach him, as an adult, how to read. As mentioned earlier it was more important who he knew than what he knew. From my perspective the Dark Ages didn't leave until some seven centuries after Charlemagne died. Historians say Charlemagne was a Renaissance man born seven centuries before the Renaissance. So some seven hundred years later the Renaissance period arrived with a movement called Humanism that allowed people to read something other than religious texts. This allowed the people to read about topics such as science without being punished. During this time people like Leonardo da Vinci, a bastard child, was allowed to study and learn scientific principles. Soon after this the Dark Ages left the present and took its place in history. I don't feel that this was by accident. Remember that society cannot evolve without objectivity and subjectivity being put in their proper balance. When these two forces become out of balance society will pay with loss of hope in the future.

You would probably be shocked if you saw how many organizations find education to be a threat and therefore discourage education among their employees. This is a strong sign that the organization is championing subjectivity. If you want to get ahead in these organizations you will need to become acquainted with the proper people, because you will quickly come to realize that it only matters who you know and not what you know.

In the end, objectivity creates power and subjectivity's job is to harness power. Now consider this: in an organization, it is dangerous to allow subjective problems to backlog. You've got to have, in your organization, the ability to solve subjective problems, or the organization will tend to fall apart. If your organization is constantly arguing about the same problems over and over throughout the years, that is an indication that your organization is dysfunctional in solving subjective problems. Almost without exception, the reason for dysfunctionality in subjective problem solving is lack of an authority figure. For example, on the world stage we have never been able to decide who can have nuclear power and when it can be used, and this is sixty-some years after the creation of this weapon. This suggests that we do not have an authority figure on the world stage, thus making subjective problem solving, on the world stage, dysfunctional. The by-product of this dysfunctionality is war, so I cannot overemphasize the importance of your organization being functional at solving both objective and subjective problems. Beware of organizations that feel threatened by objectivity to the point where they desire to destroy it. I have always refused to work with such organizations. It is very important to remember that subjectivity will always gravitate toward personify, blame, and punish. Subjectivity has no power without the force of punishment backing it up. Look at our judicial system, the ultimate organization of subjective problem solving, and ask yourself how functional this system would be if it did not have the authority to punish. The answer is that it would be a waste of an organization. As mentioned earlier, subjectivity will always gravitate toward personify, blame, and punish (PBP). If your organization is more subjective than objective, then you will see problems as people problems; if your organization is more objective, then it will tend to see problems as system problems. If you are offended by seeing problems as system problems, then you most likely see the world through the lenses of subjectivity. Objective organizations will always outperform subjective organizations, in the long run, simply because PBP is not capable of supporting sustained performance much above 95 percent. PBP is ultimately the by-product of subjectivity. In the end, the only reason human nature is subjective is because we lack knowledge. As a result, we will always need subjectivity because we are not all knowing. I am not picking on subjectivity; I am only trying to stress that both subjectivity and objectivity must be in proper balance. If we only had objective talents with no subjective talents, we would destroy ourselves because we would create power with no ability to harness it. Since subjectivity is more natural to human nature than objectivity, I have never seen a corporation that is too objective. But I often see corporations that are too subjective. Because of this, I find subjectivity to be a bigger threat to a successful transformation than I do objectivity. You should never allow one skill set to take over the other or disastrous consequences will take place. In summary, it is all about balance.

Subjective Problem Solving

- An individual with adequate authority is necessary in solving "higher level" subjective problems.
- Practitioners of subjective problem solving are lawyers, judges, politicians, etc.
- As an organization, it is dangerous if we allow subjective problems to backlog.

Figure 19

Now we're going to teach you how to be more objective. Why? Because we've found over time that we can create more wealth when we solve problems in an objective manner. So we're going to teach you more tools for objective problem solving. As a result, you will make better decisions and create more wealth for your organization and opportunity for society at large. Let's move on to the next illustration.

Converting Subjective Problems into Objective Problems

- Because our society solves objective problems more efficiently than subjective problems, it creates wealth when we convert subjective problems into objective problems.

Figure 20

Because our society solves objective problems more efficiently than subjective problems, it creates wealth when we convert subjective problems into objective problems. To do this, we use standards, procedures, and statistics to partially convert subjective problems into objective problems. However, remember that these tools continue to have the flavor of subjectivity. In other words, statistics, as I'm going to teach you, can solve many problems in a more objective manner. But it doesn't completely get rid of the subjective element. The subjective element of statistical analysis is found in the assumptions. You can argue about assumptions without losing credibility.

Let's use an example to explain this phenomenon more clearly. Let's say I drove through a community that had no speed limit. I was going one hundred mph and a policeman pulled me over and said that I was speeding. I would argue, "I was not speeding; I didn't hurt anyone, and besides that, if everyone drove as fast as I did, we wouldn't have to build as many freeways and the community would become more wealthy." The policeman would say, "You were speeding, and if you continue with this behavior, you are going to hurt someone in our community; therefore, we are going to have to fine you." Well, they could argue back and forth whether one hundred mph was speeding for a given set of conditions. To solve this problem they'd have to go before a judge. The judge would listen to both arguments and make his or her decision. The subjective problem would be solved, and society could move on.

This is not a very efficient way of solving the problem. A more efficient way would be to create speed limits. After these speed limits are created, let's say that the speed limit in that area is now sixty mph, and I go blasting through this community at one hundred mph. The policeman pulls me over with all the objective evidence from the radar gun (effectively measured data) and writes a ticket. Now I can go before the judge and argue with all this objective evidence against me, or I can just pay the fine. If I argue about it with all this objective evidence, I could easily lose credibility. Therefore, we have taken a very subjective situation, applied procedures and standards, and made it more objective. Once we have done this, it takes less time to solve the problem, because most of the time I, as the speeder, will not go before the judge. Why? Because I'm going to lose anyway and at best lose my credibility. I'm also probably going to get a fine as well. We solved the problem in a much more effective and efficient way with standards and procedures. In fact, I believe it was Montana that once had a speed limit that said, "Drive safe." Well, that was very subjective. The state ultimately overturned this law because it was costing society too much money to solve the constant subjective problems of speed. A lesson to learn here is that we can convert a subjective environment into a more objective environment by creating rules and procedures and backing them up with an authority figure.

A few more closing thoughts on the topic of subjectivity: In order for organizations to be functional at subjective problem solving they must respect the authority figure. This does not mean that you have to agree with the authority figure, but once the authority figure makes a decision it must be respected and held in high regard. If you want to see how fragile civility is, stop respecting the authority figures in your society and you will quickly learn the fragility of civility. Subjectivity working within its constructive scope is the glue that holds society together, and without it we will self-destruct.

Converting Subjective Problems into Objective Problems

- **Because our society solves objective problems more efficiently than subjective problems, it creates wealth when we convert subjective problems into objective problems.**

Figure 21

On the objective side of our world, we are always trying to create more tools to make our world more objective. As mentioned earlier in the text, to understand the mechanics of changing the probability of success of the "and" statements from, for example, 95 percent to 99.9996 percent, you must understand the fundamentals of statistics.

In an effort to explain the mechanics of improving "and" statement probabilities we will discuss the normal distribution. To help you understand the nature of the normal distribution, I have created a fictitious story. Before we get started, let's understand the importance of understanding the normal distribution. If you understand the nature of the normal distribution, then understanding the mechanics of improvement will most likely be very simple for you. If you do not understand the nature of the normal distribution, you will struggle all the way through the rest of this book. So this is the foundation of your knowledge of statistics. Please read this carefully, and if need be, go back over this portion of the material several times until you feel comfortable with the concept of the nature of the normal distribution.

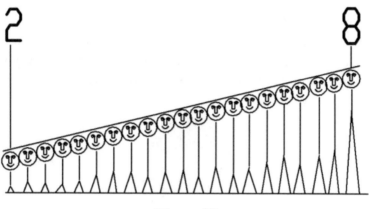

Figure 22

Here's our fictitious story. There's a king who wants to build chariots for the people in his kingdom, and he wants to build the chariots just right. He wants to have an optimum design. In order to create this optimum design, the king needs to know the average height of the people in his kingdom. So one day he has everyone take off work and come to the garden area of his kingdom. A million people show up. Remember that these are physically mature adults. He asks these people to line up according to their height. He has the shortest people line up farthest to the left and the tallest farthest to the right. Notice that the first line in the illustration is represented as the two-foot line and the line farthest to the right is the eight-foot line, and everything else is in between. So if you were two feet tall, you would line up after the person you see at the front of the two-foot line—we're just looking at the front of the mass of people that have lined up. Behind these people are longer lines depending upon how many people there are of that same height. That being the case, if you looked at the front view of this mass of people, it would be like the people in the illustration before you—at least symbolically.

Let's move on to the next illustration and talk about what it would look like if you looked down upon the top of this mass of people. Before you look at the illustration, imagine what this situation would look like if you got on top of the castle and looked down on the tops of the heads of this million people who were lined up according to their height. Whatever it looks like, we will call this "the distribution of the heights of people." What will the length of the lines look like? In other words, what will the distribution look like? Will the line for the two-foot-tall people be very long? In my experience, and yours also, I'm sure, it would be rare to have a two-foot-tall physically mature person. So out of a million people, that line would not be very long. For sake of argument I put one person in that line.

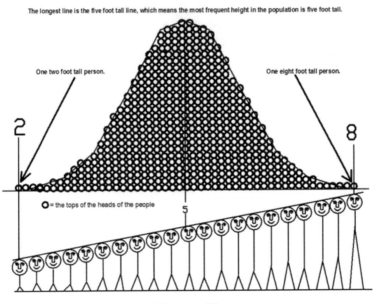

Figure 23

What about the eight-foot-tall people? Again, I don't think that line would be very long either. For the sake of argument I put one person in that line. But what if we look to the middle of the line of this mass of people between the two-foot and the eight-foot line—what would it look like? I will tell you this—the way nature lines things up, the longest line will be the line right in the middle of the distribution, which we call the "average of the distribution." So if the average height of the people in this kingdom was five feet tall (the middle line), would that line be very long? I would say yes, that would be the longest line of all. My next question would be, as you deviate from this average height of five feet, would the lines get longer or shorter? If you said they'd get shorter as you deviate from the average height, then you're correct. Take a moment and look at the illustration and make sure you are comfortable with the conversation we have had up to this point.

46

In summary the illustration shows the front view as it was on the previous illustration, and also the top view. The top view is the curve that you see while on top of the castle, and that line represents where you draw a line across the back of the head of the last person in each of the lines. Notice that the two-foot-tall line is not very long; nor is the eight-foot-tall line. But notice the average line, or the five-foot-tall line, which is the line right in the middle between the eight-foot and the two-foot line. It is the longest line of all of them. So in this kingdom there are more five-foot-tall people than people of any other height. As you deviate away from the average, whether you deviate on the right-hand side or the left-hand side, notice that the lines get progressively shorter over time. This curve that you see is what we refer to as the "normal distribution." Why? Because normally, when you're lining things up according to a value—in this case, people's height—it will take upon itself the shape of a normal distribution. It's a natural phenomenon. The normal distribution is very powerful in statistics. The king recognized that this had the potential of being very powerful because it is so common and because it is very predictable. I didn't tell you before, but each of these people standing in this line could create one hundred dollars' worth of wealth every day for the kingdom. In order to perform this study on the heights of the people, the king had to give them a day off so they could stop from their normal work to come to his garden. Because of this, the people had one full day that they did not trade, so it cost the king one hundred million dollars. The king thought to himself, *You know what? I'll bet I could determine what this curve looks like by using fewer people.* In fact, he made a hypothesis: *I'll bet I could use several hundred people to create this normal distribution. This would save me a lot of money in my studies in the future.* So the king decided to study this, which we call the normal distribution, in greater detail.

This curve, which we call the "normal distribution," is also referred to as the "bell curve," or the "Gaussian curve." It's a very powerful concept, and I'm sure you will agree as we continue on with its predictive nature.

In our society, when you want to understand a phenomenon in greater detail, what do you do? We normally break that phenomenon down into smaller elements to study them. For example, if we were to study material science, we'd break it down into molecules, then atoms, then the composition of the atoms and electron flows, and so on. That way we can really understand the phenomenon and start making successful predictions, which can create wealth and efficiency in our society.

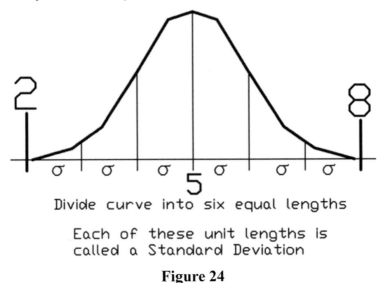

Divide curve into six equal lengths

Each of these unit lengths is called a Standard Deviation

Figure 24

That's what the king decided to do. He decided to take his normal curve and break it up into smaller components. In fact, for reasons that I don't know, he broke this curve up into six equal lengths. Remember that these lengths are the distances along the normal curve. The king took these unit lengths and called them "standard deviations," which ultimately got the nickname "sigma." That's pretty simple, isn't it? Statistics is simple if you keep it simple. Remember that the standard deviation can be referred to as nothing more than a unit of length along the normal distribution. This definition isn't complete yet, but as we go along, we'll make it more complete. But for right now, I want you to remember that the standard deviation is a unit of length along the normal curve and consists of one-sixth of the distance of the curve.

In our society we may measure length in units of inches, millimeters, centimeters, meters, miles, or whatever unit of length you're interested in. In statistics, when we measure the length from the average of the normal distribution, we use the unit called the standard deviation or sigma (the one-sixth distance). The majority of the normal curve consists of six standard deviations (or six sigma wide). I hope you'll find this easy, because statistics really is quite simple. Remember that this will be the foundation of your knowledge, so make sure you feel comfortable with this description of a standard deviation. By now you should feel comfortable with what a normal distribution is and also what a standard deviation is. Of course you should also feel comfortable with what an average is (located at the longest line on the normal distribution). In this case, the average is right in the middle of the curve at its highest point. Let's move on to the next illustration to cover this in greater detail.

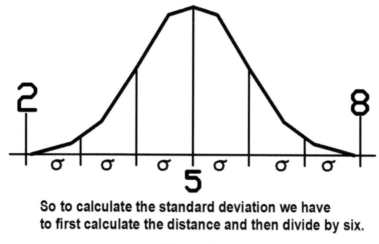

**So to calculate the standard deviation we have
to first calculate the distance and then divide by six.**

Figure 25

To calculate the standard deviation, we have to first calculate the distance along this normal curve and then divide it by six. This will give us the value of the standard deviation—at least for this particular curve. Calculating distances is very common in statistics, so we're going to spend a little bit of time on how to calculate distances. This is going to be very simple for most of you. The reason we're going over it is because we want to remind you how simple it is to calculate distances. Later it will help you understand statistical formulas conceptually, which is very important if you are going to get good at organizational transformation.

Many times in statistics we just memorize formulas without really understanding what the formula is and what it's trying to do or what it's telling us. In this book I want you to understand the formulas, not just memorize them. You must understand what the formulas are and why they are what they are, and you must understand them in depth. Fortunately for all of us, this is rather simple. As you'll see in the next illustration, the distance calculation is extremely simple. But hang with me. After only a couple more illustrations you will be ready to move on into a greater study of statistics and organizational transformation.

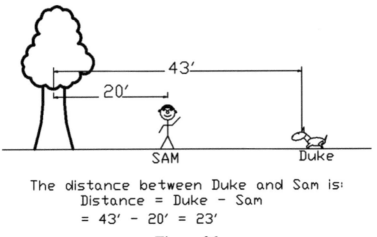

The distance between Duke and Sam is:
Distance = Duke – Sam
= 43' – 20' = 23'

Figure 26

This illustration shows an example problem. We want to calculate the distance between the boy named Sam and the dog named Duke. How do we find that distance? Well, it's very simple. To find the distance between two points, you simply subtract the value of those two points. So in this case, the distance between Duke and Sam is the distance that Duke is away from the tree, which is 43 units, minus the distance that Sam is away from the tree, which is 20 units. So the distance between Duke and Sam equals 43 minus 20, or 23 units. We spend a lot of time in statistics calculating distances between two points.

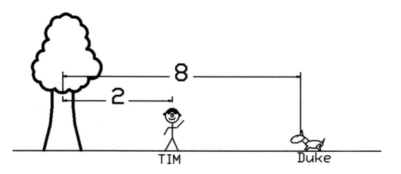

Calculate the distance between Tim and Duke.

Figure 27

Here's another example: In this one, Tim is 2 units away from the tree and Duke is 8 units away from the tree. What is the difference between Tim and Duke? The distance between Tim and Duke is 8 minus 2 equals 6—pretty simple, huh? Let's move on to the next illustration.

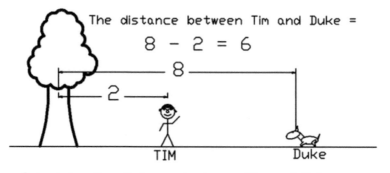

Calculate the distance between Tim and Duke.

Figure 28

Now we return to our normal distribution and a calculation of the value of the standard deviation. Now that you know how to calculate the distance between two points, you'll find this to be very simple. Before we move on, let's identify our two points at the end of the curve. That is, the value of 8 and the value of 2. We will call the 8 value the "upper control limit" and the 2 value "the lower control limit." We often abbreviate these as UCL for upper control limit and LCL for lower control limit. The upper and lower control limits are simply two points that describe the majority of the distance along the normal distribution.

The first thing we have to do in our calculation of the standard deviation is to calculate the distance between the upper control limit and lower control limit. How would we calculate this value? Remember that we're calculating a distance, and when we calculate a distance, we simply subtract the value of the two numbers. The next illustration will calculate the distance between the upper and lower control limits.

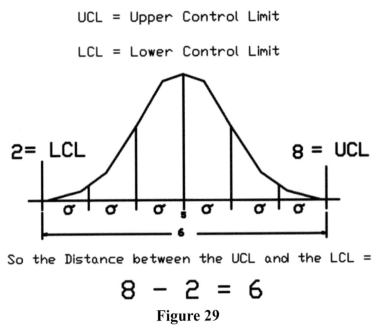

So the Distance between the UCL and the LCL =

$$8 - 2 = 6$$

Figure 29

To find the distance between the upper and lower control limits, we simply subtract the two values. Therefore, the distance between the upper and lower control limits will equal the upper control limit, which is 8, minus the value of the lower control limit, which is 2, so 8 minus 2 equals 6, and the distance between the upper and lower control limits is 6.

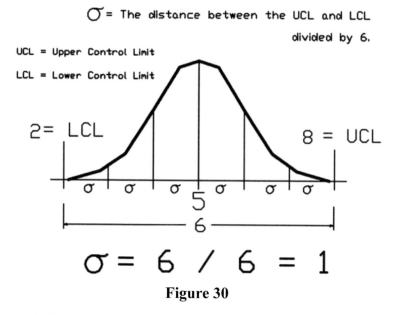

σ = The distance between the UCL and LCL divided by 6.

UCL = Upper Control Limit

LCL = Lower Control Limit

2= LCL   8 = UCL

$$\sigma = 6 / 6 = 1$$

Figure 30

And of course, there are also six standard deviations between the upper and lower control limits, so the value of the standard deviation, or sigma, equals the distance between the upper control limit and the lower control limit divided by 6. Why do we divide it by 6? Because 6 is the number of standard deviations between the upper and lower control limits. When we take that distance and divide it by 6, it gives us the value of the standard deviation. In this case, the standard deviation will equal the 6, which is the distance between the upper and lower control limits divided by 6, which is the number of standard deviations between the upper and lower control limits; therefore, the value of the standard deviation on this particular curve equals 1.

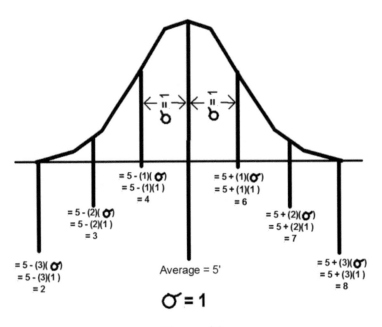

Figure 31

Now what if we take the average, 5, and add the value of one sigma to it (one sigma = 1) then the value of the first line, one sigma out, will be equal to $5 + 1 = 6$. Of course the second line (two sigmas away) to the right of the average will be equal to 7, and the third line will be equal to 8 as shown in the figure. To get the figures on the left side of the curve you simply subtract the value of sigma instead of adding it. Review the figure and make sure you understand the methodology before continuing.

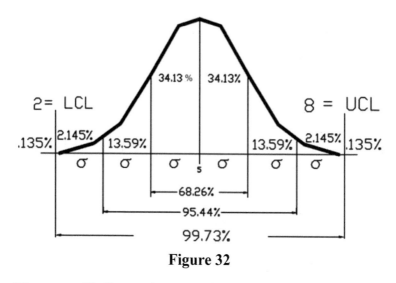

Figure 32

Now we will discuss in greater detail the nature of the normal distribution. Notice the curve shown in Figure 32. Note that the curve has been divided into six sectors of equal length, or sigma. Notice the first sector to the right of the average. That first sector is defined by one standard deviation length. Notice that the portion of the population covered in that sector is 34.13 percent of the population. The second sector out equals 13.59 percent of the population, and the third sector out equals 2.145 percent of the population. Notice also that this normal distribution is symmetrical. So the normal curve has the same shape whether you go to the right of the average or to the left. This is called a "symmetrical curve." Now all this information leads to this: if you go ± one standard deviation away from the average it will equal 68.26 percent of the population. If you go out ± two standard deviations you get 95.44 percent of the population. If you go out ± three standard deviations, you get 99.73 percent of the population. Notice that the percentage of the population that lies between the upper and lower control limits equals 99.73 percent. You should memorize this value, as we will refer to it often. Also notice that the interval between the upper and lower control limits doesn't consist of 100 percent of the population. In fact, the normal distribution is considered a continuous curve. Which means you cannot come up with two numbers that represent 100 percent of the population. The farther out you go from the average, the closer it will come to 100 percent of the population, but you can never reach it. Why? Theoretically, the normal distribution is a continuous curve. If you go out ± six sigma it will equal 99.9996 percent of the population.

I hope you feel comfortable with what you've read so far concerning the normal distribution. You should understand and feel comfortable with the shape of the normal distribution. You should also feel comfortable with the average. Remember that the average is the line of the greatest length and lies between the upper and lower control limits. And of course you should feel comfortable with the upper and lower control limits and in knowing that 99.73 percent of the population lies between the upper and lower control limits. You should also feel comfortable with the standard deviation. The standard deviation is simply one-sixth of the distance between the upper and lower control limits. You can look at the standard deviation as a unit of length. We use this unit to measure along the normal distribution all the time. In fact, you've probably heard of six sigma before. All that six sigma designates is that you're six standard deviations away from the average. Again, the standard deviation is used as a measure of length in statistics. Please don't move on with this book until you are very comfortable with all these concepts. If necessary, go back and read the material again. Read it repeatedly until you feel very comfortable with these concepts. Remember that this is the foundation of your understanding in the study of statistics. If you understand these principles, this information will be much easier to use in your organization and you'll be much more successful at organizational transformation. As soon as you feel comfortable, move forward with your studies.

Let's continue on with our discussion concerning the mechanics of increasing our "and" statement probabilities. Remember that every methodology has its limits in terms of potential. Per our previous discussions, PBP has a limited potential of approximately 95 percent. PBP is not the only methodology with limited potential. The methodology I am teaching you also has its limits. I don't know what they are, but someone out there, in future generations, will find the wall and he or she will have to figure out how to scale the wall when he or she finds him- or herself constrained by it.

As time goes along, the "and" statements continue to grow, so we have to keep increasing that probability of success just to sustain the original level of quality. When we get up to 99.73 percent, which is ± three sigma (it means the same thing), we will most likely still communicate in percentages instead of the number of sigma. But if the "and" statements kept going up, we'll start having more nines. So imagine this phone conversation: You call up your vendor and say, "What are you capable of?" He or she says, "Oh, we're capable of 99.99999 percent," and you say, "Oh, hold it … wait a minute! How many nines was that?" And then you start writing down the nines, and more than likely you'll write them down incorrectly—and remember that missing one nine can make a big difference when a lot of "and" statements are involved. In summary, the reason we speak in sigmas instead of percentages is mostly about the ease of communication. It is easier to communicate the number of sigmas than it is percentages, especially when you get a significant number of nines behind the decimal point. So eventually people say, "Hey, wait a minute, let's stop talking in percentages and start talking in sigmas instead." There's a direct relationship between the number of sigmas and the percentage. In fact, the number of sigmas you are away from something is called the "Z statistic."

What will the Z statistic be from the statement, "The spec limit is six sigma away from the average"? The answer to this question is that the Z statistic is six. The Z statistic is the number of sigmas the specification limits are away from the mean of the normal distribution. If I said, "I'm four sigma away from the average," then my Z statistic is four. And, of course, if I said, "My spec limit is two sigmas away from the average," then the Z statistic is two. So you just take the number of sigmas and cover up the sigma, and the number left over is called the Z statistic. The Z statistic is one of the most common statistics in the study of statistics. In fact, the Z table is usually the first thing you'll see in a statistics book. Sometimes they put it at the front of the book, and it's always the first table in the appendix. The Z table is simply a table that converts the number of sigmas (Z statistic) into the proportion or percentage of failure rate. So if you want to communicate in sigmas (Zs), because it is easier than percentages, but you need to know the percentage to perform some analysis, you can always go to the Z table to convert your sigma rating into a percentage. The key point here is to remember that we speak in terms of sigmas instead of percentages simply because it is easier, but in the end they are both communicating the same information.

Let's move forward and discuss the issue of how we improve our probability of success. Or, in other words, how do we improve our "and" statement probabilities?

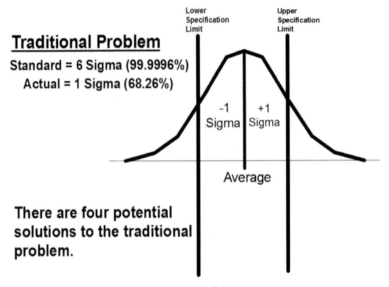

Figure 33

We will begin our discussion, on improving "and" statement probabilities by defining what I refer to as the "traditional problem." We will use Figure 33 to help describe the traditional problem. Notice that the normal distribution and the upper specification and lower specification limits are both one sigma away from the average. Which means this process is currently capable of a 68.26percent success rate on the "and" statements. Remember that the ± one sigma means a 68.26 percent success rate. So this is our process, and the customer says, "That's not good enough. Our standard is ± six sigma (99.9996 percent) and you are only ± one sigma (68.26 percent)." When people in process-improvement say six sigma, they really mean ± six sigma. Many people think that when we say six sigma, it means ± three. This is not correct. Six sigma means ± six sigma. Of course one sigma means ± one sigma unless stated otherwise.

So in this example the traditional problem is defined as follows: "They need me to build my 'and' statements at 99.9996 percent, or six sigma, and I'm only capable of 68.26 percent." Definitely a problem, which will be referred to as the "traditional problem" in this text. This traditional problem only has five potential solutions, and how difficult can it be if there are only five solutions? Let's move forward to the next illustration and discuss each one of these potential solutions.

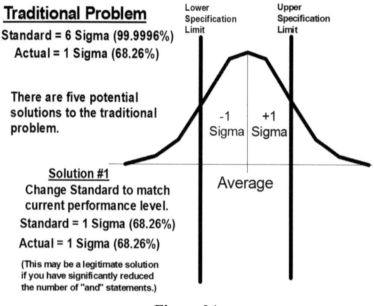

Figure 34

One of the solutions to this dilemma could be to just change the standard to match the current performance level. For example, if you're only capable of one sigma, let's change the standard to one sigma. Instead of six sigma, we'll do one sigma. While this isn't traditionally the way things work, it is a legitimate solution if you ever get in a situation where you're able to significantly reduce the number of "and" statements. When that happens, you can reduce the standard without negatively impacting product performance. This isn't traditionally what happens, because, as we have discussed, over time the assumption was that the "and" statements would go exponential, and that is a good assumption. That's how things have been going, and I'm sure they're going to continue to go that way into the future, which forces us to improve our probability. However, there are some instances in history where the opposite has happened, where the "and" statements have actually been reduced with new technologies.

One example is that when the computer first came on the scene, manufacturers built the computer with vacuum tubes. These vacuum tubes had a lot of "and" statements in them, and those "and" statements weren't really reliable. As a result, not everyone could afford a computer. However, as time moved on, people invented new technologies and ultimately came up with the transistor, which effectively reduced the number of "and" statements. Of course the transistor was also smaller, allowing me to write this book on my laptop while sitting in an airplane that is taking me around the world. So consider Solution #1. This may be a legitimate solution if you have significantly reduced the number of "and" statements. This is not a very common solution to the problem, one of those once-in-a-lifetime experiences. However, if you do discover and own technology that allows you to effectively implement Solution #1, you will most likely own the competition in that market sector. As a minimum, when you are designing processes and products you should always attempt to minimize the number of "and" statements while meeting the project objectives. If you go through a process of improvement, you should always ask yourself, can we reduce the number of "and" statements and still reach the project objectives? Can we make our processes simpler? If you do, your processes will become more robust and the overall probability of success will be higher.

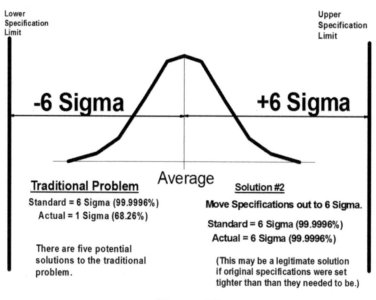

Figure 35

Now let's move on to Solution #2. Remember the traditional problem is that we are not capable of meeting the customer's standard. So in this particular example, we were at ± one sigma and the standard is ± six sigma. So why not, for Solution #2, just move the specifications out to six sigma? Remember that sigma is nothing more than a distance, so if I'm out one sigma right now, why not just move my specs out to six sigma? Thus our standard is still six sigma and we've moved our specification limits out to a distance of six sigma. This makes our actual performance six sigma or an "and" statement probability of 99.9996%. This may be a legitimate solution if the original specifications were set tighter than they needed to be. In reality this is more common than not. I went to a client once who said, "Hey, we have a machine out here that's generating hundreds of thousands of dollars' worth of scrap every month, and we need to find out what's wrong." They thought the people were doing something wrong, so I was hired to perform a capability study. Performing a capability study involves collecting data and calculating the sigma rating of the process, or the probability of success. I found the process was approximately ± one sigma and their standard was six sigma. In other words, the client was throwing away 30 to 40 percent of their product at a cost of over a hundred thousand dollars per month. The problem was rather simple—they cut metal parts to a certain length and the specification limits on this cut length was ± .005. My first instinct was that the specification limits were set unrealistically tight. I calculated that if they could move their spec limits from ± .005 to ± .125 they could meet the six sigma standard.

They thought that we were crazy, and I don't blame them. This was a huge change in specification limits. They said, "Engineering will never change those spec limits, and if you go over there you'll lose credibility and you'll be the laughingstock of this organization." Well, I'm a consultant and by definition I am a temporary employee anyway. On top of that, I don't necessarily get scared of getting laughed at, so I called up engineering and asked them if I could come over and discuss this issue with them. They let me come over, and when I explained the situation and told them that they were throwing away hundreds of thousands of dollars' worth of potentially good parts every month and that if we could just change the specs from ± .005 to ± .125, the problem would go away, to my amazement, no one laughed at me. Surprisingly enough, the head engineer looked at me and said, "John, we don't care what the specification limits are, all we do is send this product off to the customers and they re-cut it to length anyway. So if you want it to be ± .125, no problem." So I, per their procedure, had them redline the drawings, and I took them back to the plant manager, put them on his desk, and said, "Problem solved." And it was! So this was, of course, a problem where there was a little bit of miscommunication between production and engineering, which isn't that uncommon. Solution #2 becomes a legitimate solution to a problem when the specifications were set too tight in design. Solution #2 should be considered one of the first potential solutions. Why? If Solution #2 is legitimate it will be the least expensive solution to implement. I've used solution #2 in several situations and as a result saved organizations a massive amount of money. I have saved organizations more money with Solution #2 than any of the other solutions. What is the root cause of this type of problem? Like most problems it is a lack of communication. In this situation it was ineffective communication between production and design engineering. Typically organizations like to blame this problem on design engineers (PBP). In reality the problem is a system problem.

Traditionally we solve this problem by implementing a database that allows the design engineer to look up what the specification limits should be to meet the organization's standard, which is based on similar processes that are currently generating data. So when engineering designs a product, they can type up what they are designing and get information from the process that says, "You know, we have a six sigma standard here, and to get six sigma, you must design this product to, in our example, ± .125." The engineer says, "Can I make this work over that range of variability and still be successful with the customer?" In my example, they could have done that. If the information had been available, engineering would have said, "Okay, we have a six sigma standard that we have to design to, and that means we have to set the specs at ± .125, even though traditionally we set them at ± .005." Before they ever got started, they could have designed the product with those specification limits and saved the company a massive amount of money. Often engineering can do that, but they don't always know what the specs need to be. I know, because I was a design engineer once, and there were some specs that weren't that important and I could design around that range of variability if I knew what that range of variability needed to be. A lot of people talk about this, designing to standards, but hardly anyone does it, and it's a shame. Because you'll find that Solution #3 takes significantly more time and money to implement. If you don't use Solution #1 or #2, then Solution #3 will most likely be the only solution left. You're much better off solving this problem in design than you are in manufacturing, because it is usually significantly less expensive. So Solution #2 is an excellent solution to the problem, especially if it's performed at the design engineering stage.

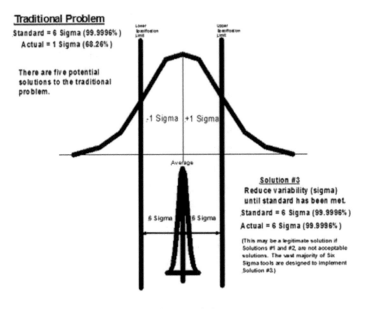

Figure 36

Let's move on to Solution #3. Remember that we have five solutions to solve the common or traditional problem. The traditional problem is that our performance level does not meet the standard. So an example of Solution #3 would be as follows. You call up and say to your customer, "Can I change the spec limits?" which is Solution #2, and they say, "No, you can't change the spec limits. The machine will not run if you exceed those spec limits." So the doors to Solution #1 and #2 are closed and you are left with Solution #3. Solution #3 is implemented when changing standards or specification limits is not an option. Instead we reduce variability (reduce the value of sigma). We do this by reducing the width of the curve. Remember that sigma is one-sixth the distance of the width of the normal distribution. So we need to reduce the width of the distribution until the one-sixth distance of the curve is so small that we can fit six sigmas between the distribution average and the specification limit. In the process-improvement industry it is called "reducing variability." That's Solution #3: reduce variability or sigma until the standard has been met. If you give me a couple of spec limits, I can easily calculate what sigma needs to be to meet those standards ((USL – LSL)/12), and then you can send out your six sigma black belt and have him or her run intelligently designed experiments until he or she reduces variability to a point that the standard is met. Now this is the most traditional solution to the problem in the world of the six sigma business strategy. The majority of tools used in the six sigma business strategy are designed to help with Solution #3. Solution #3 is one of the more common solutions to the traditional problem in most six sigma organizations. But I have a problem with it, because if you look at all your "and" statements, they have probably all been designed outside of the standards. The problem with Solution #3 is that it traditionally takes around four to six months to finish one "and" statement project. Let's assume you have ten thousand "and" statements and none of them meet the standard. This is not uncommon; actually, most companies don't even have a standard, which usually means they are operating at between one and three sigma. If you are trying to make quality your competitive advantage, one of the first things you need to do is to set a standard. Without a standard you cannot perform the math necessary to solve the traditional problem, which means you won't solve the traditional problem. If your engineering department does not design to standards, then they are most likely mass-producing projects for Solution #3, which can be like mopping the floor with the water faucet turned on full blast. This has never made sense to me, but the actions of companies around me suggest that this makes perfect sense to everyone else.

If engineering is not designing things to standard and you're trying to reduce variability with all of your "and" statements in an effort to meet a standard then you may be busy for quite some time. Before you implement such a strategy let's perform some basic math. If you have ten thousand "and" statements and each "and" statement takes an average six months for Solution #3, then you have five thousand years' worth of work, and you may not live long enough to reach the standard. I would suggest that a better approach is to use Solution #2 at the design engineering level of your organization. If the engineer cannot make the product work at the recommended specification, he or she should try a different design. If it still doesn't work, then as a last option I would use Solution #3. But the solution would be performed at the design engineering level before being released to production. The inherent variability (the normal distribution) of a product is a by-product of the design of that product, so if you are going to fix the problem it needs to be implemented in design. Most organizations try to implement Solution #3 at the production level without ever considering a change in design (problem source). Trying to fix a problem as far away from the source as possible has never made sense to me. This is a very expensive way to run a business. Too many organizations try to solve everything with Solution #3, and you'll quickly find out that you do not have enough resources to use Solution #3 on everything in most organizations. Don't get me wrong—I love performing Solution #3. I'm an engineer, and I am truly passionate about running experiments and crunching data to discover "gold mines" in process-improvement exercises. But I cannot, in good conscience, recommend financial suicide to my client. Solution #3 should be used but only when all other solutions are not capable of meeting the standard, and if possible this problem solving should be performed before releasing to production. This does not mean that design engineering runs the experiments, as they likely are not equipped with enough resources. I would suggest relocating process-improvement talent from the production floor to design engineering, but only after they are educated in such a way that allows them to succeed in such an environment. (Study topics such as Taguchi philosophies and design for six sigma methodologies.)

Now let's review Solution #3 one more time. Solution #3 is to reduce variability or sigma until the standard has been met. So if your standard is six sigma, then you reduce variability until you can reach the six sigma standard. This may be a legitimate answer if Solution #1 and Solution #2 are not acceptable. The vast majority of six sigma tools are designed to implement Solution #3 in the production process.

With all that being said, Solution #3 is the preferred solution. If I had a magic wand I would always solve the traditional problem with Solution #3 because this solution allows more of the product to be built at target value. Engineers design machines and processes to run best at target value. Japan has spent from 1950 to the present implementing Solution #3 into its automobile industry and, to a great extent, took over the marketplace due to their higher-quality automobiles.

If your organization has the drive and character necessary to make Solution #3 a reality it will serve you well. The reality of the situation is that most organizations do not, and that is why I promote the implementation of other solutions first. Ideally the easier solutions, Solutions #2 and #4 (to be discussed later), are intermediate steps to "stop the bleeding" and thus free up time to allow Solution #3 to be implemented. Japan spent approximately thirty years on Solution #3 before it was recognized as a competitive advantage by consumers and other members of the US automotive industry.

Now we will discuss Solution #4. Like Solution #2 (changing specifications), Solution #4 is potentially quick, easy, and inexpensive to implement. Solution #4 is simply centering the process.

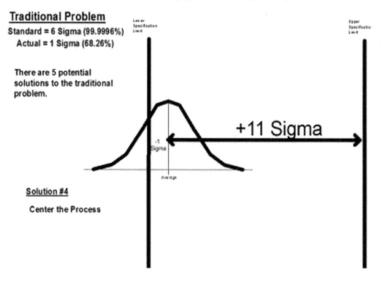

Figure 37

Figure 37 shows an example where Solution #4 would be a legitimate solution to the traditional problem. Notice that there is an eleven sigma distance from the average to the upper specification limit but only one sigma distance from the average to the lower specification limit. Often people in the process-improvement industry would call this a one sigma process or a Cpk of .333 (one Cpk unit = three sigma). Cpk is always the lower distance between the average and the upper specification limit or the distance between the average and the lower specification limit. The next figure shows how Solution #4 solves the traditional problem.

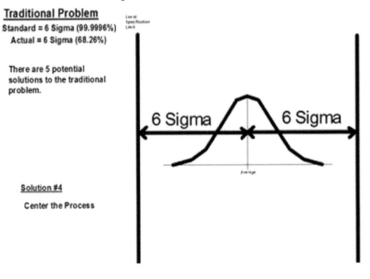

Figure 38

Now let's go on and discuss Solution #5 to our traditional problem. Solution #5 is definitely the easiest to implement; however, the results may not be what you would like. Solution #5 is to do nothing. In other words, you don't meet standards and you have no desire to meet standards; in fact, you don't even have a standard—you've hit the wall, you're not going to transform because you don't know how, and you're going to do absolutely nothing except patiently wait for extinction to take you to a better world. Solution #5 is the solution that most organizations subscribe to, and most readers will quietly recognize that they most closely follow Solution #5. In summary, Solution #5 is not one I would recommend.

Now that I have vented my frustrations through sarcasm let me define the true Solution #5. Unfortunately it is not much more effective than what I just described. The real Solution #5 is to reach the standard through inspection. So you say, "Okay, I need to get to 99.9996 percent and I am currently at one sigma (64.26 percent). This is a real problem. I know how I will solve the problem! I will just inspect the product until I deliver a 99.9996 percent good parts. Problem solved." The problem is that this solution is going to cost you approximately 10 to 20 percent of your production cost and you are working in an industry with a 5 percent profit margin. Do the math. I would estimate that approximately 97 percent of organizations choose Solution #5 because the other solutions will make no sense if you consider that all of your problems are coming from the people and not the system.

Organizations that feel their system is perfect and the only reason the system fails is because of the people who are supposed to support the system have failed. I refer to this as "people are subordinate to the system" or "people-constrained." Most organizations are "people-constrained" and "people-constrained" organizations will gravitate toward PBP (personify, blame, and punish) and the ultimate potential of a "people-constrained" organization, on "and" statement probability, is approximately 95 percent. A "people-constrained" organization will spend their budget on trying to improve organizational performance by improving the people. The problem with this is no one has ever determined how much money it takes to make people 99.9996 percent perfect simply because it has never taken place on a consistent basis. Remember 99.9996 percent is the probability of success we must have to survive in a high "and" statement, low— profit margin industry.

The alternative to a "people-constrained" organization is a "system-constrained" organization. A "system-constrained" organization sees that the purpose of the system is to support the needs of the people instead of the people being there to support the system. A "system-constrained" organization will spend their budget on improving the system. To do this, of course, they teach the people how to improve systems instead of how to improve themselves.

The logic that explains why "system-constrained" organizations consistently outperform "people-constrained" organizations is that imperfect people can create nearly perfect systems but imperfect systems cannot create perfect people. Most organizations will try to create perfect people with imperfect systems. Let me help you save some time – it does not work. The quicker you transform to a "system-constrained" organization the quicker you will be able to create and sustain improvement.

In the process-improvement industry solution #5 is called "inspecting quality into the product" instead of designing it in.

Solution #5 is also bad because, contrary to Solution #3, it does not promote building parts closer to the target value. In the 1980s the American automotive industry was heavily invested in Solution #5 and the Japanese automotive industry was equally invested into Solution #3. This is why the Japanese automotive industry created cars in the 1980s that would go 300,000+ miles without significant problems and the American automotive industry created cars that would only go 100,000 miles with significant repairs along the way. This is why they lost massive amounts of market share. The automotive industry was fortunate; many American industries were lost altogether to the competitive Solution #3 model. The important thing to remember here is that building parts at target value allows machines to run better and longer and makes the customers happier. This rule of thought will be amplified as the "and" statements continue to grow exponentially.

I have spent a lot of time talking about manufacturing processes; however, these principles apply equally to support functions such as accounting, finance, marketing, purchasing, etc., as well as the service industry at large. The difference between manufacturing and support functions, as well as the service industry is that the manufacturing operations is easy to physically observe and has specification limits on the "and" statements. Support functions and the service industry are difficult to observe. For example, have you ever watched an accounting operation and tried to figure out, through observation, what was happening? It is difficult to watch operations flow through computer systems. However, you can make this work visible by using a tool called "flow charting." What is left is putting specification limits on time, and once you add these two elements, flow charting and specification limits on time, to support and service functions, then all the tools used in process-improvement can be applied to support functions as well. Once these two ingredients are applied you will potentially witness exponential gains in productivity in these important processes. I say potentially because it will only work if you follow the rules of transformation outlined later in this book. Without knowledge of these rules and the correct implementation of these rules, placing specification limits on time will only create a revolution from discontented employees. All the principles that have been discussed or will be discussed in the book are equally valid in manufacturing, support functions, and the service industry.

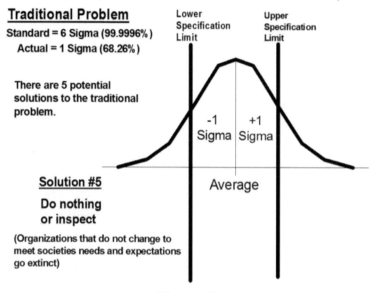

Figure 39

I hope you enjoyed and learned some new principles from our discussion of the five solutions. Remember that the most desired solution to increasing our probability on the "and" statements is to reduce variability. That is a key concept. So as we reduce variability, our probability of success goes up.

Let's think back and do a root-cause analysis on why many companies have had such a difficult time in, for example, gaining market share. Historically, the American automotive industry started losing market share to the Japanese automotive industry (Toyota) until Toyota ultimately gained so much market share that it outsold the giant General Motors. During the time period of the pre-1980s, you would have never thought that could have happened. If you go back and say, "Why? Why did that happen? Why did General Motors lose so much market share to Toyota?" there are several reasons. The biggest reason is Solution #3, but one of the reasons the Japanese manufacturer believed in Solution #3 was the cost model for quality.

Taguchi vs. Traditional Loss Function

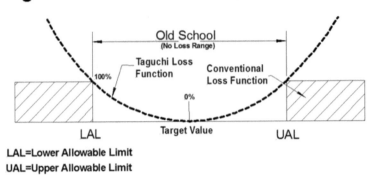

LAL=Lower Allowable Limit
UAL=Upper Allowable Limit

Figure 40

Figure 40 is a representation of the Taguchi Loss Function vs. the traditional or the American Loss Function. The Japanese cost model is shown as a dotted line. The American cost model is everything but the dotted line. Both of these models use the "target value." Now let me ask you a review question. Where do engineers desire manufacturing to build their designs? Of course given that all options are open, the design engineers would prefer to have their product designed to target value. Let me tell you why. If you can build the design to target value, the machine will run much better. The American cost model for quality said, "A part at target value is equal in value to a part that is built next to a specification limit (further away from target), and furthermore the only time production experiences the cost of poor quality (cost greater than zero) is when the specification limit is violated." We call them "spec limits," but Taguchi called them "allowable limits." Per the cost model shown in the previous figure, you will notice those cross-hatch sections, which show that the cost jumps up—usually the cost of the products being produced. And so America would operate this way and management would say, "Hey, you want higher 'and' statement probabilities? No problem—we'll just inspect the bad products out." As a result, we ended up with much more variability about the target value. This American cost model gave no motivation toward reducing variability (Solution #3). Now look at the dotted line in the previous figure. The Japanese cost model (dotted line), which they called the Taguchi Loss Function, said that "as soon as you deviate from target value, the cost of poor quality goes up exponentially." The Japanese said, "As soon as we deviate from target value, we violate our customer's trust." And furthermore, "the only way we can experience zero cost of poor quality is by always hitting target value." The Americans felt the only way to have zero cost of poor quality, from the customers' perspective, was to inspect out all the parts that violated specification limits. This ended up costing approximately 20 percent of the cost of making the product. Solution #3 demands little inspection if any at all.

That's the way the Japanese automotive industry saw things, and that mentality forced them to think about reducing variability, because if you reduce variability, you create more product closer to target value. So that's what they did. And ultimately the Toyota cars would go 300,000+ miles in the 1980s. The American automobile would go 80,000–100,000 miles and would vibrate and blow smoke all the way to the salvage site. Why? Because the Japanese cars were built with less variability about the target value, and the machines were designed to operate best at target value. In summary, the Americans tried to inspect quality into the product (Solution #5) and Japan designed quality into their processes and products in an effort to reduce variability about the target value (Solution #3). In the pre-1980s, American companies did not have quality departments; they had inspection departments. As a result the Japanese automobile cost less money to build and lasted longer with fewer problems along the way. Japan also used fewer "and" statements on those 1980 automobiles compared to the massive "bells and whistles" or "and" statements found on and within the American automobile.

The Americans were slow to pick up on this new vision of creating wealth. I have been told on occasion that I come across as being too mean to American manufacturing. I would be doing a great disservice to those companies that sincerely desire to become old companies if I were to sugarcoat the past. Also keep in mind that you're doing a great disservice to your company, to your employees, to the community, and to your stockholders when you use the traditional cost model (that promotes Solution #5 instead of Solution #3). We need to look at it like the Japanese automotive industry did—the instant you deviate from target value, you're costing your stakeholders money. If you do this, your mentality will not be to inspect quality in but to build quality into the product and process, which will reduce variability, one of the definitions of quality. To create quality, you reduce variability. The Japanese figured that out in the 1950s, and we didn't start to figure it out until the 1980s. With all that being said, we'll go back to our original model.

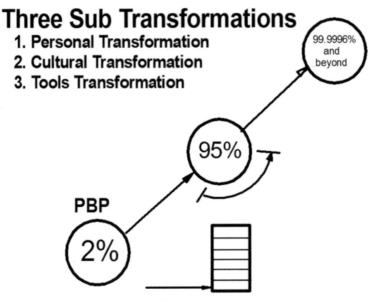

Figure 41

Three subtransformations are necessary to have a successful transformation: personal transformation, cultural transformation, and tools transformation. The previous discussion concerning the cost model would fall most closely under the category of tools transformation.

The next topic we will discuss is the importance of cultural transformation. I'm not necessarily going to tell you how to change culture or even what a good culture looks like (at this time). The objective of this discussion is just to help you understand the importance of the cultural transformation and what is necessary for it to take place.

Galileo Galilei

Three Sub Transformations
1. Personal Transformation
2. *Cultural Transformation*
3. Tools Transformation

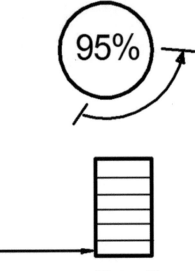

Figure 42

Let's look at Figure 42 and give you some case study examples of why cultural transformation is necessary. Let's look back to an important event in history. I definitely think February 15, 1564, was an important event in history, and that was the birth date of a gentleman named Galileo Galilei. He was an objective thinker and became a champion of heliocentric cosmology, which displaced the earth from the center of the universe.

Back then it was the popular belief that the earth was the center of the universe, which meant the most important part of the universe, and that everything else rotated around the earth. That was very much a part of the culture back then, until heliocentric cosmology said, "No, wait a minute, not everything rotates around the earth. In fact, everything rotates around the sun, including the earth." Now this was not a very popular thought to have at that time. But Galileo was one of those people who felt that the earth was not the center of the universe, a result of what he saw through the lens of his telescope.

He had visual evidence that this was the case as he viewed out into our galaxy. If I remember correctly he saw Jupiter and the moons rotating around Jupiter, and that was enough evidence for him to become a champion of heliocentric cosmology.

The zealots of the day did not agree with Galileo's heliocentric cosmology, and as a result he was put under house arrest, where his movements were restricted by the community leaders, who just happened to be the most powerful group of people in Europe. This is one of many examples where tools have to be supported by culture. The telescope was one of those tools. At the time, Galileo could see that heliocentric cosmology was correct, but the culture would not support the results of his use of that tool. On January 8, 1642, Galileo died.

Isaac Newton

The year after Galileo's death, another important event took place when, on January 4, 1643, a gentleman by the name of Isaac Newton was born. Isaac's father died before he was born, and his mother remarried shortly after the birth, leaving him to be raised by his grandparents. Eventually his stepfather died and his mother returned to raise Isaac.

Newton's mother desired that he become a gentleman farmer, which demanded that he go to grammar school, and he did. Initially there were no signs of genius, but then Isaac was given a book on mechanisms. After he was introduced to mechanisms, his genius blossomed for everyone to witness. Eventually it was time for Isaac to graduate from grammar school and become a gentleman farmer. Newton's grammar school teacher, whose name was Henry Stokes, was very passionate that Isaac should go on to college and leverage his genius to benefit society. Ultimately, Henry Stokes talked Isaac's mother into letting him go to college. Even though she couldn't afford to send him there, she gave her approval and Isaac worked his way through college.

Isaac Newton's time in college was temporarily cut short as a result of rumors that the bubonic plague had returned to his college campus. This was definitely something to be worried about. Earlier on, the bubonic plague had spread through Europe and wiped out half its population. Now, granted, this happened many years earlier than Isaac Newton's college days; however, the Europeans were still very concerned about the return of the plague. Remember that they didn't know what caused it and they didn't know what spread it. Today we know that, most likely, rats with fleas were brought in from other countries, and these fleas would jump around and bite people, which was pretty common back then, and as a result the people got the bubonic plague, and a high percentage of those who came in contact with it died. It was an ugly, painful death that destroyed approximately 50 percent of the population. This tragedy was still in the back of the minds of the Europeans, and the rumor of its recurrence ultimately shut down the campus and Isaac had to return home to his mother.

During this time, Isaac Newton experimented with mathematics and physics. He discovered the nature of light, gravity, and integral calculus. Isaac Newton was definitely, by every standard, a genius. Eventually Isaac returned to college and ultimately analytically proved heliocentric cosmology. In other words, he proved out in an objective fashion using mathematics that the world was not the center of the universe.

During the life of Isaac Newton, the culture was gradually changing. Due in part to this culture change, Isaac was never threatened with house arrest or any other punishment for his support of heliocentric cosmology. In fact, later on, Newton was knighted and became Sir Isaac Newton.

The point is that when you have tools that aren't supported by the culture, it can be very frustrating and very painful. You cannot have tools and expect the tools to work effectively unless you have a culture that supports them. Tools must be supported by an organizational culture, or the tools, again, will not work. No one gave this cultural transformation and its relationship to analytical tools a second thought until W. Edwards Deming realized the relationship and began teaching it to the Ford Motor Company in the early 1980s.

TOOLS must be supported by organizational culture or the tools will not work!!

Figure 43

The cultural relationship to analytical tools was a tremendously important discovery in the art and science of organizational transformation. Eventually W. Edwards Deming published his fourteen points, which helped Ford envision what a functional quality culture should look like – this was a culture that would support his quality tools; tools that were designed to reduce variability and increase the probability of success of the "and" statements.

Today, W. Edwards Deming is considered to be the founder of the "third wave of the Industrial Revolution." Deming is considered a hero in the art and science of organizational transformation. He was also one of the most prolific contributors toward tools transformation.

W. Edwards Deming   **Shigeo Shingo**

Shigeo Shingo was born some nine years after Deming and was a Japanese industrial engineer who was instrumental in creating the Toyota production system. Mr. Shingo was an outside consultant who taught industrial engineering classes to Toyota employees beginning around 1955. He is given credit for having created the poka-yoke system, which promotes the concept of looking at problems as system problems. Poka-yoke is often referred to as mistake-proofing, meaning to fix the system so we can exceed the 95 percent human barrier described in our earlier model.

Three Sub Transformations
1. Personal Transformation
2. ***Cultural Transformation***
3. Tools Transformation

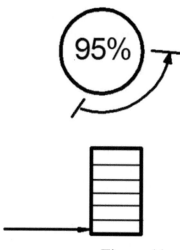

Figure 44

Here we are back at our model, and you should recognize the symbolism. Remember that you hit the wall, which takes place when your current methodologies are not capable of meeting society's needs, which results from an exponentially increasing number of "and" statements and also exponentially increased customer expectations. Remember that in our modern age of high "and" statements and high customer expectations 95 percent is no longer good enough, thus making organizational transformation an act of survival.

I hope you understand the importance of cultural transformation. Remember that if you do not have a culture that supports the tools, the tools will not work in your organization. I have never witnessed this rule being violated. Deming originally went to Japan and taught others about quality tools for Solution #3 (reducing variability). This was in the 1950s, and we'll talk in greater detail about this later. In the early 1950s Japan had a tendency to look at problems as system problems, so when Deming took his tools over there, the businesses naturally flourished. As a result, Deming, an American, spent most of his career in Japan, teaching them how to reduce variability.

When Deming was about eighty years old, the American automotive industry started "crying wolf," and Deming went to America and started teaching Americans about these same tools. And guess what—the tools didn't work. From our discussion you should know why. Deming figured it out; it was because the culture did not support the tools. So Deming went back and compared the US business culture to the Japanese business culture and came up with fourteen points. These fourteen points, at least from my perspective, describe what a functional organizational culture looks like. By a quality culture I mean one that will support the quality tools that allows Solution #3 (reducing variability) to be effective.

An important thing to keep in mind here is that changing organizational culture is very difficult. Most organizations that fail at organizational transformation fail because they are incapable of changing culture. It's a very difficult task. There have been people in the past who have changed culture, but more often than not they get assassinated! Yes, many people who start transforming organizations or countries or cultures end up getting assassinated. I think Abraham Lincoln can be classified as one of those people. He desired to end the practice of slavery, and of course the Civil War broke out, which was very ugly. Abraham Lincoln had a very difficult time. His wife was going insane, his kids were dying of alcoholism, and no one necessarily wanted to be around him at the White House. Even though we celebrate him as a success today, that isn't necessarily how he was seen by everyone back then. I feel that the following story is a good reflection of his difficulties. One day as he was going home from his work of being president, he was going through the woods when suddenly someone shot the hat off his head. If that happened today there would be secret service agents jumping all over him and pulling him from harm's way. In his day that just wasn't the case. After getting his hat shot off he just got off his horse, bent down and got his hat, dusted it off, put it back on, got back on his horse, and trotted away. To me that suggests he was saying, "The next time, shoot a little bit lower." What I am attempting to convey is that this thing I refer to as organizational transformation is very difficult; it will always be very difficult for leaders to change the culture. The definition of culture is how an organization acts out on its value system. When you start messing around with an organization's value system, watch out, because things can quickly become violent. However, there is a difference between difficult and impossible. If you do not understand the rules of transformation, then transformation is impossible. If you understand the rules and are capable of implementing them, then it is not impossible but still difficult. Of course in modern-day corporations you are not going to be seeing a lot of assassinations. However, I will say the corporate equivalent to assassination is termination. This is one reason transformation must originate and be supported at the highest level of the organization. If you try to transform an organization from the middle of the organization, you are highly likely to get terminated. Either way you look at it, organizational transformation is difficult and risky due to the element of cultural transformation.

As we all know, Abraham Lincoln ultimately got assassinated for his attempts at changing the culture of America. It is not unusual that when a leader goes about changing culture, especially within societies, assassination is the end result. As difficult as leadership is, leadership is the most important element in a successful transformation. Since leadership is so important, we should come up with a specific definition of what leadership is in this strange world of organizational transformation. In the world of transformation leadership is defined as follows: leadership is the ability to change culture.

One of the first rules of transformation is this: *leadership dictates culture.* So in the world of transformation, if you are called a leader but cannot change culture, then you are a leader in name only. Transformation cannot take place without leadership.

It comes down to this: if you don't like the culture in your organization and you are the leader of the organization, then the first place you need to go to see the source of the problem is to the mirror, because problems with culture lie at the feet of leadership. If no one takes ownership for culture, then cultural transformation will be impossible. Remember that in the world of transformation, if you are called a leader but cannot change culture, then you are a leader in name only. True leadership is a lot to ask of a person, so I hope this doesn't sound overly critical—what I am trying to do is be realistic in hopes that I can teach leaders how to be effective at organizational transformation.

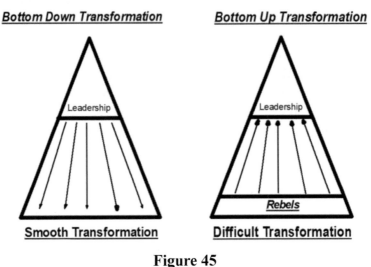

Bottom Down Transformation   **Bottom Up Transformation**

Smooth Transformation   **Difficult Transformation**

Figure 45

There are two general methodologies to create this transformation. One is called "top-down transformation," and the other is called "bottom-up transformation." In top-down transformation, executive-level individuals lead the transformation. Of course, you must have leaders capable of changing culture. If you have effective leadership, then you'll have a relatively smooth transformation, assuming you follow the rules of transformation. On the other hand, you could choose bottom-up transformation. In the vast majority of situations this would be a very poor choice, because bottom-up transformation does not work very well. For example, there was a time when I was helping a military organization with transformation by teaching transformation classes; I taught them the importance of top-down transformation. Eventually a leader came in and announced to the crowd of students that he wanted a transformation from the bottom up—which was obviously contrary to the information I was teaching. He obviously had not attended the class, and it didn't create a very good situation for the transformation. So I ask you the reader, "Do you know what historians call transformation from the bottom up?" Historians call transformation from the bottom up revolutions. Revolutions are bloody, they're violent, they're ugly, and they are seldom successful. In summary, top-down transformation is preferred over bottom-up transformation simply because we desire to improve the odds of transformation. The seeds of revolution (transformations from the bottom up), takes place when the lower levels of the organization are creating a more inspiring vision of the future than the leaders at the top. So when the more inspiring visions are being authored at the bottom of the organization, seeds of revolution are being sown. In other words, the source of revolution is ineffective leadership.

Most managers will not tolerate rebels leading a transformation, which is why revolutions tend to become violent. There is a part of me that wishes that bottom-up transformation could have higher success rates, but in reality they do not, and in something as important as organizational transformation, or organizational survival, we must be realistic. I know that when we study history we always study the successful revolutions, which can give us a false sense of security that revolutions are usually successful. The fact of the matter is that if you dig a little deeper, you'll find that revolutions are usually unsuccessful, and they are bloody and violent in every way. In the world of transformation we would rather have a top-down transformation. There is a choice if leadership gives the organization an inspiring and motivating vision of the future. If leadership cannot fulfill this need, then the seeds of revolution will be sown and evidence of these seeds will become visible within the organization.

In summary, people at the top of the pyramid must have a vision that motivates and inspires the organization. When people at the base of the organization grow tired of a stagnant existence they will naturally start creating a bigger and more motivating vision than those at the top of the organization. That's when you create the environment for a transformation from the bottom up to take place. I guess there's another lesson to learn here, that leadership must also be visionary—at least more visionary than the people at the base of the organization. If they're not, you're going to have a revolution. Revolution is the result of ineffective leadership. Leadership is a heavy responsibility, and when it fails, organizations fall and people experience problems of epic proportions. The nature of human beings is that they have to have hope in the future; if leadership can't provide it, then they will come up with it on their own and topple the powers that be, if necessary. History suggests that the desire for hope is a powerful force to reckon with. Hope is the fuel of effective transformation. Leaders who attempt to lead without hope will eventually fall from power.

Leadership will ultimately change culture. It is just a question of where leadership resides within the organization. In our transformation model the proverbial wall is analogous to cultural change. The wall is assumed to be very strong and difficult to knock down. The first step in weakening the wall is to understand the nature of the wall. The wall is constructed from bricks and mortar, and the mortar is made up of fear and ignorance. One way to weaken the mortar and thus weaken the wall in this transformation is to educate your people about transformation. Effective education reduces the ignorance level, and by reducing the level of ignorance, fear goes down. So, through education backed by leadership, we can weaken the wall enough so that when leadership decides it's time for change, it can knock the wall down, which is ultimately leadership's responsibility.

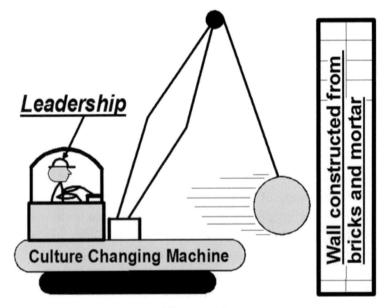

Figure 46

CHAPTER TWO

THE DEMING STORY

You may recall from the previous chapter that transformation is defined as evolving to a higher level of sustained performance.

You may also remember this model—the transformation model—and that there must be three successful subtransformations to have a successful organizational transformation. These include personal transformation, cultural transformation, and tools transformation.

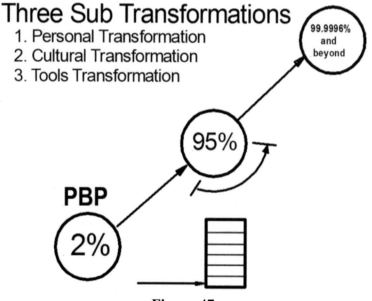

Figure 47

This chapter will concentrate on the second subtransformation, cultural transformation. The fundamental objective of this chapter is to teach you what a functional organizational culture looks like. I have never been to a family counselor, although some may argue that I should have. I would suspect that when you go into a family counselor for help, one of the first things he or she does is show you what a functional family looks like. In effect this is what W. Edwards Deming did for corporate America in the early 1980s. This chapter will go into the details of what I call the "Deming story." Ultimately you will see that corporate America did not have an organizational culture that would support the analytical tools that Deming successfully used to transform the Japanese business environment, which began in the early 1950s. With this problem at hand Deming created his fourteen points, which defined what a functional organizational culture looked like. As you read through Deming's fourteen points, ask yourself how well your organization lives up to the "functional culture" described by Deming. If your company lives up to these standards, then your organizational culture is most likely capable of supporting the analytical tools necessary to improve your "and" statement probabilities.

The Deming story begins around World War II. World War II changed some of the motivators for businesses. Edwards Deming and his friend Walter Shewhart both worked in the manufacturing effort during the war. Shewhart created the first SPC, or statistical process control charts, which were used in process control. This process control was considered a revolutionary idea at the time. It looked at processes in a more systematic approach and would eventually consider Solution #3 as the preferred solution to the traditional problem.

After World War II, American manufacturers had to decide between product inspections (Solution #5) and process control (pre-Solution #3) as a tool to create quality products. The American industries chose to use product inspection (Solution #5) as their primary tool for creating quality products. We will see later that this proved to be a disastrous decision for the United States, and, for the record, Deming passionately disagreed with it. He felt that American manufacturers needed to reduce variability (Solution #3) in an effort to improve "and" statement probabilities. The American industries felt that they could inspect out bad parts and thus improve "and" statement probabilities of good products reaching the consumer

(Solution #5). These were two very diverse opinions on how to create wealth for society.

There is a saying out there that goes as follows: "If you don't learn from history you are destined to repeat it." So let's spend some time learning from history. W. Edwards Deming is important because he was the first person I could find, through my studies, who recognized the need for a cultural transformation. Another reason for studying the history of Dr. Deming is that most organizations ignored his message the first time around. I feel I could successfully argue that the only industry that really applied Deming's thoughts was the automotive industry. The only reason the automotive industry implemented Deming's philosophy is that if they hadn't they would have gone extinct. What made the automotive industry unique? The automotive industry was unique because they had a massive amount of "and" statements and a very thin profit margin. The competitive advantage the Japanese automotive industry had over the American automotive industry, in the early 1980s, was taught to them by Dr. W. Edwards Deming, and as a result the Japanese could build an automobile that cost $2,200 less and lasted three times longer than the American counterpart due in large part to the successful implementation of Solution #3 (reducing variability). It has been pretty popular as of late to talk about bringing manufacturing back to the United States. This may happen, but those jobs won't stay long if we don't learn and implement lessons taught from the past. This book was designed to teach businesses how to return better-paying jobs to America and to keep those jobs based on more competitive methodologies. If you think we can return jobs and perform those jobs with the same logic we used when we lost them, then you are by definition insane.

Dr. W. Edwards Deming was born on October 14, 1900. By 1928 he had earned a bachelor of science degree in engineering from the University of Wyoming in Laramie, a masters of science in mathematics and physics at the University of Colorado, and a PhD in mathematical physics at Yale. So Deming was a "brain child."

In 1951, he was sent to Japan as part of the reconstruction effort to help the Japanese with surveys. Deming was an expert on using statistical analysis in surveys. At the request of the secretary of war,

Dr. Deming helped prepare Japan for the census of 1951. Before arriving in Japan, he had already established his name in the United States as the expert on quality-control activities (Solution #3).

Several Japanese businessmen heard about Deming, and when he arrived in Japan he was asked to teach statistical courses to Japanese managers and scientists. Ultimately W. Edwards Deming became a national celebrity in Japan. The Japanese manufacturers have a graded national competition for quality and productivity improvements. They named the top honor in the competition "the Deming Prize" after W. Edwards Deming.

In 1980 the American automotive industry had hit the proverbial wall that we spoke of in our transformation model. The industry had experienced some rather exponential changes in "and" statements over a very short period of time, and its methodologies at that time—personify, blame, and punish—were not capable of supporting that many "and" statements.

In 1980, Deming's techniques, which he had taught to Japan, began to receive national attention. In June of 1980, Deming was featured on NBC TV in a documentary titled *If Japan Can—Why Can't We?* At that time, the general public was well aware that the Japanese built a better automobile. The American automobile, at that time, would go a hundred thousand miles and then start blowing smoke, and then it was time to throw it away. But the Japanese counterpart could go two hundred thousand to five hundred thousand miles with fewer problems.

The American public started to fall in love with Japanese reliability and quality, and they realized that the American way of life was under threat. By 1980 Japan had become a major competitor in the global marketplace. For example, in the automobile market, Japan was capable of creating a higher-quality, lower-cost car.

This cost advantage was the result of efficiency and tax advantages. However, the greatest advantage came from quality and efficiency improvements. For the first time in recent Japanese history, the Japanese found competitive advantage in competitive markets. The Japanese not only took market share due to their competitive advantage but also took the complete market away from other countries. This new competitive advantage was in great part due to the lessons taught by Deming. He taught more than just statistics. He taught a way of running businesses in an extremely competitive manner.

Deming's business philosophies were referred to as the "fourteen obligations of management." Now, let's go back a little bit. When Deming first started teaching these analytical methodologies to the Americans in the post–World War II environment, his philosophies didn't work as well as he thought they should, even though they had all the evidence of their success in Japan. It became obvious to Deming that there was a cultural problem in the US business sector. I think of Deming's fourteen points or fourteen obligations of management as a comparison of Japanese business culture with American business culture. You have to remember that Japan had the culture to support these tools, but when Deming came to America he realized that the American business culture was not capable of supporting the transformation. In reality Deming tried to implement these tools in the United States in the 1940s (war effort) and had great success, but after World War II, Deming records, "Process-improvement went up in a puff of smoke." This is why he left for a job in Japan. There is another rule of transformation that states "You stop becoming greater the instant you think you're great." When Deming came back to America in the 1980s (when he was eighty years old), he began teaching the Ford Motor Company his lessons.

Approximately thirty years after Deming started teaching his lessons to the Japanese, the American manufacturers started giving him recognition. His seminars were highly sought after for American managers. Now we will discuss Deming's fourteen points. I want you to look at these fourteen points as a comparison between Japanese business culture and American business culture. From my perspective Deming took the elements from the Japanese culture that he felt the Americans needed to implement into their culture for his tools to work (to make organizations capable of Solution #3). And what were his tools about? The objective of his analytical tools was to reduce variability.

Deming's first point says: *Create constancy of purpose toward improvement of product and service.* Let's stop there for a minute: create constancy of purpose. I feel that Deming thought something like, *When I was in Japan they'd make a decision to do something and they would stick to it until it was complete. I come over here and you guys decide to change organizational direction, so off you go, and you leave your original comfort zone and go out there a short distance until it feels uncomfortable, and when it feels uncomfortable you come running back and say, 'Well maybe we'll go to the left today instead of the right,' so you go to the left until it starts feeling uncomfortable; then you run back to your original comfort zone.* And pretty soon the people in the organization whisper, saying, "Don't follow him or her; this is just the flavor of the month—don't worry, he or she will be back." And sure enough leadership always comes back seemingly being incapable of walking through the land of the uncomfortable and thus incapable of sustaining change. As a result there was a lack of trust in management. Let's read that again: create constancy of purpose toward improvement of products and service, with the aim to become competitive, stay in business, and provide jobs. This is the first of Deming's fourteen points.

In the world of transformation, there's a rule that you need to be aware of, and that is, "You'll never become greater than that which motivates you." And what motivated the American managers was their desire for short-term profits. They could not see beyond short-term profits, and that probably also created some problems in the world of "constancy of purpose."

So Deming's saying was "You need to come to work to provide jobs for the people." This was another way of saying you have to change your motives from short-term profits to providing jobs for the people. In Japan, there was a time when the country was having a recession and Mr. Toyoda had to have layoffs, and of course, the union didn't want layoffs, so there was a conflict going on within the Toyota organization, and ultimately Mr. Toyoda made them a promise. He said something to the effect of "I promise you that if you'll let me run this company and have these necessary layoffs, I will guarantee lifetime employment with Toyota from this day forward."

Most leaders couldn't pull that off as a plan to satisfy the unions, but you must understand that Mr. Toyoda was a very trustworthy man, and when he told you he was going to do something, you could bet on it. So the union said, "Okay, we believe you'll do that and we're okay with that," and they signed off on the contract. That may be a simplification of the actual situation, but you get the point. From that time forward, when Mr. Toyoda went to work, he went to work to provide jobs for the people. This had an impact on the Toyota Motor Company.

Remember—leadership dictates culture. So when Mr. Toyoda started going to work to provide jobs for the people, guess what. Pretty soon everyone was going to work to provide jobs for the people. Leadership dictates culture. When Deming showed up, that was the motive he was greeted with—that was the culture in Japan. And how did they ultimately create secure jobs for the Toyota employees? They provided secure jobs by implementing Solution #3 into the organizational culture, which resulted in eliminating a massive amount of inspection, nearly eliminated scrap, and created a higher-quality automobile that the world would ultimately demand. Japan's culture of management had constancy of purpose, and it went to work to provide jobs for the people. Deming did not see this motive of providing jobs for the people in the American management culture. Remember that an organization will never become greater than that which motivates it. Providing jobs for the people is a higher motive than short-term profits. So in Deming's first point he encouraged American industry to learn to stay the course, which made it necessary to walk through the land of the uncomfortable and change the company motives to the higher motive of creating jobs for the people.

Deming's second point is the following: *Adopt the new philosophy.* Part of the philosophy is to quit personifying, blaming, and punishing and start seeing problems as system problems and not as people problems. In full, Deming's second point is "adopt the new philosophy. We are in a new economic age. Western management must awaken to the challenge, learn its responsibilities, and take on leadership for change."

I think the main thing I'd like you to take away from Deming's second point is to start seeing problems as system problems and improve the system. Which means to quit personifying, blaming, and punishing. Make the system the constraint and not the people. This will help you reach the quality levels that will be required for your organization's future survival.

> # Leadership as defined in the world of transformation...
>
> # <u>Leadership</u>: The ability to change culture.

Figure 48

Now let's review some information that's important. I know we have gone through this before, but after reading Deming's second point, where he talks about leadership, I just want to make sure that you know what leadership means in the world of transformation.

In the world of transformation, leadership means the ability to change culture. A leader would be able to look at Deming's fourteen points and say, "Okay, I see we need to make some changes." And by the definition of leadership, that individual would be able to make those changes to the culture. It is a very challenging thing to change culture, but it's also a very necessary element in the world of successful organizational transformation.

> # <u>Leadership Dictates Culture</u>

Figure 49

In the world of transformation, if you are called a leader but you cannot change culture, then you are a leader in name only. As you may recall from previous conversations, there are two types of transformation. One is a top-down transformation and the other is a bottom-up transformation. Remember that Deming would promote the top-down transformation—that leadership should lead the transformation and get everyone involved in it.

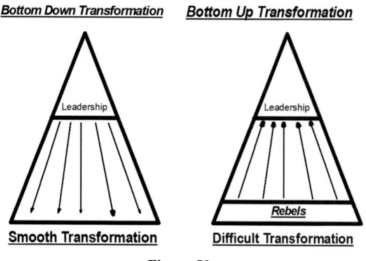

Figure 50

Now we will discuss Deming's third point: *Cease dependence on inspection to achieve quality. Eliminate the need for inspection on a mass basis by building quality into the product in the first place.* In the early 1980s, American manufacturing, in order to improve the probability on the "and" statements, just tried to inspect all the poor quality out, which we have referred to as Solution #5. There were a couple of problems with that. One, this solution was still accepting a large amount of variability—at least a relatively large amount of variability compared to the Japanese—and also, 100 percent inspection is only approximately 85 percent effective. In other words even after 100 percent inspection you will still end up accepting approximately 15 percent of the bad parts. This makes it difficult to reach the higher standards such as 99.9996 percent (six sigma).

Deming's third point takes us back to our previous conversation concerning the five solutions to the traditional problem. Deming promoted Solution #3, reducing variability or designing quality into the product, and passionately denounced Solution #5, inspecting quality into the product.

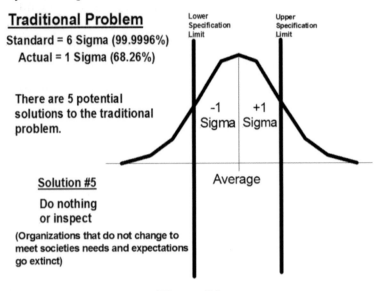

Figure 51

Solution #5 not only cost more money to create the goods and services but also reduced the quality of the goods and services. Solution #5 is a lose-lose situation in Deming's eyes.

Deming's fourth point is as follows: *End the practice of awarding business on the basis of price tag. Instead, minimize total cost. Move toward a single supplier for any one item on a long-term relationship of loyalty and trust.* When Deming was in Japan he probably felt something like the following, *You know, in Japan they treated their suppliers like they were their friends, like they were really important to running the business,* and then when Deming came over to America he probably thought, *You guys act like your suppliers are your worst enemies.* For example, Mr. Toyoda, when he'd get a supplier, would purchase stock in that supplier's company just to show, "Okay, I trust you and now we're family; let's go out and do business together." He'd form these long-term relationships of loyalty and trust. But in America, Deming found manufacturers picking the lowest price and nothing else seemed to matter. If someone sells a penny below someone else, the manufacturer will pick that supplier just based on price. They'll never look at quality or delivery or any of those other important issues that equate the total cost including the quality of the part or service. So loyalty and trust were very important in Japan in how manufacturers dealt with their suppliers. I had one client in America who was having quality problems, so the Toyota Motor Company sent out one of its most valued employees to help this supplier. That Toyota employee stayed there, I believe, for two years until the issue was resolved, which included a cultural change. Now that shows loyalty and trust!

Deming's fifth point is as follows: *Improve constantly and forever the system of production and service to improve quality and productivity, and thus constantly decrease costs.*

Deming is talking about systems thinking—constantly and forever the system. Not the people but the system. Although the definition of transformation is "evolving to a higher level of sustained performance," you should never plateau on improving your performance. Most clients that go through a nasty transformation, which means they hit the bottom of the wall and have to go through the "living hell" before ultimately having a successful transformation. Trust me—the one thing they want to make a part of their culture is continuous process-improvement so they don't have to go through a full-blown transformation again. Every day you should have incremental transformation so that you never hit the bottom of that wall again. That's a very important part to put into one's culture—to improve the system constantly and forever so that every day has continuous process-improvement.

Deming's sixth point is as follows: *Institute training on the job.* Invest in that element of the organization that is capable of improving systems. To improve systems you need training. Here's just a reminder of the importance of training.

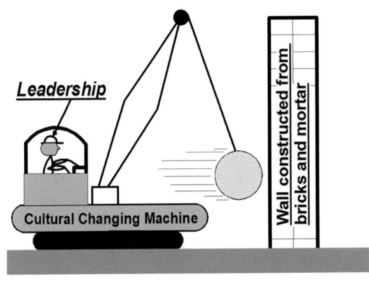

Figure 52

We referred to this illustration earlier on, and remember that the mortar is made from ignorance and fear. That makes for a pretty strong wall for leadership to knock down, but one way to reduce the strength of the wall is to reduce the strength of the mortar. And how do you get rid of ignorance and fear? It comes through education and training. You will never have a successful transformation without a successful training and education program. Remember that true education has the potential of allowing objectivity as well.

Deming's seventh point is this: *Institute leadership.* Remember that leadership is the ability to change culture. *The aim of supervision should be to help people, machines, and gadgets do a better job.* This is much different than personifying, blaming, and punishing. Deming went on to say that *supervision should be about helping people, machines, and gadgets do a better job. Supervision of management is in need of overhaul, as is supervision of production workers.* Deming's seventh point promoted just the opposite of the personify, blame, and punish methodology.

Deming's eighth point is a very important one: *Drive out fear, so that everyone may work effectively for the company.* Important point: drive out fear. The fuel for objective problem solving is data. What do you think happens in an organization when there's fear? What kind of data do you tend to get? You probably end up getting bad data when fear is a part of the culture. I'd say point number eight was one of the biggest problems with American manufacturing when it came to using Deming's tools. Part of the culture was to personify, blame, and punish, and you can't personify, blame, and punish without having the by-product of fear. PBP is totally dysfunctional without the motive of fear. There was a tremendous amount of fear in the American organization, and, as a result, you got poor data. In the world of objectivity, if you get bad data, you create bad information. That was definitely one of the reasons Deming's tools struggled initially. So just a reminder: the natural by-product of personify, blame, and punish methodology is fear. It is impossible to use personify, blame, and punish methodologies without creating fear. Another rule of organizational transformation is "You will never become greater than that which motivates you." The best an organization will do if they choose fear as their motive is the 95 percent success rate talked about earlier.

Deming's ninth point is this: *Break down barriers between departments. People in research, design, sales, and production must work as a team to perceive problems of production and use that may be encountered with the product or service.* As I mentioned earlier on in the text, I look at Deming's fourteen points as showing what a functional culture looks like that will support an objective organization, in other words a culture that would support his quality tools. Deming saw Japanese organizations working together as a team between design, sales, and production. He came to America and everyone was doing their own thing. Engineering would design a product and then push it over the wall and say, "It's no longer our problem—don't bring it back to us; now it's your baby." And there was very little communication across those walls. For years Deming was more immersed in the Japanese culture than he was in the American culture. When Deming returned he viewed things differently than before he left for Japan. This is a great way to get a new perception on the culture you came from (leave, immerse, and return). Deming was shocked at the lack of communication within American industry.

Deming's tenth point is as follows: *Eliminate slogans, exhortations, and targets for the workforce asking for zero defects and new levels of productivity. Such exhortations only create adversarial relationships, as the bulk of the causes of low quality and low productivity belong to the system and thus lie beyond the power of the workforce.*

The point here is that machines cannot and do not read banners. I know that some people don't believe that, but I do. The very fact that you hang up banners asking for better quality is an admission that you believe people are the constraint to quality and not the system. Remember the gentleman digging the trench. He'd do maybe eight feet per day, and that was as much as his system was capable of until someone went out and taught him how to use a new tool, which was a backhoe, and then he dug up to four thousand feet per day. But imagine if you were trying to dig a trench and you were given a goal that was physically impossible to reach with the current methodologies—what would you do? Can you imagine that you might get frustrated? Deming felt that the only value a banner brought to the party was frustration.

Figure 53

Deming felt that if you're going to give people those goals, also give them the tools with which they can obtain those goals. I feel that was his big point. I feel that Deming thought, *Why does management sit around the office coming up with new and clever slogans and exhortations all day when the system cannot read slogans? Evidently you don't understand that your problems are coming from the system not the people.* I feel that he thought, *Maybe you should spend more time on the floor helping them and understanding the true dilemma (the system).* Remember that the job of supervision is to help people and machines do a better job, and that's the way he looked at those things; he felt that the biggest thing you got out of slogans and exhortations was lack of morale—just making people upset. Slogans are seen as evidence that the organization is "people-constrained" instead of the preferred "system-constrained" organization.

Now even though Deming taught these points, management didn't really seem to get that the bulk of the causes of low quality and low productivity belonged to the system, and if you wanted to improve things, you had to improve the system—and not through the personify, blame, and punish technique.

American Managers did not "get it" so Deming ran the red bead experiment at his seminars.

• The Red Bead experiment helped the students understand the importance of "System Thinking."

Figure 54

As that first bullet says, American managers did not get it, so Deming ran the red bead experiment at his seminars. He had a tote of beads. Most of them were white, but he randomly put some red beads into the mix, and the job of the workers was to scoop some beads without getting any red ones. White beads were the only acceptable beads. Then he showed them how to do this. I don't know the exact procedure he taught, so I will create my own interpretation here. He had a procedure of putting the scoop at a given angle, planting his feet flat on the floor, being stable, and then thrusting in the scoop and getting the beads out of the bin. He claimed that his technique would produce only white beads, which was the ultimate objective of the exercise—at least that is what he told them. The reason he got all white beads in his demonstration is that he knew where to scoop. Ultimately Deming would ask for volunteers to come up from the audience and help him run his process. Of course, the exercise was rigged. It was just random luck, so some got more red beads than others and as a result they got fired. Eventually, because everyone was working with the same odds, everyone had good days and bad days. Ultimately Deming had to fire everyone and shut down his factory because his workers did not learn how to get only white beads. As you can probably imagine, the workers felt it was unfair that they got punished because of random variability that they had no control over. So Deming said something like but not exactly like, "Now you know what it's like working for you." He was blaming people for random luck just like they were doing in their real factories. And Deming said that random luck was from the system, and if you want to make things better, you have to fix the system. The red bead experiment was really quite effective in helping managers understand that these are system problems and need to be approached as system problems. The red bead experiment was considered a real success and is still considered so today.

Deming had two elements to point number eleven. Eleven (a) is this: *Eliminate work standards or quotas on the factory floor—substitute leadership.* Guess where the vice presidents from Toyota spent most of their time. They spent it on the floor helping to solve system problems. Deming felt this was a much more effective way to spend their time rather than sitting up in their offices creating quotas and work standards, so I feel he thought something like, *Go down on the floor and start improving the system.* Eleven (b) is this: *Eliminate management by objective. Eliminate management by numbers and numerical goals; substitute leadership.*

I feel that Deming was frustrated because he was trying to create a dynamic environment of continuous process-improvement and his clients in America were spending all of their time creating static goals for a dynamic system. This did not make sense to him, nor does it make sense to me, in most cases. Imagine if the people would take all the time they use to create standards and instead just go out and spend every day making the system better. Which strategy do you think would give the better return on investment? Deming felt that the latter was the better way to go, and his experiences in Japan backed it up. (They could build a comparable automobile, to a US model for 20 percent less, with much higher quality.)

Deming's twelfth point also has two parts. Twelve (a) is: *Remove barriers that rob the hourly workers of their right to pride of workmanship. The responsibility of supervisors must be changed from sheer numbers to quality.* So remember this: you must have a culture that supports tools. Part of the culture needed to create quality as your competitive advantage is to make quality just as important or more important than the number of parts you put out every day. In Japan they put ropes hanging from switches, and if they experienced a quality problem the worker pulled the rope and potentially shut down the production line. That is a convincing way to communicate the importance of quality to the whole organization. If you would have put such a rope in an American automobile plant in the 1980s they probably would have visualized a noose on the end of the rope. Such is the by-product of the motive fear.

And the last part of Deming's twelfth point or twelve (b) is similar to twelve (a) except that it's for management. It says: *Remove barriers that rob people in management and in engineering of their right to pride of workmanship. This means, for example, abolishment of the annual or merit rating and of managing by objective.* This may be one of those things that work very well for you. The merit rating is very common, and I've used it; it's a great tool to communicate. But again, if your culture evolves or as your organization evolves, what Deming would argue is that eventually you'll see the merit rating, or managing by objective, as a crutch to your organization. However, it may take a while for your organization to mature and evolve to the point where you see those things as a crutch. But that's the argument. Let's read that again: *Remove barriers that rob people in management and in engineering of their right to pride of workmanship.* In America we are always talking about our rights, as we should. Deming talked of another right, the right to be proud of what you created every day, from a perspective of quality.

Deming's thirteenth point is this: *Institute a vigorous program of education and self-improvement.* Remember that people create robust systems, and training is an important link to taking you from personify, blame, and punish to systems thinking.

And last, Deming's fourteenth point is this: *Put everybody in the company to work to accomplish the transformation. The transformation is everybody's job!*

Deming also came up with the Seven Deadly Diseases of Management. We'll look at those now, and you'll see that there are some similarities here to his fourteen points. The publishing of these points, I feel, reflects Deming's concern that America was lacking leadership skills in their factories, and he was hoping this would give some helpful direction.

Deming's Seven Deadly Diseases of Management

1. **Lack of constancy of purpose to plan product and service which will have a market and keep the company in business and provide jobs.**

This is very similar to the first point in Deming's fourteen points.

2. **Emphasis on short-term profits: Short-term thinking (just the opposite from constancy of purpose to stay in business), fed by fear of unfriendly takeover, and by push from bankers and owners for dividends.**

Deming considered this a disease—emphasis on short-term profits. Remember that you'll never become greater than that which motivates you. And he felt the main motive for American business was short-term profits. Another disease of management as designated by Deming was:

3. **Evaluation of performance, merit review, or annual review.**

4. **Mobility of management (job hopping).**

5. **Management by use of only visible figures, with little or no consideration of figures that are unknown or unknowable.**

For example, you may think, *I'm going to train this person*—but you can't really link numbers to it, so you decide not to train him or her. Deming says you should train him or her, even though it's not measureable, because sometimes you have to take a step of faith, do what you know is right, and reap the benefits later. He saw too much of managing only by visible figures, and he felt this was a crutch.

6. **Excessive medical costs.**

He felt that medical costs in the United States were a real burden for companies and that we needed to get that under control.

7. **Excessive costs of liability, swelled by lawyers that work on contingency fees.**

Basically Deming was teaching Americans how to create competitive advantages that the future would demand.

It's important to remember that Deming worked with a gentleman whose name was Walter Shewhart, and Shewhart really inspired a lot of the things that Deming taught—not necessarily his fourteen points, but definitely the continuous process-improvement model and SPC or statistical process control. Walter Shewhart is often referred to as the father of statistical process control, which Deming used to implement Solution #3.

The first statistical process control came from Shewhart, not from Deming, so that's important to remember—to give credit where credit's due. Shewhart also came up with a Plan-Do-Check-Act model, or PDCA model, which is a model for continuous process-improvement that Deming used while working with the Japanese. Deming actually changed the name of the model to Plan-Do-Study-Act (PDSA), but it pretty much served the same purpose. I will not spend a lot of time going over the PDSA model but do include an illustration that came from the ISO website that you may find helpful.

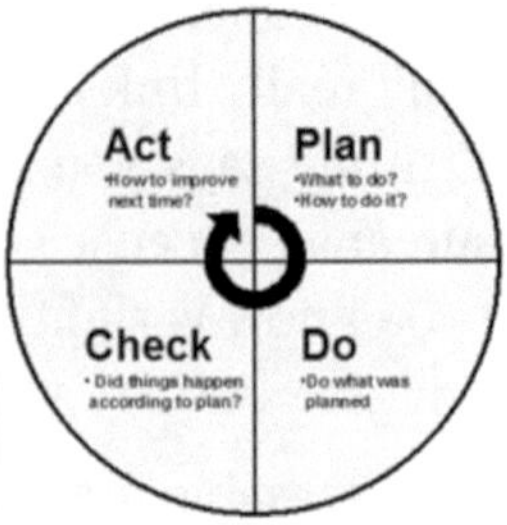

Plan	Establish the objectives and processes necessary to deliver results, for example, customer requirements and the organization's policies.
Do	Implement the processes.
Check	Monitor and measure processes and product against policies, objectives and requirements for the product and report results.
Act	Take actions to continually improve process performance.

Alpha Quality Consulting would like to thank ISO for giving us permission to copy this slide to our training module.

You can learn more about ISO by visiting their website at www.iso.ch

Figure 55

The Plan step was to establish the objectives and processes necessary to deliver results; for example, customer requirements and the organization's policies. The Do step was to implement the process that you planned. The Check, or Study if you are using Deming's model, step was to monitor and measure processes and product against policies, objectives, and requirements for the product, and to report the results. The Act step was to take actions to continually improve the process performance. So that was Plan, Do, Check, and Act. Of course, when you got through with the Act, you'd start with the Plan again—so they called it continuous process-improvement. They just went through that loop forever, basically—that's what continuous process-improvement is.

> ## 2. Emphasis on short-term profits: short-term thinking (just the opposite from constancy of purpose to stay in business), fed by fear of unfriendly takeover, and by push from bankers and owners for dividends.

Figure 56

These principles are used as a baseline in quality system standards.

Concerning Deming's seven deadly diseases, from my perspective these look closely related to Deming's fourteen points. The point is this: what a functional quality culture looks like has been defined and pretty much agreed upon among quality professionals. It may be a good time to look at your own organization's culture and see how closely it mirrors these values. Perhaps most importantly, these are the values that make it possible for objective tools to work effectively. If your organization deviates too far from these base values, then you will most likely find it difficult to effectively use tools that will allow you to reach higher levels of success on your "and" statement probabilities. This is a reflection of my experience as a quality consultant.

Now we will turn our attention to the three subtransformations. We will study them in the order given.

CHAPTER THREE

PERSONAL TRANSFORMATION

In previous chapters we defined transformation as evolving to a higher level of sustained performance.

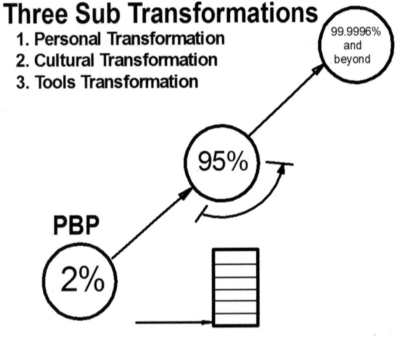

Three Sub Transformations
1. Personal Transformation
2. Cultural Transformation
3. Tools Transformation

Figure 57

You should recognize this illustration—remember that 2 percent was the initial attempt at mass production with Eli Whitney and his muskets. And remember that we talked about personify, blame, and punish as being the methodology to get better—and it worked. It got society up to approximately 95 percent of sustained performance, but in our day and age, that's not good enough, because the "and" statements have gone exponential, so we have to revisit the way we do business. Hitting the wall symbolically means that our old methodologies are no longer capable of meeting the organization's needs. When this happens we must transform. You'll also remember that when we hit the wall, the organization's first impulse is to amplify the old, dysfunctional methodology. In this case, we used the example of personify, blame, and punish. This is shown directly above the 2 percent, in the transformation model.

Most organizations do not transform well. In fact, most organizations will go extinct rather than transform.

The objective of this chapter: to define what personal transformation is, why it's necessary, and how to go about making it happen.

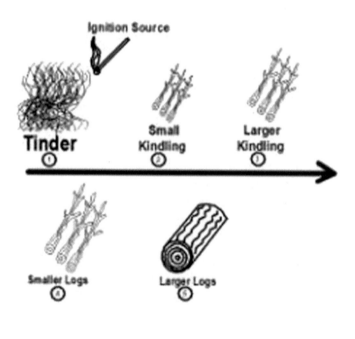

Figure 58

I feel that creating a fire is a good analogy for transforming an organization. There are several ingredients necessary to start a healthy fire. To start a fire capable of generating any warmth, you must have an ignition source (a match), tinder, small kindling, larger kindling, smaller logs, larger logs, and of course plenty of oxygen to support the combustion process. Figure 58 shows the materials needed to start a fire and the order in which they are to be used. Personal transformation is analogous to the match and the tinder. Tinder is a fuel used to get the fire started. Often you create tinder by peeling bark off of a tree and shredding it into fine hair-like fibers. The advantage of tinder is that it is highly flammable. The disadvantage of tinder is that it burns very quickly and if all you use for the fire is tinder, you will be incapable of building a large fire or in this case a successful organizational transformation. In organizational transformation you have to create the "organizational tinder" by educating the employees in such a way that they look forward to their role in the transformation. The match or ignition source is a well-planned motivational lecture on the importance and inevitability of the transformation. Personal transformation is, in large part, an emotional event that gets everyone excited about the transformation. However, like tinder, this emotional event will burn bright only for a very limited amount of time. Because this emotional event, personal transformation, will burn out quickly, you must be prepared with fuel to feed the fire. The fire is analogous to the organizational transformation. In the world of organizational transformation, the kindling is analogous to relatively easy process-improvement projects. After personal transformation, people are excited to make a difference, so you give them projects to work on that will legitimately make a difference; however, these projects cannot be overly difficult projects. At this time you are not looking for huge returns on investment, which usually suggest more difficult projects. Many organizations destroy their hopes of transformation by coming up with projects that are too difficult for the newly trained process-improvement organization, and this immediately destroys hope. In the fire example it is like throwing a huge log on the tinder. I have seen this happen more times than I desire to remember. You have to gauge the difficulty of the initial projects vs. the power of the flame; this is a very important part of a successful transformation. Remember that the first set of projects is more about small successes than it is about large returns on investment (ROIs). If your organization has significant talent in the area of running projects and solving difficult problems, then you can feed the transformation with bigger projects. The ability to run projects must also include the ability to get people involved in working the projects. If you have people who can solve problems but can't get people involved in helping solve the problems, then they will be more of a hindrance to the transformation than they will be an asset. Like it or not the American culture does not value people solving problems and then shoving the solution down their throats. If you want to transform you must be able to get the people to see problems as system problems and then find a system solution and implement it as a system solution. In the end the people must see the solution as their solution. If they see it as their solution, then they will be successful in implementing it and maintaining it over time. Most organizations do not do a good job at implementing solutions because they hire someone to solve the problem and then shove the solution down the throats of the workers. You must have the ability to get all the stakeholders involved in the problem if it is to have a lasting impact on the organization. Organizational transformations are starving for success, and the transformation will starve to death if you don't properly nourish it. As Deming said, everyone must be involved in the transformation, so don't make it an engineers' transformation; this would be a big mistake. Get everyone involved in the transformation. Everyone should be involved in the projects, and not all projects should necessarily be headed by engineers. It is very important that the people who lead the projects are more concerned about team dynamics than they are about project completion, at least early on in the transformation. Remember that we are creating people who are capable of creating better systems, and they're probably not used to this way of thinking, so you will need to be patient, at least through the kindling stage. Eventually you will identify the team as "log burners," which is to say they can handle more advanced and difficult types of projects (Solution #3 projects), with the accompanying high ROIs. The people who are trained to gauge the power of the fire and correctly select projects accordingly are called "facilitators." Facilitators are people who understand team dynamics, are very talented using the analytical tools necessary to solve problems, and are more concerned with the people than they are with the projects. They are also excellent communicators. I call them freaks of nature—just kidding, kind of. Actually I call them Phase III, which is the ultimate compliment in the world of organizational transformation. Facilitators provide the proper nourishment to the team, and without them you will not have a successful transformation, end of argument. Before beginning personal transformation, upper management, middle management, and facilitators must be effectively trained on how to effectively manage the transformation. Before these smaller projects are handed out, the infrastructure has to be built up to properly support the transformation. Everyone on the transformation team must be on the same page, and any subjective arguments, of which there are bound to be some, must be taken care of and put to bed. I call this "the transformation team must be as one." Some healthy arguments and education are usually necessary to make this happen. Another rule of transformation is that you stop becoming greater the instant you think you're great. I have never seen an organization go through a successful transformation that thought it was great. I have never seen an organization successfully transform until after it hit the proverbial wall that we discussed in the transformation model.

At the center of personal transformation lies the second rule of transformation, which is this: *you will never become greater than that which motivates you.* Transformation is very difficult, and it is impossible if you're trying to transform an organization filled with employees who have grown indifferent. In order to have a successful transformation, you must have employees who have a purpose and a desire to transform. The standard motives within organizations include financial needs (remember that we all have bills to pay), short-term profits, and pure survival (fear). I call these types of motives "standard motives." They're not the kind of motives we need if we're to successfully transform an organization. We stand in need of "higher motives"—a higher purpose for the existence of the organization. Ultimately, it is leadership's responsibility to create the proper motives within an organization.

In this chapter I will give some examples that I have used in organizations to help them find those higher motives or that higher purpose that will help them accelerate into higher levels of organizational performance. As an example of the destructive force of lower motivators, let's look at short-term profits. I once heard of a CEO who sold all of his manufacturing facilities worldwide and then leased them back just so they could have a good financial quarter. Now obviously, this did help him reach those short-term goals, but it came at the cost of long-term security for the organization. Remember, you will never become greater than that which motivates you.

One of the reasons for organizational existence is to create wealth in an efficient and effective manner. Most people do not understand the importance of wealth creation. In this chapter we will explain the nature of wealth and why it is important. Every employee must understand why wealth creation is important. We will explain that through the creation of wealth we create opportunity for future generations. This will ultimately evolve into a higher motivator that will allow us the power to transform our organization (light the tinder). In summary, personal transformation is about changing the motives of the organization from the "standard motivators" to the "higher motivators"; in other words it is changing the reason people go to work, and it has to start at the top of the organization. I would recommend performing personal transformation in three steps. First perform personal transformation on upper management, middle management, and finally on the general workforce. This allows you to take care of concerns before publishing it to the masses.

For profit organizations, the reason for their existence is to create wealth in as efficient a manner as possible. For nonprofit organizations, one of the reasons for organizational existence is to use wealth more efficiently and effectively in reaching the organization's objectives. Transformation is a necessary activity for both profit and nonprofit organizations. So if wealth is such an important concept, we'd probably be wise to define it.

So what is wealth? Wealth is an abundance of those things that we value. It can often, but not always, be effectively measured in monetary units, such as dollars. One of the more common measurements of wealth is how many widgets we can make per person in our society. In the world of transformation, a widget has a specific definition. A widget is defined as a product or service that improves the human condition.

So what happens when you create more widgets per person in society? Remember that a widget is a product or service that improves the human condition. So what happens when we create more widgets per person? Well, in theory, if we create more widgets per person, then the human condition should improve because widgets are things that improve the human condition so if we make more of them it should naturally improve the human condition. This is a key concept: *if we create more widgets per person in our society, then the human condition will improve.*

Let me give you an example of using higher motives and how they work. When I am traveling around I often listen to the radio and look at the billboards along the highway as a method of staying alert. In doing so I always found one advertising campaign more interesting than most. The company was the Workmen's Compensation Fund of Utah (WCF). From what I understand, WCF is an insurance company of sorts, so they obviously had a financial interest in workers being safe while on the job. I witnessed their various advertising campaigns over the years but didn't pay a lot of attention to them until one day I was speeding down the highway (a bad habit I have always had) and noticed a new billboard that had a picture of a cute little kid standing in a construction zone with a sign in his hand that said, "Daddy, please come home tonight. I need you." I immediately dropped my speed down by about ten mph. Turns out it not only had an impact on me but was an extremely successful advertising campaign at bringing a higher level of safety awareness to the citizenry of Utah. Your organization will never become greater than that which motivates it, so be sure to choose your motives carefully. This is of strategic importance and should be discussed at a strategic level.

As a transformation consultant I play many roles in a successful transformation, but one of my favorite roles is to be the one that creates and lights the tinder, in other words identifying the needed motives and then giving a lecture that will instill the new motives into the organization (Light the tinder on fire). Before creating the lecture I do my homework on the background of the company and determine the best way to light the fire. Remember that it has to be an emotional event. Some of the lectures I have used in the past, to light the tinder, have been made a part of this important chapter.

Now I will tell you a story in an effort to help you understand the importance of creating wealth or using wealth wisely. Before we go through this story, let me remind you about the objective of the story. I tell this story, among others, when I am hired to help organizations transform. This story and other stories like it are designed to light the tinder within the transforming organization. Lighting the tinder means to create an emotional experience that gives people the desire to make a difference. Let's go through the stories so you have an idea of the types of material used to light the tinder. This story is simply the match in the fire analogy.

This story takes place in the Dark Ages. The Dark Ages was a time in history when there was very little social, artistic, or scientific advancement—much like an organization that has just "hit the wall." In fact, not only was there no significant advancement, but society slid backward in the Dark Ages.

This was a period of history that, for the most part, started with the fall of the Western Roman Empire and continued until the European cultural transformation that we often refer to as the Renaissance. Most historians consider the time period between 410 AD and 1400 AD as the Dark Ages. If you dislike change, then perhaps the Dark Ages was your time.

Before you decide to fantasize about the beauty and lack of change that occurred in the Dark Ages, perhaps we should study this time period in greater depth. Did you realize that during the Dark Ages one-half of the children died before they reached adulthood? And that one-quarter of the children died as newborns and one-quarter died before they reached the age of twelve years? Most children would lose one or both parents before they reached adulthood. Many people would wear their clothes until they rotted off their backs. All of a sudden, the Dark Ages don't seem so great. But you haven't heard anything yet!

Another unique thing about the Dark Ages is that there was not a lot of opportunity in those times. You pretty much did what your parents did, public education was nonexistent, and most of the people were malnourished. There was no real room for advancement in life, and life was about survival. The story that I have been referring to is a story about a young girl born toward the end of the Dark Ages.

She was born in Fife, Scotland, into a family of coal miners, who were often referred to as colliers. I found her story as I read through some family journals; this makes this story about me. The name of the girl in the story is Margaret. I was rather shocked when I learned that all of her family members were slaves in the coal mines of Fife, Scotland. For whatever reason there was a high demand for coal that started in the 1300s, and there weren't enough people who were willing to stay around and work in the coal mines. It wasn't exactly a fun job! Because they could not sustain a labor force to work in these mines, the coal mine owners took the people who knew how to mine coal and made them slaves. So the parliament in Fife, Scotland, basically made slavery legal, and whole families worked in the coal mines as property of the mine owners.

Often the parents would go down into the coal pit and knock coal from the walls. The children would then pick up the coal in buckets and carry these coal-filled buckets up ladders where they would be stockpiled for the community. The family would usually work six days a week, fourteen hours a day. The children were referred to as "coal bearers." School and education were nothing but a pipe dream. Legal and social degradation by many acts of the Scotland parliament caused the rest of the population to look upon the miners or colliers as something less than human. They were herded together in miserable hovels and villages close to the pits. In Fife, a dead collier was not allowed to be buried in the same ground as a free laborer. It was a rather sad situation. Then I came across this letter from six-year-old Margaret Levitston (which later became Livingston, my great-grandmother's maiden name). She was a coal bearer, so she carried the buckets of coal out of the mine and she wrote:

> **"Been down the pit at coal carrying for six weeks – make 10-14 journeys a day. Carriers a full 56 lbs. of coal in a wooden backit. The work is no gaid: it is so vary sair. I work with sister Jesse and mother: dinna ken the time we gang it is gae dark. Get plenty of broth and porridge and run home and get a bannock. Never been to school it is so very far away."**

Figure 59

Notice that there are many misspelled words (at least I know where I get it from). I'm going to try to interpret the letter for you the best I can. This is what I believe it says: "Been down in the coal pit for six weeks—make 10–14 journeys a day. Carry a full 56 lbs. of coal in a wooden bucket. The work is no good; it is very scary. I work with sister Jesse and Mother: by the time we get finished, it is way dark. Get plenty of broth and porridge and run home and get a bannock. Never been to school; it is so very far away." Well, school *was* far away. I'm sure it was far away geographically, but it was an eternity away idealistically speaking. From Margaret's letter I sensed a strong desire to go to school. These people had zero opportunity to improve their situation.

Something had to happen between that time and the time I am living in today. I have more opportunity than I have time to take advantage of, a deep contrast compared to the life Margaret lived. I would argue that the story I am about to tell you is fairly realistic in describing what must have happened for society to evolve to where I find myself today. Well, one day these colliers lives were about to change drastically as a direct result of a gentleman who came to the mine and explained to the mine owners that he could hook up a conveyor system powered by a water wheel or animal power (whichever they preferred) and this power could be used to haul the buckets of coal out of the mine. He explained that by using this new mechanism, they could send all the coal miners home except for the fathers. The mine owners decided to give the man a chance to prove out his idea. The idea worked! The machine could pull coal out of the mine with fewer people. The next day the mine owners called all the colliers together and told them about this new mechanism and how they could haul coal out of the mine with this machine. They announced to the workers that the only people that would be allowed to continue their labor in the coal mine were the fathers.

As a result of this conveyor system, all the other workers were laid off except for the fathers. What do you think? Do you think they were happy with this layoff? Imagine that! They no longer had to go to these dreadful coal mines. It turns out that most of the workers were very depressed. Why? Why would people be depressed if they didn't have to go to that dreadful coal mine anymore? Well, there's something unique about human beings, and that is that they desire to participate and make a difference. The only way these people knew how to participate in society was to dig coal. They also lost the short-term ability to work for their food. So they felt that the rug had been pulled right out from under them. When they could no longer participate, the people felt discouraged and depressed.

So back at the coal mine, everyone was pretty discouraged and depressed except for one man, who was somewhat of a visionary and was Margaret's dad. He called Margaret over to his side, knelt down on his knees, and looked into his daughter's coal-stained face. He then told Margaret that this was the greatest day in all his life. He told her that he never dared dream of having a daughter who would not have to live and die in the dreadful coal mines. He also told Margaret that he had a plan and that he needed her to help him realize this dream. Margaret agreed to do all that she could to help with her father's plan. Her father told Margaret that instead of going to the coal mine the next morning, she should go to Isaac's house. Isaac was a neighbor who lived some distance down the street. Margaret was to go and work at Isaac's house instead of going to the mine. He said that Margaret must work fourteen-hour days, six days a week, at Isaac's house (the same hours she worked in the coal mine). She was instructed to sweep Isaac's walks, wash his windows, take care of the cattle, mend fences, and fix whatever else appeared to be in need of repair. Margaret's father told her, "It may take a while," but she was to continue working on Isaac's property until she found favor with Isaac. She was then instructed by her father that it was extremely important that as soon as she gained favor with Isaac, she was to excuse herself from her labors and run to the coal mine and find her father, who would be anxiously waiting to give her further directions.

The next morning around 4:00 a.m. Margaret was awakened by her father. For the first time in Margaret's life, she took a different path than her father. Not only did she go a different direction physically, but idealistically the girl's life was about to change relative to her father's. Margaret went to Isaac's house, and her father returned to the coal mines. Margaret did as her father instructed and worked six days a week, fourteen hours a day, taking care of Isaac's property. Several weeks went by and Margaret was faithful to her father's plan. Then one early afternoon, Isaac came out on his porch and looked around at his property. He was amazed at how great it looked. He had been watching Margaret for some time and greatly respected the young girl's work ethic. Ultimately, Isaac called Margaret over and told her he had never seen his property look so good. He told Margaret he would like to reward her for her hard work. He asked her, "Would you like some candy? Would you like some clothes"—you have to remember that the colliers would wear their clothes until they rotted from their backs—"or perhaps some money? What can I do for you, Margaret, for all the service that you have provided me?" Throughout the whole conversation Margaret realized or recognized that this was her cue to go back and talk to her father. So Margaret asked Isaac if she may be excused, as she needed to talk with her father. Isaac laughed at the indecisive young girl and said she could come back whenever she was ready to claim her reward.

Margaret had never been so excited in all her life. She felt that she had truly succeeded. She knew that her father would be so very proud of her. Margaret ran as fast as she could to the coal pit and scooted down the ladder as fast as she could and from there ran into the depths of the coal mine where she found her father literally slaving away in a dark corner of the pit. Margaret looked at her father with a big smile on her coal-stained face and told him, "Father, I have found favor with Isaac!" Margaret's father ran over to his daughter and fell to his knees. Margaret had never witnessed her father crying before and felt a little bit nervous. With tears of optimism running down his face, Margaret's father looked into his little girl's coal-stained face and told her, "This is the greatest day in our lives!" He told Margaret,

"This is what I want you to do: you must go back to Isaac and ask him if he wouldn't mind attempting to teach a poor little 'collier' girl how to read."

Filled with her father's optimism, Margaret ran back to Isaac's home and knocked on his door. As Margaret heard footsteps approach the door, she began to be afraid—what if Isaac rejected her request? She was afraid that would crush her father for life. She knew people were prejudiced against the colliers. What if he didn't feel that Margaret even had the potential to read? That was the way many people felt back then. It was not hard to see the gravity of the moment and how disappointed her father would be if this didn't work out.

After what seemed like an eternity, the door slowly opened and there was Isaac standing at the door. In an intimidating voice, Isaac asked, "Well, girl, what is it?" With all the courage a young girl could muster, she looked right into Isaac's eyes and quietly and sincerely asked him, "Would you mind attempting to teach a little peasant girl, even a collier girl, how to read?" To Margaret's disbelief, Isaac smiled, stretched out his hand, patted the young girl on the head, and told her, "I would be honored to attempt to teach a poor little peasant girl—even a collier girl—how to read." With Margaret's heart pounding, she followed Isaac into his kitchen, where she was instructed to sit down at the man's dinner table. Isaac then went to another room got a book, sat down by the girl, and began the miraculous act of teaching the poor little collier girl how to read.

While Margaret was finishing up her first reading lesson, her father had arrived home from the mine. He was very nervous when he realized that his daughter had not returned. Finally he could wait no longer and started walking down the long road toward Isaac's house. As he reached the midpoint in his travels, he noticed the dark shadow of a little girl with her hair bouncing up and down in an expression of her excitement. With his heart about to break, the next thing her father knew, his daughter was flying into his open arms. Hugs were exchanged as her father gained courage to ask the question of her success or failure. When Margaret yelled out, "He is teaching me how to read!" the excitement ripped all the strength from the young father and they fell to the ground in celebration of their good fortune.

As the years went by, the father got black lung disease and was on his deathbed. He decided to look out the shack's window one last time before slipping away into what he hoped would be a better tomorrow. In the far distance he noticed an individual walking down the road. He saw that it was a woman with a book in her hand. Back then, having a book in your hand really meant something—it suggested that you could read, and that demanded respect from all those around you. If you could read, people would listen to you and they'd believe you. You were a respectable person if you knew how to read.

As the image grew closer to the father's fading vision, he noticed that it was his daughter. It was Margaret! Shortly after that proud moment, Margaret's father died in his daughter's loving arms. He died that day with one of the greatest gifts in his heart—the gift of knowing that his life had made a difference.

The important question to ask and for you to answer is what was the nucleus or central event that allowed Margaret the opportunity to read? This event was the gentleman coming to the mine and setting up the conveyor belt to haul coal out of the mine. It was the layoffs. Why? Because the mechanism allowed society to create more widgets per person—and remember that a widget is a product or service that improves the human condition. And it indeed improved the human condition in Margaret's life!

The mine was now capable of fulfilling society's need for coal with fewer people. In doing so, the act created what we call opportunity. There's no such thing as opportunity, as we know it, without the creation of wealth. Thus, the creation of wealth becomes an extremely important activity. By creating wealth more efficiently we too can make a difference in not only our own life but perhaps more importantly in the lives of our children and their children's children. And perhaps someday someone, perhaps many years from now, will stand up and tell a story about your life and how your sacrifices created a better life for them. Eventually the colliers were no more, but many of them continued to mine as the demand for coal continued to increase. Eventually they received a call, in their hearts—the call of freedom to go to another land and start a new life, and many of them came to the United States and helped start the mining industry. But Margaret's grandchild, James, came to America and at a very young age (grade-school age) worked in the granite quarries. Eventually James grew up and ran the granite quarry; there is now a plaque there that honors his sacrifices (one of his arms was blown off by dynamite). Every morning when I wake up I see the granite quarry from my front window and I remember Margaret and her descendants' sacrifices and how they have impacted my life. I go to work every day and work my hardest in an effort to pass on the blessings of those sacrifices, and more if possible, to my children in hopes that someday I too will make a difference. And what exactly am I trying to do to make this difference? I try to create more widgets per person every day, with every breath, so I may be the author of opportunity for others yet unknown.

So the third rule of transformation is this: *you will never realize a future that you cannot envision, and you cannot envision a better future without an appreciation for the past.*

I have a difficult time finding a more destructive element in the world of transformation, whether it is personal or organizational, than fear. Fear is a reflection of a loss of hope. Sadly most organizations are motivated by fear, and where there is fear there is no hope. The point is that you can't obtain a better future without the hope of a better future. I feel that the real cause of general fear in society, and in our own personal lives, is a lack of appreciation for the past as well as a lack of education. Fear is destructive enough to destroy the greatest economies in the world. It is also powerful enough to destroy the greatest organizations in the world, including yours. Remember that a natural by-product of personify, blame, and punish is fear. So we have to overcome that; we have to start looking at problems as system problems, and if we do that, we'll notice that fear will go away and thus allow us to perceive a better future.

If you cannot appreciate the past, you cannot envision a better future. In other words, if you cannot appreciate the past, you will fear the future. Lack of appreciation for the past creates fear for the future.

Oh what the world could be if only we could master the art of appreciation! Great people have usually mastered the art of appreciation. Remember what Isaac Newton said: "If I have seen further than most, it is only because I have stood on the shoulders of giants." We all stand on the shoulders of giants. We must learn who those giants are, and we must learn to appreciate them. By doing so, we will master the art of appreciation just as Isaac Newton did, and just like Isaac Newton, we will see further than most.

I spend a fair amount of time teaching about the art of appreciation in helping people get through their personal transformation. I tell my students that they will know when they have appreciated enough when the future looks bright again. If we, as a generation of Americans, feel that we do not have anything to be thankful for, then no one in all of written history had anything to be thankful for, for no one has had more opportunity than we have. Sometimes people, myself included, act like these are the worst times in all of history. I have read history, and these are not the worst of times, relatively speaking; these are the best of times, and the only reason we see them as anything but that is our inability to appreciate the past. Run an experiment by taking a day and attempt to appreciate all you are capable of imagining, and when you are full of appreciation look into the future and see if it looks brighter than it did the day before.

After I lecture on the art of appreciation, it is not unusual to see individuals working their way through the crowd so they can visit with me. Ultimately, these people will tell me life stories to help express their appreciation for what they have. To date, these people who come and tell me their stories come from a single demographic group. Can you guess what group that is? They always come from the demographic group of immigrants. Ultimately, they tell me they are appreciative of their humble beginnings, which allows them to appreciate what they have. I have found that appreciation is like salt, as it enhances all the human experiences.

Wealth without appreciation does not necessarily create happiness; again appreciation enhances all the human experiences. Wealth creation has the potential of creating opportunity only when it is enhanced with the ingredient of appreciation.

Remember that life is like a book, and you only get to write one of them; you are the only one authorized to write it, so let's make it a great one.

I have one client who manufactures medical devices. The company workers go to the hospital every year and visit patients to see them use the devices that they are instrumental in creating.

This brings the employees a sense of purpose greater than money. So always remember: you will never become greater than that which motivates you. And finally, don't forget your preferred motives: Go to work and create opportunities for future generations. Look around you and figure out how you can create more widgets per person. Remember that it is your legacy! This is the end of the story that I use to "light the tinder."

So what is the outcome of a successful personal transformation? You will have the ability to envision a better future, and you will be going to work for the right reason. Work will be filled with purpose, and your motives will be to create more widgets per person. Why? So you can create opportunity for those who follow you. In other words, you will go to work to create opportunity for future generations just like past generations have done for you. Your whole organization has to experience this new sense of purpose-centered work if your transformation is to be successful. Remember what Deming said: "The transformation is everybody's job. Get everyone involved in the transformation."

Over the years I have gotten pretty good at using stories like this one to "light the tinder" in the personal transformation element of organizational transformation. Always remember that the weakness of personal transformation is that it is an emotional event and will burn out quickly just like tinder. Before personal transformation takes place you should have some basic projects prepared and assigned to the individuals who participate in personal transformation. If projects are not strategically chosen and assigned before personal transformation, then the fire will be started but will quickly burn out and the transformation will have a short life. This is not meant to be a motivational speech. It is meant to kick off a successful organizational transformation, and there is a big difference between a motivational speech and a personal transformation.

Ultimately, the result of a successful personal transformation is that you and the people you are responsible for desire to make a difference. Making a difference will come in the form of a project followed by education that will help them complete their project successfully. After they finish their project, celebrate with them and then give them another project. This is how you keep the fire (transformation) burning. You will know you are doing everything correctly when you notice that work has become fun again.

As a leader of the transformation don't forget why you should be going to work every day. It should be to (and I quote from Deming) "help people, machines, and gadgets to do a better job" and create more and higher-quality widgets per person. Remember that as we create more widgets per person, we will ultimately create opportunities for our communities. This is the higher motive.

Without a successful personal transformation, trying to transform an organization is analogous to leading the dead. You have to have people who are filled with passion and the desire to make a difference in the world. This can happen, but it will take a great deal of leadership to motivate the people, so don't be afraid to ask for outside help where needed. Always remember that we will never become greater than that which motivates us.

Chapter Four

Cultural Transformation

If we are to have a successful organizational transformation, we must also be successful with the three subtransformations: personal transformation, cultural transformation, and tools transformation.

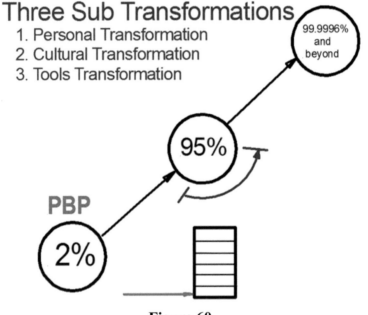

Figure 60

In the last chapter we discussed personal transformation, and in this chapter we will cover perhaps the most important topic of all, cultural transformation. This is the second of the three subtransformations.

A successful personal transformation will bring momentum to the cultural transformation. Deming's fourteen points identified some of the important elements that must be part of a functional culture. However, we have not yet talked about how to change culture and how to sustain it over time. The ability to change organizational culture is also called leadership. And leadership must take full responsibility for culture if the transformation is to carry on successfully. This suggests that if executive leadership does not like the culture of their organization they must be willing to look in the mirror and understand that this is where the problem lies. This attitude is referred to as owning the culture. If leadership does not own the culture, then organizational transformation will fail before it gets started.

Cultural transformation will be the most difficult element of your transformation. It is also the highest-risk element in the organizational transformation. The vast majority of organizations will fail at cultural transformation. This is the biggest reason we don't see a lot of old companies around (older than one hundred years).

Most companies go extinct for two reasons. First, they do not know how to transform. Second, they put the transformation off until it's too late. Remember that transformations take time. Transformations are less painful if the organization can effectively practice continuous process-improvement. Continuous process-improvement is similar to small incremental transformations that take place on a daily basis. Effectively using continuous process-improvement will keep you from hitting the bottom section of the wall, and future transformation will not be as painful.

Culture is based on the belief system of an organization. It is witnessed as an organization acts on its belief system. Attempting to change belief systems has been known historically to start wars. Culture is sometimes referred to as an organization's personality. An effective culture is one of the best competitive advantages because it is nearly impossible to copy. Have you ever tried to copy someone's personality? It's very difficult, if not impossible.

Every organization has its own unique culture, as unique as the personality of the leader who started the organization. Remember that culture is dictated by leadership. If you are to change culture, you must be capable of changing, in part, the value system of an organization, such as seeing the system that supports people instead of people supporting the system.

Abraham Lincoln   **Martin Luther King Jr.**

Many individuals throughout history who have effectively changed culture have paid with their lives. Abraham Lincoln and Martin Luther King Jr. are examples. The point is that leadership is not easy. Most leaders of significant transformations of countries, get assassinated, and the equivalent of assassination in corporations is termination. This is why executive management (the most powerful people in the organization) must lead the transformation; starting a transformation in the middle of the organization (middle management) is not something I would recommend.

Of course Abraham Lincoln ended up getting assassinated, and so did Martin Luther King Jr., who picked up where Abraham Lincoln left off by going against the Jim Crow laws.

You don't have to be a Christian to understand that Jesus changed world culture, and look what happened to him!

Just to give you hope I will give you an example of a leader who did survive a major transformation. His name was Martin Luther. You may recall that he created the Protestant Reformation, so that's changing a belief system of a significant part of the Western world, which resulted in many battles and many deaths. It was very difficult for Martin as well; in order to survive he faked his own kidnapping and changed his name. If you need help changing your name let me know and I will try to help you out (just kidding!).

As was mentioned earlier, leadership is about the ability to change cultures. That's putting up a pretty high bar for the definition of leadership. You will not be capable of changing culture if you do not understand the nature of human nature. Even Deming said, "If you are to have a successful transformation, you need to understand human nature." The main objective of this chapter is to help you understand the nature of human nature and how to be influential enough to change it.

So let's begin. I have identified three levels of human behavior:

- Phase I behavior
- Phase II behavior
- Phase III behavior

This model uses two basic assumptions. The first assumption is that the mother of all motivators is survival. We do amazing things just to survive. There is a program called *Survival Stories* that goes over the amazing things people do just to survive. A few years back, there was an individual who was hiking in the state of Utah when a rock somehow fell on his forearm. As a result of this misfortune, he stayed pinned under that rock for three or four days, at least until he felt he wasn't going to last much longer. Finally, just to survive, he took out his pocketknife and cut off his arm and then managed to hike out to get help. That shows how strong a motivator survival is. Remember, the first assumption is that the mother of all motivators is survival. The second assumption states that if people do not perceive they stand out in a crowd they will die. Using these two assumptions I will attempt to explain the nature of human nature.

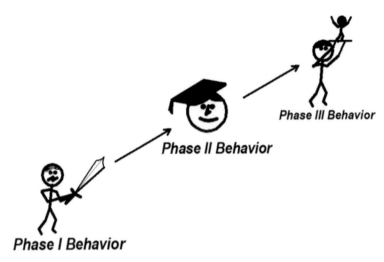

Figure 61

This model will be symbolized, as shown in the illustration above. Phase I behavior is symbolized by an individual holding a sword, Phase II behavior is symbolized by an individual with a graduation cap, and Phase III is symbolized by an individual lifting someone up.

Phase I Behavior

Figure 62

In Phase I behavior, we tear other people down in an effort to help us perceive that we are standing out in a crowd. If we cut everyone down around us, then, relatively speaking, we will be standing out in a crowd—it's all relative. Phase I behavior is the starting point of human behavior. For example, what happens to a child who goes to grade school and is different in some way? Phase I behavior identifies unique characteristics, magnifies them, and belittles them. Imagine the shock of the child who has been taught that his uniqueness makes him special and then goes to school and his uniqueness is amplified and belittled by the other students. The child then comes home believing that the message that his uniqueness makes him special is nothing but a big lie and that in reality his uniqueness only qualifies him for some kind of freak show. That's what Phase I behavior does—it amplifies uniqueness and then belittles it. Such organizations tend to gravitate to the center. Everyone tries to be the same so no one will belittle them.

An important thing to understand here is that Phase I behavior doesn't just take bad characteristics and belittle them. It doesn't matter if it is a positive or a negative characteristic; it just needs to be a unique characteristic. I've heard of children who went to school, and just because they got good grades they'd be teased and belittled. Then they would go back and purposely get bad grades just so they could belong to the crowd. That's the nature of Phase I behavior. Remember that it doesn't have to be anything bad; it just has to be something different—something unique. Phase I behavior will always amplify uniqueness and belittle it.

To continue on with the story, of course the child comes home and is usually crying, and the response of the mother is, "How can children be so mean?" I tell my students, and I'll tell you, that you're not children anymore and you must turn away from childish behavior.

Phase I behavior, by its very nature, tends to be insecure, and thus the starting point of human nature tends to be to believe the critics. Critics are very powerful in a Phase I environment because everyone cares what they think. For example, when the child goes to school and the other kids say he's a freak because he gets good grades, he tends to believe them; we tend to believe the critics in Phase I. Why? Because humans tend to be very insecure, and insecure people tend to believe critics. This gives Phase I behavior the power to do negative things, especially if it happens within a Phase I organization that values and supports Phase I behavior. If your skin is a different color than the norm or your eyes have a different shape or your beliefs are different from the norm, then watch out if you are in a Phase I organization.

Phase I behavior will attempt to keep people from evolving out of this behavior. It will attempt to convince people that they are incapable of improving. Phase I behavior is inherently destructive. Culture change in this book is referring to a constructive exercise. Thus, Phase I behavior is inherently incapable of changing culture for the good. People who exhibit Phase I behavior are incapable of being leaders in the world of transformation. Remember that the definition of leadership in the world of transformation is the ability to change culture for the good.

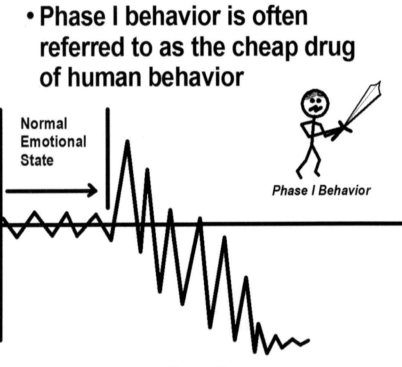

• Phase I behavior is often referred to as the cheap drug of human behavior

Figure 63

I will begin to describe the nature of this drug. We'll begin by describing the normal emotional state of a human being. It goes up and down within a reasonable amount of variation. When a person hits the lower side of this reasonable amount of variation in his emotional state, he may desire to have a "high," so he takes a cheap drug. This drug does give him the high he's looking for. Of course, the nature of the cheap drug is that after he has the high he has a steep drop-off afterward. Now he really wants to get a high because now he's lower than his original state, so he takes another hit and the cheap drug gives him another high. However, the nature of the drug is that the new high is lower than the last. This cycle continues until eventually his new high is lower than his old norm.

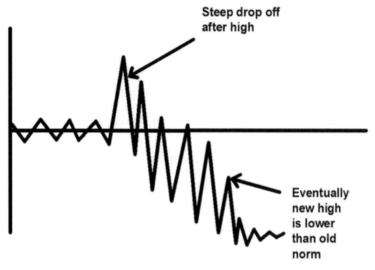

Figure 64

This is the nature of Phase I behavior. To stand out in a crowd, you chop other people down. This gives you a high, but it's followed by a steep drop-off. If you keep performing Phase I behavior, eventually your old high will be below your norm.

***Phase I Behavior is the starting point
of human behavior but it should not
be the ending point of human behavior.***

Figure 65

Remember that Phase I behavior is the starting point of human behavior. If you decide to habitually practice Phase I behavior, your reward will be jealousy, enviousness, and hatefulness. You will be easily offended, and you will experience a lack of influence for good. These are the fruits of Phase I behavior. In hindsight, Phase I behavior will always look stupid. Cultural change will always demand courage and character by constructive participants—especially if you are trying to change culture in a Phase I organization.

Phase I Behavior
Figure 66

Every phase of behavior has its own decision-making processes as well as its own set of motives. Phase I behavior solves problems with the PBP methodology—the personify, blame, and punish methodology. Phase I behavior is motivated by fear. Remember that you'll never become greater than that which motivates you, and Phase I behavior is motivated by fear. This behavior also lacks the influence that is required to evolve to higher levels of performance.

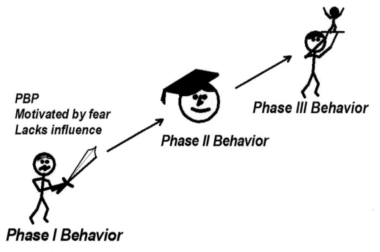

Figure 67

Now you can see that I have upgraded our model on human behavior. I have put in the personify, blame, and punish problem-solving methodology, and motivated by fear, and that phase I behavior lacks influence. Now if you're going to lead Phase I behavior, you have to remember that it's motivated by fear.

I have been a plant manager for several companies, and sometimes I would go into an organization that had just been purchased by an unfriendly takeover, or something similar to that. I'd notice that these organizations were very much a Phase I organization. Initially (my rookie season) I thought that if I was nice to everyone then eventually they would be nice back. In reality that never happened, and I learned fairly quickly that Phase I behavior respects fear. So eventually I changed my style. I would go into these organizations and say, "Hey, listen, you may not like me, and I don't blame you, but the fact of the matter is I am your boss and I have rules." And then I stated the rules. I would say, "If you disobey the rules, I want you to know that I will terminate you immediately." And so they feared me—and all of a sudden I realized that Phase I behavior type organizations respect fear, and therefore they respected me. Remember that you cannot lead if you do not have the respect of the organization you're trying to lead and Phase I behavior is motivated by fear.

Obviously this is not where you want to keep the organization. Your job in a leadership role is to evolve the organization to higher levels of human behavior. But this is a starting point, and you do have to deal with reality. Reality doesn't care what you wish the organization was or is; you have to deal with where you currently are. You ultimately want to evolve the organization from Phase I behavior to the point that the organization is not motivated by fear. This change in culture demands leadership.

Remember that one of the elements that take place if you habitually exercise Phase I behavior throughout your life is that you tend to develop a sense of hatred toward things. Remember, though, that as a leader, you cannot effectively beat hatred with hatred; thus you must rise above it all—you must rise above the behavior of the organization that you're trying to transform. So even though Phase I behavior is a starting point for human nature, it does not have to be the ending condition. The good news is that human nature is capable of evolving. Evolving to higher levels of human behavior usually demands help from those who have matured out of Phase I behavior. It also demands personal courage, strength, and a belief that the seemingly impossible is possible and doable. In other words, you must be capable of going against the critics.

In summary, Phase I behavior is good at creating problems but dysfunctional at solving them, which is another way of saying it is a destructive behavior.

Phase II behavior is when you develop skills and talents that allow you to stand out in a crowd based on those skills and talents. If your skills and talents allow you to stand out in a crowd, they allow you to meet the needs of human nature to stand out in a crowd so that you can start walking away from Phase I behavior. As you develop skills and talents, you have less of a desire to use Phase I behavior to stand out in a crowd. Why? Because the high you get from standing out in a crowd based on skills and talents is a higher, more sustainable high than you get from Phase I behavior. Phase II behavior does not have the steep drop-off like the cheap drug of human behavior. Ultimately you evolve out of lower levels to higher levels of human behavior simply because it feels better. Pretty basic.

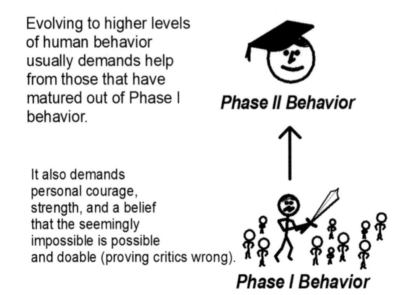

Evolving to higher levels of human behavior usually demands help from those that have matured out of Phase I behavior.

Phase II Behavior

It also demands personal courage, strength, and a belief that the seemingly impossible is possible and doable (proving critics wrong).

Phase I Behavior

Figure 68

Phase II behavior is relatively constructive, so that's a good thing. We can develop skills and talents through formal education or informal education, which is what the graduation cap symbolizes. But we have to develop skills and talents to evolve to Phase II behavior.

When this model was being realized in my mind, I was a father with relatively young children. I have four boys, and at the time, the oldest one was in second grade and the youngest one was a toddler. Through observation, I noticed Phase I behavior developing in my children, so I decided I would try introducing them to the joys of higher-level human behavior, such as Phase II behavior. I felt I needed to find a lonely person for my kids to stand out in a crowd with based on their limited skills and talents.

One evening after work I dropped by the local elder-care facility. I went up to the lady at the front desk and asked her, "Is there anyone in this facility who is extremely lonely?" She responded without hesitation and told me about Mary. Mary had not had a visitor in twelve years! I quickly told the lady at the front desk that this would be perfect and then left the facility, went home, and told my wife about Mary and how I felt it would be a good opportunity for the kids to experience the joys of serving others with their skills and talents. I figured Mary was so lonely that the slightest amount of talent could pull this one off. My wife agreed and immediately started working on the project. She taught the kids some new songs.

Within a couple of weeks she had the kids perform their dress rehearsal. I felt that they did an excellent job and was certain that it would be especially effective for someone who had not had a visitor for twelve years. Generally speaking, loneliness tends to tame overly critical behavior, not that it was needed in this case. After a little polishing of the production, my wife informed me that they were ready for the big performance, so on a Sunday afternoon we got the kids dressed up in their cute little outfits and headed out to the care center.

We arrived at the front desk and announced to the attendant that we had come to see Mary. She was shocked that someone had actually come to visit Mary. She happily led us back to Mary's room. When we arrived there she was in a deep sleep. I told the young lady not to wake her up and that we could come back later. The lady quickly responded, "Are you kidding me, sir? This wonderful woman has not had a visitor for twelve years. Do you really think I'm going to let you escape?" I couldn't really think of a counterargument, so we stayed.

With the persuasive efforts of the young lady, Mary eventually woke up. The attendant told her, "Mary, you have company." I could tell by the look on her face that Mary was shocked. Mary informed us that she needed to get ready and made me promise that we would not leave. I gave her my promise and left her room. While my young family was waiting outside the room I rubbed my hands together and told them that Mary was on her way. After we waited for ten or fifteen minutes, Mary walked out of her room dressed in what I perceived to be her best clothing. She had a warm smile on her face as she sat down, and my wife started asking her questions about herself.

Mary started talking and an hour flew by—and then she stopped and asked us about the children. This is where their practice was to kick in. So I brought the children forward, straightened up their clothing, and reminded them of what they had practiced to do. To my relief, the kids performed as planned. Each child went up to Mary, looked her right in the face, and introduced himself. Then my wife announced to Mary that the kids had prepared some songs that they wanted to sing to her. My wife brushed each of the kids down and had them line up in front of Mary; then they started singing their songs. They were doing a great job. Wow, those genes must have come from their mother! Soon I noticed tears building up in the corners of Mary's eyes. The next thing I knew, tears were flowing freely down her face. I thought to myself, *This is exactly what the kids needed.* When the first song was over, Mary asked if they could sing another song. My wife informed her that the kids had practiced four songs and that they desired to share all of them with her. By the time they had finished all four songs, my wife and Mary were openly crying.

I don't really like crying in front of people, so I was exercising every tool that has evolved over time to keep men from crying. I bit my lips, licked my lips, spun circles, went for a walk, and blew my nose, and in the end I survived. But the point was that it was a very touching performance. At the end of the fourth song I watched my children scanning the two women in front of them, their mom and

Mary. I gave my sons high fives for the great performance, and my oldest boy looked at me and said, "I think we did a good job." I told all the boys that they had just done an excellent job. I asked them, "Do you feel good?" and they responded in the affirmative. I could tell that the boys had just learned how to stand out in a crowd based on their skills and talents. The exercise was a success!

Eventually, all the boys went up and gave Mary a hug, and we began to leave. As I looked around, I was shocked at what an impact this performance had on everyone around us. It seems that everyone was in tears. As we exited the building through the various hallways, I noticed that at the corners of the hallways were various nurses, and all of them had red and puffed-up eyes from the emotional experience they had just witnessed. I must admit that I was greatly surprised at the influence this small act had on all these people. At that moment I started to realize the power of this kind of behavior.

In Phase II behavior
we learn to stand out
in a crowd by developing
our skills and talents.

Phase II behavior
does not have the
nasty after taste
of Phase I behavior.

Phase II Behavior

Figure 69

In Phase II behavior we learn to stand out in a crowd by developing our skills and talents—not only by developing those skills and talents but by exercising them in society. Phase II behavior does not have the nasty aftertaste of Phase I behavior.

From this experience, I can tell you that it felt good to my kids to stand out in a crowd based on their skills and talents. They exercised those skills and talents and wow—they really stood out in the crowd! I noticed that they recognized this and found that this was something good. It made them feel great, and it was my hope, as a father, that they would start practicing that form of behavior to stand out in a crowd and start divorcing the Phase I behavior.

I wish I could tell you as a parent that you only need to do that once, but I've learned, not only in teaching children but really in teaching anyone, that redundancy is a powerful and necessary tool in teaching people. Obviously you don't just do this once for your organization—you give people many opportunities over and over to learn to stand out in a crowd based on their skills and talents that can improve systems.

Individuals desire Phase II behavior over Phase I behavior because it naturally feels better. The good feelings from Phase II behavior are a powerful motivator, and people will dedicate their lives to improving skills and talents so that they can spend more time in Phase II.

Phase II behavior still has some of the stains of Phase I behavior. The relationship between the two behaviors is that Phase II behavior secretly desires others to fail but only if they are developing the same skills and talents that the Phase II currently uses to stand out in a crowd. What makes Phase II different from Phase I is that Phase I wants everyone to fail. Phase II behavior finds those with the same skills and talents to be threatening to our ability to stand out in a crowd, and thus it threatens our very survival. Symbolically speaking, when no one is looking, Phase II behavior will throw out the proverbial banana peel and hope the "competition" slips.

Phase II behavior respects skills and talents. Phase II organizations will allow you to lead them as long as they perceive you have more skills and talents than they have. Organizations will not allow you to lead them unless they respect you. So remember that Phase II respects skills and talents. As soon as Phase II people perceive that they have more skill and talent than their leaders, they will no longer respect them and they will not allow themselves to be led by those leaders. In other words, once Phase II people perceive that they have more skill and talent than their boss, they will attempt to undermine the boss's authority.

Phase II behavior seeks self-glorification. When Phase II behavior does something good, it desires to share it with others in an effort to bring attention to itself. What people are doing here is trying to stand out in a crowd based on their skills and talents so that they bring attention to themselves (self-glorification). Phase II behavior is relatively constructive. It is a big improvement over Phase I behavior. Because people with Phase II behavior expend a great deal of energy letting as many people as possible know of their skills and talents and good works, a natural by-product of Phase II behavior can be to make other people feel inadequate in their presence based on their unique skills and talents.

Phase II behavior may even realize that the feeling of stupidity exists. The main priority of people with Phase II behavior is to make themselves stand out in a crowd based on their skills and talents. As a result, they will not compromise this value to compensate for others' perceived insecurities.

In summary, Phase II behavior is a constructive behavior that respects skills and talents and desires to be recognized for the social benefits that are achieved during the implementation of those skills and talents. An organization can go a long way on Phase II behavior.

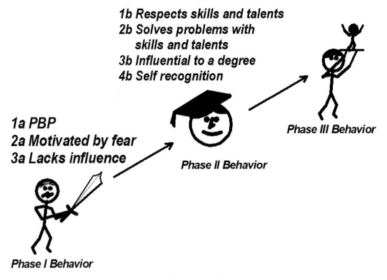

Figure 70

I have again upgraded the information in our human nature model. Notice that it says: respects skills and talents; solves problems with skills and talents; influential to a degree; and self-recognition.

Eventually human nature has the potential to master Phase II behavior to the extent that this former behavior becomes boring and unfulfilling. When this is experienced, then human nature is capable of evolving to Phase III behavior.

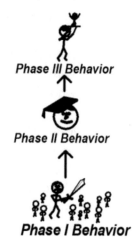

Figure 71

Phase III behavior is the crowning achievement of human behavior. The key phrase for Phase III behavior is "to lift up." Phase III behavior can only be realized after overcoming Phase I behavior and mastering Phase II behavior. You cannot evolve from Phase I behavior to Phase III behavior. This model shows that you must evolve through lower levels of behavior to higher levels in an orderly fashion. It is an evolutionary experience.

Now I'd like to tell you a story in an effort to illustrate Phase III behavior. It is a story about athletes with special needs. One of the organizations that support these athletes is the Special Olympics. So why was this Special Olympics organized?

I believe it was organized to give people a chance to stand out in a crowd. It was designed for a group of people whom we perceive as incapable of standing out in a crowd with their own natural skills and talents. The organization appears to be very successful.

Now here's the story: I believe it was based on an actual event, but it came from the book *Chicken Soup for the Soul*—a rather inspiring story. I have added to the original story in hopes that it would be more effective at teaching you the desired lesson. Specifically I have added the father and the coach characters to the story.

As the story goes, a group of young men lined up in the final race of their Olympics. The stadium was full of enthusiastic fans. The coaches were at the end of the track prepared to motivate their athletes. It was considered to be a once-in-a-lifetime opportunity for these young athletes to stand out in a crowd. The starting gun sounded and the athletes took off with all the effort their talents could afford. It soon became obvious who the winner of the race would be as he pulled out yards ahead of the second-place runner. Then, unexpectedly, the last-place runner twisted his ankle and fell to the ground, screaming out from the excruciating pain. The first-place runner heard his screams and stopped. The second-place runner quickly responded and took over the desired position of first place.

The father of the athlete who was originally in first place threw his hat on the ground and said, "This handicap stuff is very difficult—here my son had an opportunity to stand out in a crowd and he blew the opportunity. Damn it!" The coach at the end of the lane stomped his foot on the ground and walked away in disgust. Soon all the athletes stopped in an attempt to figure out the cause of the screaming. With everyone witnessing the event, they watched as all the athletes stopped and walked back to the injured athlete. Eventually the original first-place runner reached out his hand to the injured athlete and lifted him up. The audience gasped as they watched the athletes put their arms around one another's shoulders and walk down the track, all crossing the line in "first place." I often ask my leadership students, "Makes you wonder a little bit, doesn't it? Doesn't it make you wonder, just a little bit, who the truly handicapped ones are?"

Phase III behavior is willing to sacrifice its own glory to allow others to stand out in a crowd. In other words, Phase III motives are pure. By "pure motive," I mean the only reason for Phase III action is to lift others up, not to draw attention to oneself. When Phase II behavior performs acts that benefit society, it does so for its own self-glorification. Phase III behavior performs acts to benefit society; however, it does so strictly for the benefit of others—not for self-glorification. This is what makes Phase III behavior unique.

There was a time when NBA Jazz tickets were given away anonymously in the Salt Lake Valley area. (The Jazz are an NBA basketball team.) I was a witness to one of these occasions when I met a young lady who worked for one of my clients. This young lady was the biggest Jazz fan I had ever met. Her cubical was totally decorated in Jazz memorabilia. On occasion I would stop and talk to her about the recent Jazz games. She loved to relive the biggest plays of the game. I once asked her if she had ever been to a Jazz game. She replied that she could never afford such a luxury. Later I found out that she was a single mother, and besides that, she didn't make that much money (she was just scraping by). As the years went by, I would stop and visit with her about the latest information on the Jazz team's performance. One day I was walking by her cubical and noticed that she had her head in her hands and was crying. I went in and asked her what was wrong. I asked her several times, and she wouldn't answer. Finally I decided that it must not be any of my business, so I apologized and was starting to leave when she called out my name. When I heard my name I turned around and an envelope hit me right in the chest. I caught the envelope and then opened it up and looked inside and was shocked to find what appeared to be thousands of dollars' worth of Jazz tickets. Not only were there a lot of tickets, but they were in excellent locations. So I stopped and looked at them for a moment, and then I sat down and asked her if I could have one. (Just kidding—I didn't really ask her that, but I must confess the thought crossed my mind.) I asked her where she got all of those tickets. She said she had come to her office that morning and they were sitting on her chair. I then asked her, "Who gave you these tickets?" She said there was no note or anything that would allow her to identify the Good Samaritan. She desired to thank someone, so she called up the Jazz ticket office and told them she had found some tickets and desired to return them to the rightful owner. She read off the tracking number of one of the tickets. The lady on the other end of the phone line asked her to hold while she investigated. Eventually she came back and told my friend that she could not help her as the owner had paid cash for the tickets. Whoever the sly dog was who purchased those tickets had made himself or herself untraceable! I don't know who gave those tickets away, but I assumed it was one of the vice presidents, as they were all paid well and never seemed to be shy about sharing their wealth with others on occasion.

This story is a good example of Phase III behavior in that someone sacrificed for someone else with no apparent desire to be recognized for the good deed. Phase III behavior demands sacrifice, and sacrifice demands character. Character is defined as the ability to follow through with a decision long after the emotion of making that decision is gone.

For example, imagine yourself being a child again, and everyone is always asking you, "What are you going to be when you grow up?" You notice that you get a pretty good response when you tell them you are going to be a surgeon someday. Enjoying the attention, you start telling everyone you are going to be a surgeon when you grow up. Eventually the thought of becoming a surgeon becomes an emotionally packed dream. Then you grow up and finally go to college and take your first difficult class. It is the first time you have ever had to sacrifice for the dream. When sacrifice meets emotion, emotions evaporate. Now, that's an important concept to remember: when sacrifice meets emotion, emotions evaporate. And the only thing that will determine whether you continue on with the dream is if you have enough character. So you start sacrificing, emotions evaporate, and the only thing that will determine if you move forward or not without those emotions is character. Remember that character is the ability to follow through with a decision long after the emotions of making that decision are gone. Whether this young man will ever realize his dreams to be a surgeon will depend upon his ability to follow through with his decision long after the emotions of making that decision is gone. In other words, his dream will not be realized unless he has enough character.

I can still remember the day the movie *Rocky* arrived at the local theaters. I went with all my neighborhood friends. When we got out of the theater, everyone was on an emotional high and wanted to be Rocky. Now, if you haven't seen *Rocky* it's a rather emotionally action-packed film about an underdog fighter who goes out and fights for the championship. And I think there were several *Rocky* movies, but if I remember correctly, the first one he may not have won, but he came close to winning, and it really got people emotional about the sport of boxing, especially a group of young boys.

One of the things Rocky did when he was working out was that he'd drink raw eggs. So the next morning my friends and I got up and knocked down some raw eggs and took off running. We ran until we started hurting. Remember that when sacrifice meets emotions, emotions evaporate. Well, as soon as the sacrifice began, the emotions left, and we stopped running. We did not have the strength of character to become like Rocky. Life can be that way if we let it.

Remember that Phase III behavior demands sacrifice, and sacrifice demands character. If you are incapable of sacrifice, then you are not capable of performing Phase III behavior—it's impossible. Sometimes Phase III behavior even demands that you sacrifice your own popularity. I love to read the books from Jack Welch. Jack Welch is an ex-CEO of General Electric, and in his book *Jack Straight from the Gut* he told of an experience he had as a young man. It was the last game of the hockey season for Jack, and his team desperately wanted to end it on a positive note. As the story goes, the game went into overtime and ultimately they lost. Jack was very upset and vented his frustration by throwing his hockey stick across the rink. He then skated out, picked up the stick, and went off to the locker room. As Jack tells it, he entered the locker room and saw his friends stripping off their pads when all of a sudden his Irish mother crashed through the locker room door and grabbed him by the jersey. Jack tells how the place fell silent. Quoted directly from his book, he said, "Every eye was glued on this middle-aged woman in a floral-patterned dress as she walked across the floor past the wooden benches where some of the guys were already changing. She went right for me, grabbing the top of my uniform. 'You punk!' she shouted in my face. 'If you don't know how to lose, you'll never know how to win. If you don't know this, you shouldn't be playing.'" Obviously this could have been a rather embarrassing moment for Jack, but we have probably all experienced similar situations in life. You know, it's "the Mom thing." I don't know exactly how Jack felt about this, but I know how I have felt in similar situations. I would have thought, *You are the meanest woman on the face of the earth—how dare you embarrass me in front of my friends like that?*

But as we mature, we realize that our mother's desire was to lift us up to our true potential (that only they can perhaps see) and that they are willing to sacrifice their own popularity on our behalf. So remember that Phase III behavior demands sacrifice, and sacrifice demands character, and sometimes we must sacrifice our own popularity to lift others up. This is especially true when we have a larger vision than the organization we're trying to lift up. In other words, in the organization's current state they are incapable of perceiving our vision of a better tomorrow. When this is the case it is pretty standard that the group receiving this Phase III behavior perceives it as Phase I behavior.

Now, back to our beloved Jazz ticket story. I don't know who bought those tickets for that lady, but I do know this: on his or her way to the ticket counter, that person's emotions evaporated, and the only thing that allowed him or her to follow through with the good deed was the strength of his or her character. It is worth repeating again: character is the ability to follow through with a decision long after the emotions of making that decision are gone. Remember that you cannot perform Phase III behavior if you do not have the character demanded by the specific task.

I always give my students a homework assignment that I cannot grade. The homework assignment is to go out and do something good for someone else and never, ever let anyone know about the service provided or the sacrifice involved. This is the only way I know to prove that they are capable of Phase III behavior or have evolved to the point that Phase III behavior is a possibility.

The next story is what I call a composite story. A composite story is where you take people you have met and experiences you have had or witnessed and combine people and experiences into a story designed to teach an important lesson. There was a time in my life when I was fortunate enough to become a plant manager. On my first day on the job I went around and introduced myself to all of the employees. I met one young man whose name was Tom. I called him Tommy. I introduced myself, shook his hand, and asked him how everything was going. He told me that "things would be a hell of a lot better if those bastards on the other end of the line would pull their heads out." Tommy went on and on—and it felt very good to finally get away from him. Tommy was the most Phase I person I had ever met in my life. I never really went around Tommy after that day; it was just too depressing. I would always stay about fifty yards away, and if he looked at me, I would wave. That is pretty much how everyone treated Tommy. Don't get me wrong: Tommy was a hard worker; it was just his attitude that I had a difficult time stomaching. I once asked one of the employees who grew up in the town Tommy was from if he had known him growing up. He said, "Yes, I knew him all right. I used to feel sorry for him until he beat me up a few times." He then looked me right in the eye and said, "To be right honest with you, if Tommy died tomorrow, I wouldn't even shed a tear." In summary, no one liked to spend time with Tommy; he was just too much of a downer.

The manufacturing plant where the majority of this story took place had a problem. It was not just a plant problem; it was an industry problem. Whoever solved this problem would gain market share, increase profitability, and achieve job security for all the employees. This problem had been worked on for years before I ever arrived at the plant. At every production meeting for the last several years the plant manager would always ask for updates on a solution to this problem. Out of respect for this tradition, I would ask the same question, day in and day out. I was so accustomed to asking the question and getting the same answer that I stopped listening for the response from the production supervisor. Then one day, during the traditional production meeting, I asked the question, "How are we doing on the problem?"

The production supervisor quietly said, "Problem solved."

It didn't register, and I skipped to the next bullet point. Then the meaning of what he had just said struck me. I stopped, looked up, and said, "What did you say?"

He smiled back and said, "Problem solved!"

I threw my pen across the table and said, "You have got to be kidding me."

He then said, "No it's true."

Then, while rubbing my brow, I looked up and said, "Who solved the problem?"

The supervisor quickly answered, "Tommy solved the problem."

I gasped and then quietly laughed and said, "You have got to be kidding me."

I thought in my mind, *What is this, April Fool's Day or something?* Then I looked over at the production supervisor with a look that said, *We shouldn't be joking around about this.*

He then took his hat off, ran his fingers through his hair, and said, "No, really, John—Tommy solved the problem."

I put my elbows up on the table, rested my chin in my hands, looked him straight in the eye, and said, "Tommy solved it?" I then said, "Maybe I misread the kid."

The supervisor responded, "Maybe." The supervisor explained the solution to the problem, and all of a sudden it made so much sense. I thought to myself, *Why didn't I think of that?*

After the meeting I reluctantly swallowed my pride and went out to Tommy's workstation and told him, "Hey Tommy, I heard you solved the problem. Is that true?"

He responded harshly, "Who told you that?"

I swallowed my pride for the second time and said, "That's what your supervisor told me."

Tommy then stood up a little taller, and with his typical, angry-sounding voice said, "Yeah—so what's it to ya?"

I swallowed my pride again, for the third time now, and said, "Thank you for all that you have done for this company; you have created job security for everyone."

He then quickly looked at the ground and turned away from me and said, "Sounds like a bunch of bullshit to me."

I then swallowed my pride again, now the fourth time, and said, talking to his back, "I am going to talk to the VP and see if I can't come up with a reward for you." Tommy didn't respond, and I took a drive to go break the good news to the VP. Ultimately, the VP was very excited about the news and agreed to give Tommy five thousand dollars for his successful efforts. However, he told me I was not allowed to present the check to Tommy until the company Christmas party.

Before we go any further, I probably should give you some background on Tommy. You see, Tommy was born to a drug-addicted, prostitute mother. He never knew his father. Growing up, he lived in a camp trailer with his mother and younger brother. They lived right off the bottom edge of a huge lake, and in the winter when the winds would come off the lake, it would get extremely cold. The poorer people in town would heat their trailers with kerosene lanterns or heaters. One evening Tommy's mother was out doing her thing and Tommy and his younger brother were in the camp trailer playing with a ball. When the younger brother threw Tommy the ball, it accidently hit the kerosene heater. The heater fell from the shelf and broke open when it hit the floor. The floor was covered with burning kerosene. Tommy's brother escaped out the front door without injury, but Tommy was not so lucky. He had to run through the slick, burning kerosene. In doing so, he slipped and fell, burying the left side of his face in the burning kerosene. He got up and ran around the trailer screaming with one-half of his face ablaze. He eventually jumped in a snow bank and put out the fire. By the time he jumped into the snow bank, the damage had already been done. Half of Tommy's face was melted. It was so damaged that he would never fully recover. The left side of his face looked like melted plastic.

From time to time we would provide plant tours for customers, suppliers, and others. I would always warn them about Tommy's face in hopes that they would not gasp and embarrass themselves. I told the visitors that if they did gasp, not to worry. It seems that Tommy had learned how to deal with it over time, but despite the warning, they would gasp anyway. Tommy didn't seem to notice. Imagine how Tommy must have felt going to grade school! Eventually, he found out how he could stand out in a crowd. He could be ornery and nasty and beat people up if they as much as looked at him sideways—and he became rather good at beating people up.

You know, most people have parents or other significant people who can champion them through life. Tommy did not have that luxury. He had to become tough; he also had to learn how to effectively use Phase I methodologies to give himself a feeling of value. Remember the two assumptions of the model. The first one was, "The mother of all motivators is survival." And number two was, "If you can't stand out in a crowd, you will die." Tommy was just trying to survive the only way he knew how.

Anyway, back to the story. Tommy had supposedly solved the problem. In reality, I never really believed that he had solved that problem. I felt the only person in that plant who had the skills and talents necessary to solve that problem was Tommy's supervisor. This supervisor was in my office once, and I told him that I didn't think Tommy had solved that problem. I told the supervisor that I thought *he* was the one who had solved the problem. After I communicated this to him, he got mad; he went ballistic. He told me that if I wanted to believe my own lie, then go ahead, but it was just that—a lie. He then stomped out of my office. Now I have to tell you, I'm not real sharp all the time, but I did realize that was a subject I didn't want to visit again. I never brought up the topic to Tommy's supervisor again.

Time went by, and we eventually had a company Christmas party. We rented the local high school auditorium and everyone showed up for the anticipated annual event. I went to the party, stood up on the stage, and made some generic announcements, and then I told them we had someone to honor this day. I told them there was a young man who had gone the extra mile and solved an important problem for the company. I told them that this young man had brought job security to everyone in that auditorium, and we should be appreciative of what he had done. Then I told them it was Tommy—that Tommy had solved the problem that brought job security to everyone in that auditorium. I called Tommy up to the stand and ushered him up to the podium next to me. I paused a minute and told the audience, "This is the young man who made the difference." I wasn't really expecting what happened next. The audience stood up and gave Tommy a standing ovation.

I never told anyone, but I saw tears well up in the corner of Tommy's eyes as he stared at the floor and walked from the stage. Looking back, I realize that was probably the first time Tommy had ever stood out in a crowd based on his perceived skills and talents. Tommy got a lot of pats on the back that night and eventually seemed to rise to the occasion.

One morning I had to go in especially early to the plant; it was approximately 4:00 a.m. As I passed by Tommy's supervisor's office,

I noticed that his light was on. Out of curiosity, I peeked through the window on the door. I was shocked at what I saw; the supervisor was in his office with his hat off, lecturing Tommy on problem-solving methodologies. Now I knew for sure who had actually solved that problem. Past experience suggested that I dare not mention it to anyone, which I didn't until I wrote this book.

Being a little humbled from past experience, I decided to give Tommy another chance. I was pleasantly surprised when I went up and asked him how he was doing, and all he wanted to talk about was problems he was working on. Unbelievable! Tommy had actually learned how to stand out in a crowd based on his new skills and talents, and he loved it. He was, no kidding, a different person. Tommy had evolved to Phase II behavior right before my eyes.

I learned a couple of lessons from this experience. First, don't look at Phase I behavior as bad or evil; look at it as people just trying to survive the only way they know how. The second lesson was that I was taught the power of Phase III behavior. I witnessed Phase III behavior, from that supervisor, changing a person right before my very eyes. I learned that changing culture is ultimately about changing people.

In summary, Phase III behavior is the only form of behavior capable of changing culture in a positive way. Phase III behavior, then, is the essence of leadership. Remember that leadership in the world of transformation means the ability to change culture, and the ability to change culture is the ability to change people. Phase I behavior is not capable of changing culture for the good; neither is Phase II, at least to any significant extent. So if we are to become capable of changing culture (which is leadership), we must learn to master the art of Phase III behavior.

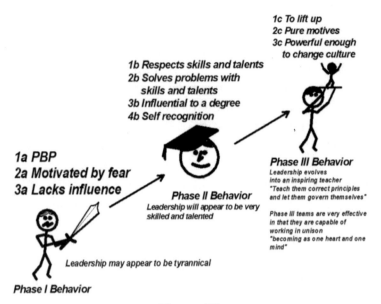

1c To lift up
2c Pure motives
3c Powerful enough
to change culture

1b Respects skills and talents
2b Solves problems with
skills and talents
3b Influential to a degree
4b Self recognition

1a PBP
2a Motivated by fear
3a Lacks influence

Phase III Behavior
Leadership evolves
into an inspiring teacher
"Teach them correct principles
and let them govern themselves"

Phase II Behavior
Leadership will appear to be very
skilled and talented

Phase III teams are very effective
in that they are capable of
working in unison
"becoming as one heart and one
mind"

Leadership may appear to be tyrannical

Phase I Behavior

Figure 72

Now let's update our model and review it again. Remember that Phase I behavior tends to solve problems with personify, blame, and punish methodologies. Also remember that personify, blame, and punish has the natural by-product of fear. In addition, Phase I behavior is motivated by fear and lacks influence. Often it is hard to tell on the leadership side when you first go into a Phase I organization whether the leader is exercising Phase I behavior or not. Does the leadership have higher motives but realize that the organization has to be managed with fear because its members respect nothing else? After a short time, however, you can tell which kind of leader you have, because if he or she is a Phase III leader, he or she will use fear to get the organization under control, and then he or she will evolve the organization. So if you see an individual come in using fear as his motivator and then he evolves the organization into higher levels of behavior, such as Phase II, then he is a good leader. Bad leaders motivate the organization by fear just because they are Phase I individuals and haven't evolved yet. An indication of this is that they can never sustain a performance rating much over 95 percent. And if that's the case, they will never evolve their organizations beyond the point where they just want control and are willing to exercise fear in the long term to keep that control. Remember that you never become greater than that which motivates you. If I tour a plant and notice they are using Solution #3 effectively and as a result inspection is at a minimum, I also know what kind of person I will find in the front office, and this isn't by accident.

Now, Phase II behavior. Phase II, remember, respects skills and talents, so if you're going to lead a Phase II organization, the workers have to respect you if they're going to let you lead them. And so you have to show them that you have skills and talents—even greater skills and talents than they have. If they perceive that they have better skills and talents than you do, they will stop respecting you, you will not be able to lead the organization, and they will most likely try to undermine you because they no longer respect you. Remember that Phase II individuals solve problems with their skills and talents. Also remember that Phase II is influential to a degree and likes self-recognition. So these individuals will do a lot of things to make themselves look good in the end—self-glorification is their motive.

Now, Phase III behavior. Remember that the key words to Phase III behavior are "to lift up"—lifting others up with a pure motive of lifting them up, making people feel better about what they can accomplish, but you do this just for them, not for you. You do not try to draw attention to yourself for your good deeds. Phase III behavior is powerful enough to change culture. In other words, it's powerful enough to change people. And Phase III behavior, if you'll recall, demands sacrifice, and sacrifice demands character. So what does a leader do in a Phase III organization? Well, if you're talented enough to get an organization up to Phase III behavior, leadership becomes rather easy for most people. You see, the leader becomes the teacher. That's right. To lead a Phase III organization, you must evolve into a teacher. In other words, you teach people correct principles and then let them govern themselves. Phase III behavior will never embarrass you, which means it will never fail you.

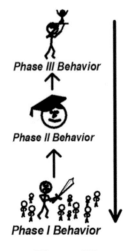

Figure 73

Thus far I have taught that once you evolve upward from Phase I to Phase II, and ultimately Phase III behavior, you stay at the higher levels of behavior. This is not true. Once you achieve higher levels of behavior, you can still slide down to lower levels of behavior. If you ultimately evolve to be capable of Phase III behavior, there are forces that can cause you to act out in lower levels of behavior. What are these forces? Well, remember that Phase III behavior demands sacrifice, and sacrifice demands character. The problem source is that no one has infinite character, so you can only stay in Phase III behavior according to the amount of character you have achieved. If the sacrifice demands more character than you currently have, then you will slide down to lower levels of behavior.

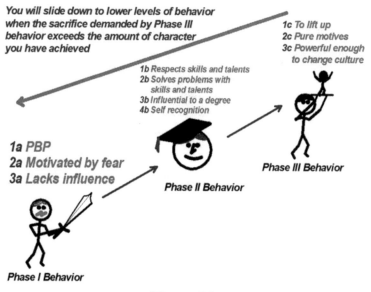

You will slide down to lower levels of behavior when the sacrifice demanded by Phase III behavior exceeds the amount of character you have achieved

1c To lift up
2c Pure motives
3c Powerful enough
   to change culture

1b Respects skills and talents
2b Solves problems with
   skills and talents
3b Influential to a degree
4b Self recognition

1a PBP
2a Motivated by fear
3a Lacks influence

Phase III Behavior

Phase II Behavior

Phase I Behavior

Figure 74

Let's add another element to our model. Remember that you will slide down to lower levels of behavior when the sacrifice demanded by Phase III behavior exceeds the amount of character you have achieved in life. So in your Phase III behavior, you start experiencing stress. By stress I mean that you're asked to sacrifice more than you're capable of sacrificing. At this point you go into Phase II where you may think or say something like, "Okay, get out of the room. I'll solve this problem myself." If the pressure keeps building, the sacrifice demands more and more, and you don't have enough character to sustain it, then you can fall into Phase I behavior, where you start acting out personify, blame, and punish. In other words, the more character you have, the more influential you are capable of becoming because you will be able to sustain higher levels of human behavior under higher levels of stress. Now remember what character is: the ability to follow through with a decision long after the emotions of making that decision are gone.

Concerning human behavior, infinite character equals infinite influence. The problem is that none of us has infinite character; thus we will not have infinite influence. However, we can raise our character and increase our influence over time. We often refer to the

157

act of reaching our limits of character as stress. If you do not have infinite character, you will have a natural breaking point.

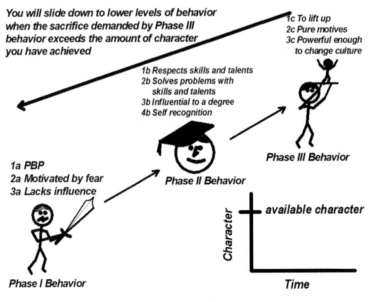

You will slide down to lower levels of behavior when the sacrifice demanded by Phase III behavior exceeds the amount of character you have achieved

1c To lift up
2c Pure motives
3c Powerful enough
to change culture

1b Respects skills and talents
2b Solves problems with
skills and talents
3b Influential to a degree
4b Self recognition

1a PBP
2a Motivated by fear
3a Lacks influence

Phase III Behavior

Phase II Behavior

Character

available character

Phase I Behavior

Time

Figure 75

Notice that down in the right-hand corner of Figure 75 I have added a little chart—the XY axis—and it shows the available character. You can maintain the higher level of behavior as long as your available character is above the character that is needed to perform the task. But as the task increases and more sacrifice is demanded of you, it works its way up that axis until eventually the character needed is above the character available. That is the point where you'll start sliding down into lower levels of behavior. I refer to it as "the breaking point." The good news in all of this is that through life's experiences, we can achieve or we can "grow" our character.

I'm going to teach you a very important lesson, so read carefully. When I was just a young boy, I had a problem. Like most little boys, I desired to be courageous. The problem was that even though I desired the attribute of courage, I was just a big chicken, and everyone knew it. One day I sat down and talked to my grandfather, to whom I was very close, and I told him I had a problem. He sat down and asked me to describe my problem to him. I quietly told my grandfather that I desired to be courageous. He looked at me for a moment in shock and then said, "You do have a problem." Again, everyone knew I was a "chicken." I looked at my wonderful grandfather and said, "What do I need to do to become courageous?"

My grandfather then got a serious look on his face and started rubbing his chin. This was a sign that he was thinking hard, so I just sat there and watched him do all the work. Then, to my great relief, I saw the countenance of his face light up and I knew he had the answer for me. With excitement, I told him, "Give me the answer, Grandfather; please give me the answer."

He said, "The answer is in the movie you watched last night."

I asked him, "What movie was that?" and then he reminded me that I had watched *The Wizard of Oz*. He reminded me that one of the characters in the movie had the same problem I had just described. I thought back for a moment and then remembered that it was the lion. The lion wanted to be courageous, but he was a natural-born chicken just like I was. My grandfather encouraged me to come up with my own answer. He helped me by asking, "What did the lion do to get courage?"

I thought for a moment and then responded, "He went to Oz—the lion went to Oz, and Oz gave him courage—I remember now!"

My grandfather slapped his forehead and said, "Good grief, kid— you missed the whole meaning of the movie."

So I shot back at him, saying, "Then tell me the meaning of the movie."

After looking around the room and making sure my mother wasn't listening, he bent down by my ear and whispered, "The lion gained courage from his voyage to Oz, not from Oz; he overcame his fears by facing his fears." Then he paused for a moment and said, "You need to do everything that scares you over and over again until it doesn't scare you anymore." He said, "That was the point of the story. That's how the lion obtained the attribute of courage—by going against his fears, even though it was very uncomfortable for him."

So I did as my grandfather said. I made a mental note of all my fears, and I went out and began to face them. I ended up with a lot of scrapes and bruises, and slowly but surely I started developing within myself the attribute of courage.

By the time I went to college, I had overcome many of my fears. Among my favorite hobbies was riding motocross bikes across the deserts of Idaho and racing stock cars on Saturday nights. By the time I went to college, I had won two series championships and one track championship at the local dirt track. I had overcome a lot of fears. With all that said, I still had one phobia that I needed to overcome, and that was my fear of heights. So while in college I picked up the sport of skydiving. To be honest with you, it was so scary to me that I can't even remember my first four jumps.

On my first jump, which I believe was in Antioch, California, there was a camera attached to the wing, so it took a picture of me falling from the plane that very first time. And I can tell you this—I looked like a scared cat—and I felt like I looked. The scariest jump I ever remember was approximately my tenth jump. It had me so concerned that as I was walking across the campus to get to my next class I would remember that I was scheduled to jump on the weekend and as a result my palms would sweat—and my palms don't usually sweat. It was a sobering week as I considered it may be my last week.

On Saturday morning, the morning of "jump day," also remembered by me—in my mind, anyway—as "death day," I got up and cleaned my room thinking I may not be coming back and wanting to let my mom know she had taught me something. Then I got in my car and picked up my friend, who was also scheduled for his tenth jump. I could tell he was scared also, as nothing was said on our way to the airport. As we rode in the car I started thinking strategically and reasoned that if I could get to the airplane first, then I would be the last one to get out of the plane; that would give me a few more breaths.

As we arrived at the airport, I quickly implemented the strategy and was the first to put on my parachute and get in the airplane. If I recall correctly, the plane was just a small Cessna Skyhawk 172, so there was not a lot of room; however, there was enough room for the pilot, the jumpmaster, and two jumpers. I was sitting on the floor with my knees up against my chest facing the back of the plane as the airplane began its climb to jump altitude, which was approximately six thousand feet above the ground.

I was attempting to enjoy what I perceived as the last moments of my life when I heard the door being pulled up on the old Cessna aircraft. This was always a violent experience, as the open door allows approximately one-hundred-mph winds to enter the aircraft. I always wondered why the battered-up old plane had such clean floors. Out of curiosity, I looked around at the front of the plane and noticed that the jumpmaster was hanging out the side of the plane, and I thought to myself, *This guy is nuts!* However, I was impressed at how he came in and out of the plane with no apparent fear; I hoped to have that level of courage someday. I also knew this was not going to be that day, as I was so scared that I was shaking.

The reason the jumpmaster was hanging out of the plane was that he was looking for the target. They actually put a target on the drop zone, and yes, it looked like a bull's eye—which was kind of strange—but that was what he was doing. I personally never felt comfortable with the bull's-eye thing, I am not sure why; it just always made me feel uncomfortable. After getting over the target the jumpmaster tapped my friend on the shoulder and told him it was time to get out. For beginners like me, getting out of the plane was not that easy. You had to first go from a sitting position to putting one foot out of the plane onto the landing gear. This is rather difficult with a one-hundred-mph wind—and especially with seeing the ground some six thousand feet below your foot, which does not help matters any.

Remember that my friend was facing the back of the plane, and the jumpmaster tapped him on the shoulder and told him it was time to get out, so he got his one foot on the landing gear. Then he had to twist his body out of the plane and quickly grab the diagonal structural strut with his left hand. Then he had to extend his right hand up further on the strut. All of this had to be done in some high-wind velocities, and, yes, I have seen students slip, fall, and yes, scream, understandably, as it is not a short fall.

Anyway, back to the story—my friend was now out of the plane and, as instructed, he had two hands on the strut and one foot on the locked landing gear. Sometimes they will joke around and not lock the wheel and when someone steps on it, well, good-bye and adios. I always found that pretty funny—unless, of course they did it to me; then I was fit to be tied. By this time, my friend's other foot, his right foot, was now dangling in the wind. I had moved into jump position, so the jumpmaster was leaning over me as he prepared to give instructions to my friend. I was now just a couple of feet from my friend, who was about to fall out of the airplane—at least that was my assumption.

While all this was happening I had not mustered up the courage to look outside, so I was just looking at the jumpmaster. After directing the plane directly over the drop zone target, the jumpmaster yelled out, *"Ready, set, go!"* My friend did not respond. As I glanced out, I noticed that his foot had slipped off the landing gear, but he still had a hellish grip on the strut. I could not believe my eyes when I saw him just swinging back and forth on the wing. I was thinking, "How can you do this to me?" and I was thinking these people were nutcases.

Finally the jumpmaster went through the countdown again, only louder this time. He said *"Ready, set, go!"* I looked out of the plane again and nope, he was still hanging out there. He was in his own world; he would not even look at the jumpmaster. I was now completely covered in sweat; this was worse than I had expected! I would prefer a quick death rather than dragging it out into infamy.

Anyway, the jumpmaster tried a couple more times with no response, and I said, "Bye-bye, mental function." I was now watching the jumpmaster and wondering what he was going to do next. He looked over at the pilot and smiled and winked, and I thought, *You pervert, here my friend is hanging out there on the wing and you are enjoying yourself at his expense.* The next thing I remember is the plane going into a rather aggressive dive, and I was thinking, *What are you doing? Don't tell me you are going to try to land the plane with my friend out there.* The next thing I knew, we were pulling out of the dive and I was being pushed into the floor of the plane by some respectable G forces. At this point in time I started getting concerned about my friend again. I noticed that he was putting up a valiant fight as his knuckles were nearly transparent. As I saw it, it was now my friend against the pilot, and I must admit I was proud of the fight he was putting out. If I had not been so scared I would have been cheering for him out loud.

I then looked over at the jumpmaster and saw him look at the pilot in a way that said, "This guy is pretty good. Okay, not pretty good—this guy is amazing." Then I felt the response as the G forces pressed me into the floor of the plane so hard I could no longer sit up straight. Lying on the floor, I now looked out at my friend, and what I saw was not pretty. He was still hanging in there, but you could tell it was only a matter of time; it appeared he was having convulsions out on the end of that wing while he was searching for the all-natural fetal position. Eventually the G forces got the best of him and away he went—good-bye friend. I watched him as he faded away into the blue skies; as he fell away he was reaching for the plane, and his pleading eyes were directly attached to mine and were clearly asking for help. I wish I could tell you I wanted to jump out and help him but that would be a fallacy, I was more in the mood of saying, "You poor bastard." Okay, okay, I said I wanted to be courageous. I was not yet courageous; these things take time—be patient.

Moving on with the story—the jumpmaster now looked into my mentally fatigued face and uttered the horrifying words, "John, it's your turn." He then followed it up by patting me on the back and saying, "You can do this—just focus." Just focus on what? The ground, which is six thousand feet below me? That is really smart—why don't I do that! Okay, I tend to get sarcastic when I think I'm about to die—sue me. Maybe he meant to focus on the warmth running down my leg? In the end I am proud to tell you that I did as my jumpmaster told me and dug into my guts and got out on that wing. Before I left the plane I noticed something that I had not noticed before. The strut was covered with a reddish transparent plastic cover and it had scratch marks all over it; I even thought I saw a piece of fingernail—no kidding.

Now, finally, I want you to know that I did jump out of that plane. In fact, I jumped out of planes some one hundred times after that, until I no longer feared the experience. But the point of the story is this: when you slide down the slope from higher levels of behavior to lower levels of behavior, remember—leave scratch marks.

I have been trying to live this model most of my life, and even though I have a full understanding of the model, when I feel myself slipping again, even though I know what is happening, I cannot stop it, as I have reached the capability of my character and I helplessly fall to lower levels of behavior. But I have also learned that if I leave scratch marks all the way down the curve and then aggressively claw my way back up, then my efforts are rewarded with an increase in character, which gives me the potential to be more influential in future situations.

I must admit that the model is rather ironic in that you must fail to succeed. I know of no other way to gain additional character except by failing. If you don't fail and fall down the curve, then you cannot put forth the effort to climb back up the curve. Fighting the fall and climbing back up the curve is what builds character.

I guess that makes Jack Welch's mom a genius when she said something to the effect of "you must learn how to lose before you can learn to win." If you're afraid to lose, then you will probably never leave the perceived comfort of Phase I behavior, "because what if I fail?" Remember that you can never become greater than that which motivates you, and if fear is your motivation of choice, then you will never climb out of the misery of Phase I behavior.

So if you ever do evolve and find yourself capable of Phase III behavior, but you build a life that never challenges your limited character and never allows you to fall down the curve, then you will no longer grow your ability to influence others—what a shame! Don't be afraid to fail. Remember that failure is ultimately what allows growth to be realized. Always remember that a weakness is nothing more than a potential strength. If you go against a weakness long enough, it will eventually become your strength. In other words, the act of fighting to overcome your weaknesses creates strength, until someday you will have enough strength to overcome the weaknesses, and thus the weaknesses become strengths—quite simple really. A weakness is really nothing more than a potential strength; however, beware that Phase I behavior does not see weaknesses that way. Phase I and some elements of Phase II will say that it is a flaw that should condemn you and because of your weaknesses you can never become great. To that I say ignore the critics and deal with the truth, and the truth is that without weaknesses you would be incapable of creating strength. Weaknesses have the potential of being your greatest blessing in life, but not until you see them as potential strengths.

Remember that Phase I behavior will belittle other people's weaknesses and hide its own. Thus, Phase I behavior does not allow personal or organizational growth. Phase I behavior is incapable of transformation. Phase III behavior, on the other hand, sees weaknesses as potential strengths. Phase III behavior does not hide weaknesses but puts them out in the open and works them over in an intelligent manner. Phase III behavior will not make fun of people or organizations for weaknesses. It makes no sense to Phase III behavior to belittle potential strength—where is the logic in that? When you bottom out on Phase I, the Phase I environment will say, "I see you have bottomed out in Phase I; you are worthless and can never climb the curve of human behavior again." I have always argued, and I must say successfully so, that God gave man the middle finger for a reason, and this is one of those moments when it should be used. Nothing is more destructive to the human soul than to believe, incorrectly so, that because of your weakness you can't get better. In reality it is just the opposite—you can become stronger because of your weaknesses. In my opinion we shouldn't call them weaknesses at all—that has a negative context—but we should call them potential strengths. I honestly feel that my weaknesses are gifts from whoever created me. My greatest gift back will be to rise above them all and bring them back as strengths, which is my goal in life. If he didn't want us to have weaknesses he would have created us accordingly. So in short, tell the critics to go to hell and get to work and climb the curve. Haven't you figured it out yet? The only reason critics have power over you is because you care what they think. Rise above it all.

Now a little clarification on the middle-finger thing. I have found from experience that this is not necessarily, usually, the most socially acceptable thing to do; however, it is still okay to use it in your mind. At least, that's the way I feel about it. Don't worry—the critics will see it in your eyes, at least with a little practice. Now that I have vented, the goal should be to teach yourself not to care what they think. The above discussion suggests that you do care what they think. If you don't care what they think, then you will be indifferent. Also, criticism can be a good thing;; however, people can only handle it constructively in the right doses and perhaps the right timing. So if you find yourself being criticized and you're not ready for it, just become indifferent to it and critics will learn rather quickly that they have no power over you and will leave you alone, because they realize that you won't give them what they want. The only reason negative critics have power over you is because you let them. Rise above it all.

Just so you know, I kept jumping out of those planes (over one hundred times) until eventually I was not afraid of heights anymore. I can still fondly remember the day I realized I had gained the attribute of courage, which resulted from overcoming my weaknesses—I mean my potential strengths. It took a lot of work getting there, and I came within fractions of a second of dying on multiple occasions, but for me, it was worth it.

The evening I remember overcoming my fear was when I was jumping in Northern California, and I was standing on the edge of a beach craft ready to leap into another skydiving experience, from twelve thousand feet. I just stood there for a moment and looked at the beauty of the California sunset; then, without fear of death or anything else, I sailed into the beautiful blue sky. I never remember experiencing such freedom as I did that day, as I had freed myself from the most enslaving and crippling practice of all, fear. Fear is ultimately nothing more than a lack of hope, and in the end I discovered that I didn't really need to jump out of planes to gain courage. I could have just taught myself to appreciate the past; it gives me the same rush and feeling of a freed soul.

If you really desire to piss me off, try motivating me with fear. I consider that the biggest insult anyone could give me. The gall to think I would choose such a poor motivator is truly insulting to me, as it should eventually be to you. I have worked too hard to be motivated by such a stupid motive. Rise above it all!

In the world of skydiving, they use the term "blue skies." "Blue skies" is a saying that means "have a great day" or perhaps a great jump, or in certain special situations "have a great life by living a great life." On that day, the term "blue skies" seemed to have more meaning to me. I had finally risen above it all.

Phase III behavior, by its very nature, is free of fear. Once you taste Phase III behavior, you will never want to go back to lower levels of behavior, and you will do whatever you can to return to its peaceful and productive environment. Why? Because it feels better, again pretty simple. For the most part everything around us is simple. Usually the reason something is difficult is because someone is trying to explain it who doesn't really understand it. Another thing to remember: Phase I behavior will always make fun of Phase III behavior. Phase I behavior fantasizes about destroying Phase III behavior. The bigger they are, the more enjoyable it is to see them fall. It is a natural conflict. Phase III behavior is unique in that it is willing to help those who, at times, desire to destroy them.

Now I would like to review some very important thoughts. Remember that if you are afraid to fail, you may not fail, but if you do not fail, you cannot succeed, for at some level success demands failure. Redundant failure ultimately allows success to be realized. By not giving up on overcoming weaknesses, you will forge the weaknesses into strengths. Effort is your hammer; weakness is your raw material. Get to work—rise above it all. Ultimately, Phase III behavior is about rising above it all. So rise above it all. Don't be afraid.

Flight Photo #1

Flight Photo #2

Flight Photo #3

Flight Photo #4

Flight Photo #5

Flight Photo #6

Flight Photo #7

Flight Photo #8

Flight Photo #9

Flight Photo #10

Flight Photo #11

Race Car Photo #1

Race Car Photo #2

Race Car Photo #3

Race Car Photo #4

Race Car Photo #5

Race Car Trophy Photo #6

Other things you need to realize is that a leader can never raise an organization above his or her predominant level of behavior. A Phase I behavior leader is incapable of raising an organization up to Phase II behavior, and neither is a Phase II leader capable of raising an organization up to Phase III behavior. Phase III organizations are not easy to find; through all the organizations I have toured throughout the world I have found a few that I would say are Phase

III. One such company is a division of US Synthetic, a company that manufactures synthetic diamonds in Orem, Utah. The top value of their organization is to "change lives". When I toured this plant I knew I had found something special, so I tried to find out more about their leader. It didn't surprise me, nor should it surprise you, when I found out the CEO had just retired. I asked where he retired to and was told that he had moved to Africa and was helping to build schoolhouses for the children. I rest my case.

One phenomenon that is fairly common throughout history is when a Phase II leader decides to create a utopia, utopia being defined as a society where everyone exhibits Phase III behavior. Remember that Phase II behavior tends to seek self-glorification. So the objective of creating a utopia is so that he or she can get recognized for being great. I refer to it as "fantasy statue building." The leader will attempt to force Phase III behavior upon the people. This is foolishness, for Phase III behavior cannot be forced; it can only be nurtured. In the end these utopias will always fail unless there is an influential Phase III leader. So remember that Phase III behavior cannot be forced and attempting to force Phase III behavior is a moral perversion that will ultimately create destructive behavior.

One reason for this phenomenon is that leaders must lead by example to lead organizations to higher levels of human behavior; leadership is the constraint of social evolution.

Chapter Five

Rules Of Phase III Behavior

Another rule of transformation is this: *You will not change the organization's personality or culture by "accident." If you are going to change culture, you had better understand and implement the principles of influence.* Remember that culture is very difficult to change. It is the most difficult of all the elements of transformation.

One of the objectives of this lesson is to teach you the principles of influence, often referred to as the principles of leadership. My experience has dictated that there are certain rules that leaders of organizations must follow to have the influence necessary to transform to what I call a "level of greatness." Transformation to greatness demands leadership at the proper place, at the proper time, and with the right vision. It also demands passion and belief that the seemingly impossible is possible and doable. Transformation to greatness demands that an organization exercise passionate appreciation for its own legacy.

The objective of this chapter is to teach you the rules of influence (rules of greatness) in hopes that you will exercise them in your life and, as a result, find your true potential and the ultimate potential of your organization.

Rule #1 of the fourteen rules of greatness says: *You will never become great if you never desire to be great. Greatness is defined as reaching one's ultimate potential, or the potential of that organization. We are currently in the dark ages of our human potential.*

Desire: what creates desire? What is desire? There is an evolution of human thought. The thought starts as a hypothesis. If the hypothesis proves to have predictable abilities, it may then evolve to a theory. If the theory is never found to be incorrect in its predictive abilities, then it becomes a law. Laws will ultimately breed objectivity, and this objectivity will ultimately serve human needs. Laws have the potential to improve the human condition. One such law is referred to as the "law of entropy." Entropy is a measure of disorder. The law of entropy states that a system will become more and more disorganized over time unless energy is added to the system. The scientists have never found an exception to this law. That's why it is referred to as a law. For example, if you leave your living quarters alone, it will tend to become more and more disorganized over time. No one in all of history has witnessed his living quarters becoming cleaner and more organized while doing nothing. People do not necessarily appreciate the law of entropy. It means that we have to perform work if we're to maintain things or to make them better. Laws are generally simple statements and difficult to argue with. So becoming more and more disorganized is only natural. Desire is ultimately the decision one makes to create a more orderly environment.

Desire is not a natural state. This is why desire ultimately has to be a conscious choice; it will not happen by accident. The by-product of desire is sacrifice. If someone says he has a desire, then you should be able to witness that person performing sacrifice. If a person says he has desire but is unwilling to sacrifice, then the conscious decision of desire has not yet been made. Desire is the fuel that drives transformation.

Somehow human beings are more capable of conscious desire than other creatures, and as a result, we are more capable of improving our environment. Why some desire to rise above nature and make things better and others are content to let things degrade into natural destruction is a question that has been asked and unanswered throughout the ages. Ultimately, desire is the decision to rise above it all, whatever the sacrifice may be. The cycle of tyranny to anarchy and back to tyranny again is a natural state of affairs.

Freedom is not a natural state of being. Freedom from tyranny is only realized when people desire to be free. As soon as people lose their desire to be free, then nature will take over and freedom will be lost. Ultimately, freedom demands desire and desire demands sacrifice. The founding fathers of the United States desired freedom. They made a choice to rise above the natural cycle of tyranny to anarchy, no matter what the cost.

One such individual, who was one of wealthiest people in the colonies, chose to make a difference in the cause of freedom, whatever the sacrifice was. This individual volunteered his time and energy in the cause of freedom. He did not accept a salary, nor did he receive a salary; he only accepted expenses after his efforts proved successful. When his inexperienced troops seemed fearful on the eve of battle, he stepped up to the challenge and rode his horse back and forth in the front of the line. The adversarial army opened fire on him with both cannons and muskets; his men were inspired by his courage as he led them into the sacrifice for freedom that we call war.

Miraculously, this person was never pierced by the enemy's bullets. This person sacrificed on the field of battle for six long, discouraging years. Toward the end of the war he went home for the first time. During this short visit home, his only son practically demanded that his father let him become part of this war for freedom. Ultimately, his father gave in and allowed the son to join the war effort. After the war was won and everyone was celebrating the seemingly impossible victory, this person went home, and alongside his wife, the mother of his child, he mourned the death of his only son, who had died in the fight for freedom.

Oh—I forgot to tell you that this person also led an army that seldom got paid, or properly fed, for that matter. There was a point in time when it got so bad that his valued military leaders decided to attack the Congress, which was incapable of living up to the contract it had signed with the soldiers concerning pay. It seemed that the unnatural act of freedom would have to wait for another day. This individual knew that he must act if the cause of freedom was to be realized.

He entered into the hall where everyone met before moving on to take over the Continental Congress. He tried to reason with them, but he could tell by their body language that they refused to be softened. Out of desperation, he thought of what he could do to save the situation. From his perspective, the results of all their sacrifices and the unnatural act of freedom were about to be lost.

After talking at length with these military leaders, it appeared to him that nothing he said was going to change their minds. He then remembered a letter that he had tucked away in his coat; he felt that this letter may soften the men. He quickly pulled the note out of his coat and tried to read it, but he could not—his eyes were worn with age. He quickly dug for his spectacles as the men watched; this shocked the soldiers—they had never seen him use spectacles before. They considered him to be somewhat immortal; they must have thought to themselves, *Is this not the same man who rode into battle before us and could not be hit by the bullets of men? Why would such a man need spectacles?* In that silent moment they realized he was human like they were.

As the man began to put on his spectacles he said something like, "I'm sorry. I fear that I have worn myself out in service to my country." All the military leadership knew that this man had volunteered his time and energy and that he would give up everything he owned to serve this ideal of freedom. The fact that he had sacrificed more than they had turned out to be very influential.

I am not certain what that letter said; I do believe it was from a congressman or a senator, but in the end it didn't really matter, for when they heard the words, "I have worn myself out in service to my country," all the men began to cry, for they all knew that no one had sacrificed more than he. The thoughts of destroying the fragile new country and falling back into the natural cycle of the human condition, that of tyranny, anarchy, and back to tyranny, would have to wait, for desire had been restored. The fall to nature would have to wait for yet another day.

I have had people argue with me that this person had flaws of his own and therefore did not deserve the accolades that I so freely give him. I studied deeper and found it to be true—this person was very much human. But instead of discouraging me, it only inspired me more. What I found is that imperfect people can do perfect things; you do not have to be perfect to do great things. This discovery was very liberating to me. Perhaps even I could make a difference for the good! Remember that you do not have to be perfect to create perfection; you can be successful at something bigger than yourself. You do not have to be perfect to do perfect things.

For all that is spoken of concerning perfection, I must confess that I have never met a perfect person. That is correct—not even one. Even though I have sat through many meetings demanding that people be perfect, I have never witnessed the goal of perfection being obtained and/or sustained. From this perspective, I must say that perfection is overrated, and the journey to perfection is underrated. This man of whom I speak was definitely human; I cannot deny that. But never have I witnessed or read of an individual who so valiantly desired to walk the path toward perfection for the cause of freedom from tyranny.

The journey toward perfection is what allows the raw material of humankind to rise above it all. This journey is filled with potholes, turns, curves, uphill climbs, and downhill slopes; there seems to be no real certainty to the journey, at least as the journey is being made. But in the end, this journey, should we choose to stay on its seemingly uncertain path, converts this raw material that we call humans into something more than that; perhaps even into this man of which I speak—even the father of freedom himself, George Washington, an imperfect person who did something perfect.

Remember that imperfect people are capable of doing perfect things, so don't wait to be perfect to make your mark. If you do, you will not amount to anything of value to society; you will never obtain your true potential (or greatness), and you will never rise above it all.

Now the question begs to be asked, "What is the gatekeeper of this journey to perfection?" The answer to the question is, of course, desire. Remember that desire is the decision to rise above it all, whatever the sacrifice may be.

Always remember the important concept that the gatekeeper to perfection is desire. Yes, that is right. Desire is a conscious decision that must be made if transformation in its various elements is to be realized. Desire is the catalyst of action, and without it the human experience will fall back into the destructive acts of natural phenomena. Ultimately, desire is the conscious decision to care about something bigger than yourself.

The by-product of a successful personal transformation is desire. The journey to greatness cannot begin without desire; those who do not possess it will have to go on various other journeys, which, in the end, will not be nearly as fulfilling. Desire is the genesis of all greatness. I will end our discussion on desire with a quote from Vince Lombardi, who said, "The difference between a successful person and others is not a lack of strength, not a lack of knowledge, but rather a lack of will," or desire. The only prerequisite for desire is the desire to find it. If you diligently search for it, you will find it. Desire and character ultimately bring results.

Now we will discuss Rule #2 of the rules of greatness. Rule number two says the following: *you will never become great if you are unable to appreciate the past.* You will envision the greatness of your future by standing upon the shoulders of those who preceded you. Appreciation is an impossible concept in the environment of ignorance. If you want to appreciate something, you are going to have to educate yourself. True education will ultimately bring about the realization of appreciation. If you say you are educated but you do not appreciate, then you are in truth, not educated, just well studied.

There was a time in my life when I decided, for whatever reason, that I would study history in an effort to gain awareness and an appreciation of people around me. I decided to study the history of World War II. The following pictures will show you a little bit of what I learned about World War II. The first picture is defined as "Preparing for Death." This picture shows men, who, I believe, are sitting in a ship, and they are reading some literature. The books they are reading are their religious scripts. Thus they were preparing for death. This was pre-D-day, World War II.

Preparing for Death

Soldiers Headed toward Omaha Beach on D-Day

This picture shows the soldiers coming in on a boat to the beaches of Normandy. Notice how curious they are as they peer over the side of this ship. One thing you should keep in mind is that about now they are hearing the mortars going off and the shells firing at them, and they may even hear shells ricocheting off their boats. This was a very nervous time for them, I'm sure. Once that ship opened up to let the soldiers out, many of them were killed by the flying bullets. Many others died when they jumped out of the ship and found that the ship hadn't come far enough up on the beach, and they sunk to the bottom of the ocean due to the weight of their gear and died there.

Storming Normandy

The rest of the soldiers, who didn't die that way, ran up on the beaches of Normandy. They called it "Storming Normandy." Many of these soldiers were given painkillers in the form of a syringe before they went up on the beach. The soldiers were told that as they ran up on the beach, they may run into a mine and it could blow their limbs off. They were told that when that happened, they were to inject themselves with this painkiller and direct the other soldiers through the mine field while they died. This allowed the rest of the soldiers to run up on the beaches of Normandy, and they did.

While crossing these beaches of Normandy, there was no cover. They were open targets for the machine guns of the Nazis. The lucky ones, if you want to call them that, went to the cliffs of Normandy. Here they could lie underneath the cliffs and have a little break from all the gunfire.

A Shell-Shocked Soldier on the Cliffs of Normandy

This picture was entitled, "A Shell-Shocked Soldier." This was one of the soldiers who made it to the cliffs of Normandy, where he sat down to rest. What he experienced there on that day would haunt him for the rest of his life. We should never forget this young man's face. We should never forget what other people have done to give us the gift of freedom from tyranny.

In the end, through my studies, the soldiers of World War II came alive and became my heroes. The problem was that I never really knew any veterans from World War II—I did not come from a military family, so I was left to honor people whom I had never really met. Then one day I went to a New Year's Eve dance with my wife, Rita. We entered the dance hall and sat down by an older couple. We exchanged introductions, and my wife began a conversation with Betty while I started a conversation with her husband, Floyd.

As the conversation with Floyd evolved, I discovered that he was a World War II veteran and that he had stormed the beaches of Normandy and fought in many of the major battles of World War II. Needless to say, I was speechless; I was sitting across the table from my hero. I honestly never believed that such a day would ever arrive. I was so excited that I started investigating Floyd's role in World War

II. Then his wife came over and asked to talk to me. She told me that I needed to stop talking about the war as such conversations made it difficult for her husband to sleep at night.

I quickly apologized to Betty and went back to Floyd and talked about topics other than the war. Sometime later, my wife and I went out and shared some time on the dance floor. By the time we returned to the table, Floyd and his wife were nowhere to be found. I couldn't believe I let such an opportunity go by without expressing appreciation for this individual who I held in such high regard. In desperation I excused myself and ran out in the parking lot hoping to find Floyd. There I saw him and his wife slowly walking across the parking lot toward their car. I ran over to Floyd and tapped him on the shoulder. He turned around and looked at me, and I finally took the opportunity to say "Thank you."

Eventually I looked up Floyd's phone number, and the evening before Veteran's Day I asked him if he would mind dropping by and talking to my children. Floyd agreed and came by and introduced himself to my children, and then he told them a couple of stories about World War II and why they should appreciate the people who sacrificed their lives on that battlefield.

After Floyd left, I expounded on the importance of appreciating what others have sacrificed so much for. To be honest with you, I didn't think much about it after that until several months later when a friend of mine said, "Hey John, did you see your son's report hanging up in the entryway of the junior high school?" The only child I had in junior high school was my oldest boy, Craig. Thanks to his mother, Craig had a respectable grade average in his schooling. However, Craig had never enjoyed reading, and as a result I assumed that he was not much into writing either. In all sincerity I responded back to my friend with "Are you sure it was Craig's?" He said, "Yes, and with all the reports written, his is the only one hanging in the main lobby of the school."

He recommended that I go look at it. I was certain that he must have misread his name as I was sure that it could not have been Craig's. To make sure of these assumptions, I dropped by the school to research it for myself. I was shocked when I walked into the school and there it was right at the entrance—one report for everyone to see—and it was written by my son, Craig Lee. It was a report about Floyd, which is shown on the following page.

The report was simple and sweet. It said, as you can see in the picture below:

"Floyd, World War II veteran, was just 16 years old when he entered the service. At 18 years of age he stormed Utah beach, and fought in Normandy for world freedom. His courage and the courage of other Veterans are appreciated daily. The freedoms we all enjoy are the outcomes of their courage."

Floyd, World War II veteran, was just 16 years old when he entered the service. At 18 years of age he stormed Utah beach, and fought in Normandy for world freedom. His courage and the courage of other Veterans are appreciated daily. The freedoms we all enjoy are the outcomes of their courage.

The Legacy and the Hero

I rushed home and asked my wife if she knew about Craig's report hanging up at the school. She told me she didn't know it was hanging up in the school, but she was aware of the report. My wife told me that Craig had come home and asked for help on an assignment that his teacher had given him. The report was to be about a hero of his choosing. He had chosen to write about Floyd. This was one of the proudest moments of my life! I later learned that all the other students had written about sports stars and celebrities and my boy was the only one who wrote about a veteran.

If you ever feel lost when contemplating what around you is worthy of appreciation, perhaps you can remember those who were willing to give up everything so you could enjoy freedom from tyranny. Obviously, there are many things around you worthy of appreciation. Pick a couple and become an expert at those topics; this appreciation will give you the courage to rise above it all.

Staff Sergeant Gregson Gourley's Funeral

In my local area I recently learned of Staff Sgt. Gregson Gourley, who sacrificed his very life so that I could continue to inhale a breath of air enhanced with the elements of freedom and opportunity. This is a picture of Gregson Gourley's casket as they draped the American flag over it. You may think, well, Gregson Gourley sacrificed his life; however, Gregson Gourley sacrificed more than just his life.

In the following picture you can see the image of a young widow and her fatherless son. This is Gregson Gourley's wife and son. I don't know about you, but to me that woman looks too young to be a widow, and that little boy looks too young to be fatherless.

Staff Sgt. Gregson Gourley's Wife and Son

After you practice a bit, you will find there are reasons to appreciate things all around you, for through all of written history no one has had more to be thankful for than the people of our generation. May I repeat Isaac Newton's inspirational phrase, and I quote, "If I have seen further than most, it is only because I have stood on the shoulders of giants."

We all have giants from our past whose shoulders are ready to support us in our quest for greater vision; we just have to find them. Remember what was written earlier: "True education will ultimately bring about the realization of appreciation; if you say you are educated but you do not appreciate, then you are, in truth, not educated, just well studied." Remember that a lack of appreciation for the past will leave you blind to opportunities of the future. You will know when you appreciate enough because the future will begin to look bright.

In my opinion, there is no greater gift that you can give to future generations than that of appreciation. The other day my wife told me that my boys were going on something called a "trek" and would be gone for several days. I didn't know what "trek" meant, but the boys seemed relatively excited about it, so I thought, "Well, whatever." A few days passed and my wife instructed me that I needed to go pick up our boys from the trek. I said, "No problem." She told me to take the truck so I would have room for all their equipment. I did as I was told, but on the way out the door I asked her, "What is this trek, anyway?" She told me it was where all the young people in the area would get a handcart, load it down with what would be needed to cross the plains, and push it across twenty-plus miles of desert in Wyoming along the actual pioneer trail. They actually traveled sixteen miles in one of those days.

On the way out the door, I thought, *Why would they be so excited to do that, especially since the last couple of days have been in the high nineties?"* As I headed toward the location where I was instructed to pick up my boys, I was thinking I would meet someone in an old rusty pickup truck where I would reload my sons' belongings into my vehicle and come home. When I got to the pickup point, I was shocked to see five buses of young people exiting and standing around the bus. At first I thought I must have gone to the wrong location, as this looked more like a rock concert than what I perceived the return from a trek would look like.

However, as I looked around, I realized that these kids (from fourteen to eighteen years old) were sun-beaten and limping; that's when it hit me that this was a big deal. With all the kids around there, I was not able to find my boys right away, so for about fifteen minutes I wandered through the crowd looking for them. It was rather inspiring to see these beat-up kids meeting up with their parents after experiencing such a journey. For the most part, the kids looked pretty bedraggled. Everyone had been browned by the sun, and all seemed to be limping from walking on blisters; some cried when they saw their parents.

Eventually, I found my boys back at my truck waiting for me; they looked as beat-up as the rest. On our way home, I asked them if it was fun, and to my surprise, they said, "Yes." However, they admitted that it was a lot of work as the trail went up and down hills, through mud puddles, and across rivers. They mentioned that they had even crossed an old graveyard where some pioneers had died as a result of difficulties in crossing the plains.

After a little bit of silence, I cautiously asked them if the experience made them appreciate the pioneers more. They both responded with a confident yes, and I thought to myself, *Job well done.*

Rule #3 of the rules of greatness is this: *you will never become greater than that which motivates you.* We have already talked a fair amount about rule number three. In summary, if you let fear be your motivator, then the best you will ever become is average. Many people allow short-term profits to be their motivator; this will only take you and your organization so far. I find it rather interesting that the less you let money be your motivator, the more money you tend to receive. Henry Ford once said, "A business that makes nothing but money is a poor kind of business." Henry Ford was a very rich man.

The ultimate motivator that can lead you to the crowning achievement of human behavior (Phase III) is the desire to lift someone up, not from the desire of self-glorification, but for the pure desire to lift people up, to help them succeed, even if it means the sacrifice of one's own popularity. You will find that each motivator also comes with its own unique cost or sacrifice.

Now we will discuss rule #4 of the rules of greatness, or the rules of Phase III behavior: *you will never become great if you spend time blaming other people for your inability to reach greatness.* If you desire pity more than greatness, then pity is what you will get. Pity and greatness are mutually exclusive characteristics.

This is a very difficult rule to teach, because ultimately you will meet people who are truly victims of life's situations, and those situations demand a sense of sadness. However, for the betterment of even these people, they must gather their strength and overcome these difficulties. Sometimes people may need to sit down with someone in confidence and just lay it all out on the table until they can "get the monkey off their back." Whatever it takes, the individual must overcome pity for one's situation, for he or she cannot move forward on life's journey until he does.

Helen Keller was born in 1880. At the age of two years old, she became ill, and this illness robbed her of her ability to see, hear, and speak. Ultimately, Helen Keller refused to be a victim in her own mind. Through great faith, courage, and optimism, and with a lot of sacrifice from others (for example, Miss Sullivan, her teacher),

Helen Keller learned how to read, write, and communicate with the outside world. She also became a sought-after speaker worldwide. Helen Keller once said, "When one door of happiness closes, another opens, but often we look so long at the closed door that we do not see the one which has been opened for us."

I believe that everyone feels a little pity for his or her own situation from time to time, but if you are to reach your true potential, you must learn to rise above it or it will stop you along life's wonderful journey; in effect, pity is an anchor to progress. Remember that the most beautiful part of life's journey lies ahead of you. Cherish the past and reach for the future. You cannot do this if you allow yourself to be stuck in life's pity. Pity comes at too great a price.

Some people desire to play the role of victim, which is different from being a victim, as it seemingly allows one to be irresponsible for the consequences of their own decisions.

Rule #5 of the rules of greatness is this: *your ability to reach greatness is directly dependent upon the strength of your character.* As we discussed in an earlier chapter, the good news is that you can increase your character. Remember that character is the ability to follow through with a decision long after the emotions of making that decision are gone. This is a result of the relationship between sacrifice and emotions. As mentioned earlier, when sacrifice meets emotions, emotions evaporate. And when performing tasks of value, sacrifice will always be demanded—so if valuable tasks are to be performed and sustained, then character must be part of the recipe for success.

Rule #6 of the rules of greatness is this: *you cannot become great without sacrifice—and you cannot sacrifice without character.*

Rule #7 of the rules of greatness is this: *you will never become great if you don't believe you can become great.* You must believe. You have more potential than you know. Belief, in part, tends to be a by-product of desire.

Rule #8 of the rules of greatness is this: *you will never become great if you do not have passion for what you do.* You must have passion. Passion, in part, tends to be a by-product of desire and appreciation.

Rule #9 of the rules of greatness is this: *you will never become great if you do not find within yourself the desire to serve others.* If an individual is to rise above it all, he or she must learn the desire to serve others. Serving others is the ultimate motivator and will allow greatness to be realized. Don't make your life about you; make it about something bigger than you. As you do, you will discover the true nature of happiness.

Eleanor Roosevelt said it well: "Happiness is not a goal; it is a by-product."

Rule #10 of the rules of greatness is this: *you will stop becoming greater the instant you think you're great.* People who think they're great never become great. I have never witnessed an exception to this rule. Once you perceive you have become great, the motive to move forward dies. Why try to become greater if you have already achieved your goal? It doesn't take a lot of achievement for most people to perceive their own greatness and destroy their ability to move forward.

Figure 76

Rule #11 of the rules of greatness is this: *you will never become great if you are afraid to fail.* If you let fear of failure motivate your actions, the best you will ever become is average.

Rule # 12 of the rules of greatness is this: *patience.* You must have patience, for every great destiny has a specific journey. Lack of patience will cause you to attempt a shortcut on that journey, which may not allow the destiny to be realized. One of the important ingredients in rising above it all is patience. The element of patience that you must be most concerned with is the patience you exercise toward yourself. Remember that we all start at the bottom of the model (Phase I); evolving takes time. Enjoy the journey, for when all else is done, what else is there to enjoy but the memories of that journey?

Rule #13 from the rules of greatness is this: *you will never become great if you are unable to focus on the important.* I have been fairly involved in high-risk sports for the majority of my life. Unfortunately, I have had friends die while participating in these activities. I have nearly died on several occasions myself. One of my near-death experiences took place during the early spring months when I was jumping at a drop zone located in the heart of the Rocky Mountain range. It was a beautiful place and a beautiful day.

On this particular day I had left my wrist-mounted altimeter back at my apartment, so instead of driving back, I just borrowed a chest-mounted altimeter from the drop zone. An altimeter is used to tell skydivers what their altitude is—in other words, how high up in the air they are. The jumpers have a targeted deployment altitude so they know when to deploy their parachute. The deployment target is usually around three thousand feet. The goal is to watch your altimeter to know when it's time to deploy.

The first jump I made that day was a solo jump. During that jump, the altimeter blew under my chin and I could not see it during free fall, so I simply deployed early. I went back to the drop zone and attempted to fix the problem. With the new alteration to the altimeter, I got back on the plane and performed another solo jump. The new alteration did not work, so I played it safe and performed a slightly early deployment again. Nothing is more agonizing to an experienced sky diver than a long boring ride under canopy. When I arrived back at the drop zone, I performed some other procedures to the altimeter. At this time some of my buddies came up and invited me to participate in some relative work. Relative work is where several skydivers get together, jump out of the plane, and create formations such as shapes of stars, triangles, whatever. I was excited to have the opportunity to have a lot of fun with my friends, so we jumped in the plane and off we went.

During our ascent to jump altitude (approximately ten thousand feet), I told my friends about the problem I'd been having with my altimeter and asked them to let me know when we had reached deployment altitude, which was approximately three thousand feet for this particular jump. They came up with a signal they would use to communicate when deployment altitude was reached. We all practiced it, and once we reached jump altitude, we bailed out of the plane together. As we accelerated to the ground, we began creating our formations in the sky. We had a lot of fun!

On our last formation before deployment altitude, one of the jumpers got separated from the group. Just as we approached deployment altitude, the missing jumper closed the gap and bumped into the side of me. As a result of this mild collision, I went tumbling out into the "wild blue sky." Now I must tell you that about every three months or so I received a sky diving magazine in the mail. In the back of this magazine was a very important report entitled, "Fatality Reports." It would always contain the latest fatalities in the sport. It was published in an effort to educate sky divers on how to save their lives in difficult situations.

The fatality report would always go over the incident and then explain what the sky diver could have done differently to avoid the fatality. In a recent report, I remembered a group of people doing relative work. Somehow one of the sky divers fell below the rest of the team and then, around deployment altitude, deployed per plan. Little did the diver know that there was one individual still in free fall, right above him. After the lower jumper deployed, the one above him fell right into the deployed parachute; as a result both members of the team died after violently crashing into the ground. It's called "bouncing" within the skydiving community. You probably don't want to know why they call it that.

So back to my free-fall story, I quickly realized the potential danger and decided to free fall to the point that if someone above me waited any longer, they would have waited too long. I knew from past experience that I would experience ground rush between 2,000 and 1,500 feet. So I decided that I would watch the ground until I felt ground rush; then I would give it a second or two count and deploy.

From the many fatality reports I studied and learned from, I was aware of a couple of other dangerous phenomena. The most dangerous one was where some people would get fixated on what would kill them, such as the ground, in my case, and never focus on what could save them. The result of this phenomenon, of course, is death. I know because I once had a friend with whom I shared an evening jump in Northern California, and the next day I came back and they told me she had died earlier in the day. She was in a position similar to mine, and when she started getting ground rush, she couldn't think about anything but the danger—and as a result she bounced.

In my story, I began to experience the ground rush. By ground rush, I mean you can see and feel the earth rushing toward you at one hundred-plus mph—and, yes, it is rather scary looking. I was so close to the ground at this point that I could see a car cruising down the road and I could see the driver inside. I can still remember turning my attention away from the ground and focusing all my efforts on what could save me. I can still remember watching my hand as if it were in slow motion as I reached for my pilot chute, grabbed the knob, pulled the pilot chute out of the pocket, and threw it out into the wind stream—resulting in a successful deployment.

I used all of my energy in concentrating on my body position in hopes that the deployment would be both efficient and effective. Ultimately, everything went as hoped, and the deployed parachute slowed me down just as I hit the ground. My timing was perfect—not a second to spare!

The owners of the drop zone had been watching the jump and noticed several deployments at the horizon line of the mountain, and then they saw a dot (me) drop well into the mountain range before the successful deployment—they thought I was going to die. They were always proud of the fact that they had never had a fatality. Needless to say they were not happy with me when I got to the ground.

As a person who participated in high-risk activities, I had plenty of things I needed to work on, but one strength I had was that when circumstances evolved into dangerous situations, I would naturally keep my awareness of the danger but I would focus my energy on what had the potential to save me. This skill has saved my life on several occasions. If you do not develop this skill in the competitive world of business, then you leave your organization at risk of extinction.

One of the phenomena I have noticed in organizations that put off the transformation until it is too late and they are about to fall into extinction is that they are focused on what will kill them instead of what could save them. The dying organizations most commonly focused on the personify, blame, and punish methodology, which is the biggest reason for their soon-to-be extinction, instead of focusing on systems thinking, which could have saved them. In reality, this makes sense, because when an organization is about to become extinct, the pressure becomes so great that individuals snap and slide down the curve to lower levels of behavior where the preferred problem-solving methodology is personify, blame, and punish.

In summary, remember to focus on that which can save the organization and don't get hypnotized by what can destroy it. Also remember that every organization has its unique level of character, and after that level is exceeded, the organization will slide into lower levels of behavior. The most common reason for organizations to exceed their level of character is managers asking them to perform more than they are capable of.

Organizations should have two visions—a published vision and an unpublished vision. The published vision should not overload the organizational capacity. Remember that every organization has its own unique level of character, and after it is exceeded, it will slide into lower levels of behavior and practice personify, blame, and punish.

To summarize, remember to focus on that which can save the organization—not on that which can destroy the organization. You must be aware of danger but not intently focused on it. A sky-diving analogy is that people become mesmerized by the ground rush to the point that they "freeze up." What we need to do is be aware of where the ground is but focus on the deployment mechanism. Focus on that which can save.

Rule #14 of the rules of greatness is this: *remember, never ever, ever, ever, ever give up!* You can do it! I once taught a Six Sigma green belt class for a client. The objective of the class was to prepare the students for a very difficult national certification exam. The pass rate on this type of exam was somewhere between 60 percent and 70 percent. After the class I was very satisfied that of the twenty students, only one had failed. That is a pass rate of approximately 95 percent—much higher than the national average.

From my many failures in life, I have always tried to learn something from each of them. One of the things I have learned is "Don't forget the one." In other words, go ahead and celebrate with the nineteen, but when it is all over, don't forget the one. The supervisor of this student sent me a letter telling me how devastated the student was, being the only one among his peers who failed the exam. In the letter, the supervisor told me he was going to give up, as failure was just too painful. The supervisor asked me if there was anything I could do to help him keep from feeling so bad and to talk him into not giving up.

In response I wrote something similar to the following:

Dear Adam,

I heard that you struggled on the green belt exam. Please don't feel bad—many people have to take these exams more than once. I have also failed certification exams, more than once, so I just keep moving along and retaking them until I pass them. I had one student take the certification exam seven times before he passed it. After all was said and done, the student told me he was glad he didn't pass it the first time, as he learned more and more every time he took it. In the end, it is about learning, so don't give up. Knowledge comes at a price, and everyone has their own price. Don't compare your price to other people's prices. The price other people have to pay for knowledge is no one else's business. Comparing your price to others can be very destructive in reaching your true potential.

I don't tell many people this, but I used to be in resource mathematics when I was in junior high school. In fact, I never really understood mathematics until I continued my studies after high school, as I will explain later. No one seemed overly concerned as they just realized that I wasn't all that smart. Unfortunately for me, I always enjoyed learning, but learning was very difficult for me. I started my educational career in the Head Start Program. From what I understand that was a program for high-risk children. I'm not sure who determines high risk; I never felt I was high risk. I had a good family—what else is needed? I remember in junior high school a teacher by the name of Mrs. Ransom who decided she was going to teach me math. There were only two of us in her class. (Most would have considered us the two dumbest students in the school.)

Mrs. Ransom was a very successful teacher, and she would always remember the "one." In this case, I was the "one." Every day she would try to teach me the principles of mathematics and every day I would fail; eventually she had to let me go as I moved on into high school. After high school I started studying a simplified mathematics and physics book called *The Nature of Automotive Dynamics* by Steve Smith. It was a technical book about race cars. I found the book just the other day as I was cleaning up my office. It fell off the bookshelf onto the floor and the pages went everywhere—what a mess it made! When I saw it, I was ashamed, as it reminded me of how dumb I was. I quickly bent down and picked up all the pages and stuffed them back into the book. You see, there was a reason why all those pages fell out. I would read that book everywhere I went. I took it to the factory with me, and during breaks I would read it; I would read it at stoplights, and I would read it before and after work. At the end of each reading I realized I did not understand any of its contents. That's right, nothing—zero.

I knew that everything came at a price, and the price of knowledge for me was extremely high. It was all right, though; I kept reading it anyway. Sometimes I would get teased for reading that book so often, especially when people would ask me what it was about and I would have to tell them I didn't know.

Anyway, I kept reading this book for literally years. After about twenty reads I still didn't understand it, but on the twenty-first time, yes, on the twenty-first time, it all made sense to me. I couldn't believe it; I understood everything in the book. I had to understand it in my own way, an easier way, but I didn't see anything wrong with that; in fact it helped me understand it in a way that allowed me to understand it deeper than others. To me it was miraculous—the floodgates had finally broken down. I would go to the local racetrack (where I raced stock cars) and listen to the engineers talk about automotive dynamics. I understood everything they said and even recognized their misunderstandings of the concepts (eventually I authored the book *The Nature of Dynamic Weight Transfer*). I didn't argue with them, as I lacked the credibility to do so. This new understanding had a great impact on me. It made me believe that, maybe, I was smart—well, at least not as dumb as I thought I was. In fact, I started to think that perhaps, just perhaps, I was smart enough to go to college.

I still understand things in simplified ways. That is why I was able to explain the nature of human nature to you. Most things around me look simple. My weakness became my strength. Remember that effort is the hammer, weakness is the raw material, and the output is strength. You can't create the output if you are missing any of the inputs.

So anyway, if you desire to pass the test, step up and don't give up—no matter how many times it takes. If it is not something you are interested in, then I understand that also. Mostly, I just wanted to tell you not to feel bad about it.

Thanks,
John Lee
President of Alpha Training and Consulting
BSME, MBA, CMQ/OE, CQE, CRE, CQA, CQIA, CQI, CCT, CQPA, CQT, CHA, CBA, CSQE, CSSGB, CSSBB, AQC Six Sigma Master BB
www.alphaTC.com
801-942-9274
Cell: 801-599-1579
Fax: 801-942-9280
    John.lee@alphatc.com

He responded with something like the following letter:

John,
Thank you so much. I really appreciate you taking the time to send me this e-mail. It is inspiring and very kind. I will take the test again. I am going to join a study group and take it in October.
Thank you so for all your help.☺

So to you readers out there, don't forget the fourteenth rule of greatness, and please, never give up on yourself or others. If you do, you will never know your true potential. Remember that you are in the dark ages of your true potential. And if any of you know where Mrs. Ransom is, please tell her, "Thank you for not giving up on the one." Tell her that my children are all really good at math, most took two semesters of calculus while in high school, and I am so very proud. It took a couple of generations, but we finally rose above it all.

Remember that to become great is to change. Winston Churchill once said, "To improve is to change—to become perfect is to change often."

In the most difficult and discouraging days of World War II, Winston Churchill said to the people of England, "To every man there comes that special moment when he is figuratively tapped on the shoulder and offered the chance to do a special thing unique to him and fitted to his talent. What a tragedy if that moment finds him unprepared or unqualified for the work which would be his finest hour."

Dear reader, prepare to make a difference; once prepared, you will know what to do from there.

Chapter Six

Tools Transformation

We have finally made it to the last element of the three elements of transformation. After your organization has successfully completed personal transformation and begun cultural transformation, you are ready for the final element of organizational transformation, which is referred to as tools transformation. If you are not interested in tools training at this time, then feel free to skip to the final chapter of this book. Realize that this is just an introduction to tools transformation, and the list of analytical tools is nearly endless. By reading this chapter you will be able to communicate at a functional level concerning basic analytical tools.

Many organizations ignore the first two elements and go directly for tools transformation. This is why most transformations fail. Remember that you have to have a culture that supports the tools or the tools don't work. If you don't believe this, then try it and you will come to a realization that the principles are true.

I have a friend that was an IT consultant when computers were first populating corporate America. She said it wasn't unusual that when the computers were shipped out to the various corporations they would get delivered and the employees would hammer in the computer screens. The point being that the computers were a new tool and the organizational culture was not ready to support them. The computers represented unwanted change to many of the employees. So when she arrived to install the computers they were damaged beyond repair. I think you get the point.

Some elements in this chapter are a review of previous topics covered in the book, so if you do not need the redundancy then please skim through until you find something that will benefit your organization.

Let's begin our discussion on tools transformation. You may recall that there are two general types of problem-solving models. The first one is called objective problem solving, and the second one is called subjective problem solving. Though conceptually this is very easy, it is extremely important that you understand the difference between objective problem solving and subjective problem, understand the benefits of both, and understand what role each methodology plays in the world of transformation. It is also extremely important that you understand the relationship between these two problem-solving methodologies.

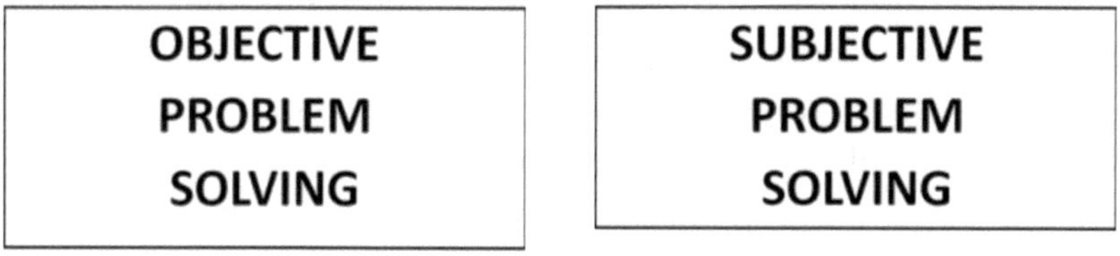

OBJECTIVE PROBLEM SOLVING	SUBJECTIVE PROBLEM SOLVING

Figure 77

Remember that the acid test to objective problem solving is this: if you argue about a properly solved objective problem, you will lose credibility among your peers.

An important concept to keep in mind is this: the fuel of objective problem solving is data. Without data that has been collected properly, you cannot solve problems objectively. And data comes from measurement. Objective problem solving promotes a system approach to problem solving. Remember that we have two approaches: we have the system approach, and we have personify, blame, and punish. Objective problem solving promotes a systematic methodology for solving problems and subjectivity promotes PBP.

As a society, we do not solve subjective problems as efficiently or effectively as we do objective problems. Organizations tend to create more wealth as they become more objective and less subjective. An interesting question to ask in our study of subjective problem solving is this: what is a telltale sign that an organization is dysfunctional at subjective problem solving? Organizations that are dysfunctional at subjective problem solving will argue about the same problem over and over and over again. You could leave an organization and come back years later and you'd find that they are still arguing about the same thing. This is a telltale sign that an organization is dysfunctional at subjective problem solving. The next question logically comes into place: what is the cause of this dysfunctional condition?

The main reason for this dysfunctional condition in subjective problem solving is the lack of an authority figure.

So what do we learn from this conversation? It's this: effective subjective problem solving demands an authority figure. The authority figure's job is to listen to the counterarguments and make a decision. Once the authority figure makes the decision, then society must respect that decision.

Selecting authority figures is considered one of the most important jobs within an organization. You want to select the wisest of the wise to be your subjective problem solvers so that your authority figures are effectively solving subjective problems, because they will have a huge impact on the company. You don't want someone who doesn't reflect the value system of the organization he or she is to represent.

Respecting authority is difficult in the American culture, as our very existence as a country evolved from rebelling against authority. You'd think that in the United States, subjective problem solving would be a very difficult thing to come by, since we tend to rebel against authority. I feel that history would suggest that Americans know how to argue, but they also know when it is time to stop. Rule of law suggests that society in general will respect authority figures.

The most effective way to implement authority in our culture is to spread the authority across many individuals. If everyone has authority in the problem-solving process, then we are less likely to feel we are being ruled with tyranny. Our very government was designed to govern a people that tends to rebel against authority. The designers of our government solved this problem by spreading the authority over many branches of government. In the American workplace, it usually works best if we give everyone some authority to solve subjective problems in their area of expertise.

Organizations that feel a lesser sense of tyranny in their environment tend to be more innovative. For example, America is one of the most innovative countries in recorded history; it is not accidental that it also has the lowest sense of tyranny in its culture and the lowest tolerance level for tyranny. Now let me ask you another question. Have we, as a society, become more objective or more subjective over time?

There is not an easy answer to this question. The early scientists actually referred to themselves as philosophers. Philosophy teaches you how to systematically and constructively argue, with respected logic and fundamental truths, in such a way that you will ultimately realize the evasive truth—at least that is the objective. Eventually, the fundamental truths in subjective problem solving became numerical in nature, and with the advancements in mathematical logic, philosophy gave way to physics and some philosophers evolved into scientists. This argument would suggest that we have become more objective over time. However, per our earlier discussions we understand that objective solutions create subjective problems and thus society has become both more objective and more subjective overtime. We also came to the realization that this is not necessarily a bad thing as long as we can keep the objective and subjective powers in the proper balance. The less ethical organizations become, the more subjective they need to become if they are to survive.

Dysfunctionality in subjective problem solving always comes at a high price; it destroys countries, families, and companies.

Most of the subjective hot-button issues that we are attempting to deal with today are the results of successful objective problem-solving exercises; these include areas such as abortion, cloning, and other controversial topics. In the end, our organizations must be functional at both objective and subjective problem solving. If you are good at objective problem solving and dysfunctional at subjective problem solving, then your organization will eventually destroy itself.

If you are dysfunctional at objective problem solving but functional at subjective problem solving, then your organization will never evolve (transform), and the best it will be capable of is to maintain its status quo. The reward for not being functional at either is a downward trend toward ultimate organizational destruction or extinction.

So the ultimate goal for your organization is to become better at both, as objectivity creates power and subjectivity harnesses power—one without the other is not capable of transformation. Let's review again the definition of transformation. Transformation is "evolving to a higher level of sustained performance." Objectivity allows evolving to a higher level; subjectivity allows that new level to be sustained performance over time. So we must be good at both if we are to transform our organizations.

If objectivity is what makes cutting-edge organizations move forward, then what is the constraint in objective problem solving? The answer to this question is measurement. Measurement ultimately creates data, which is the fuel of objective problem solving; without good data, objectivity quickly becomes dysfunctional and subjectivity takes over.

This relationship between data and objective problem solving is one reason that a functional organization must remove fear from the workplace. We talked about that in the cultural transformation chapter. If your organization has a culture of fear, then you will get bad data and objectivity will not be functional, so subjectivity will take over. Remember that personify, blame, and punish is only capable of around a 95 percent success rate on the "and" statements. So becoming more objective is extremely important, and we cannot become objective without data, and we cannot get data without measurement, and we cannot effectively record measurement in an environment of fear.

I have taught many classes on tools transformation over the years, and what I often tell my students is that you will know you understand tools transformation when you realize that the only problem you have is a measurement problem and a culture capable of supporting that measurement. With modern-day, objective problem-solving tools (analytical tools) with the accompanying software, hardware, etc., there are not many problems that cannot be solved, assuming you fully understand the tools and you are capable of measuring the critical variables.

I suspect that we could solve most diseases that challenge the well-being of the human condition if we had the critical data for those diseases. The problem is that it literally takes a lifetime to collect this critical data. Why did we not collect the data earlier? There are two traditional answers to this question. One is that past generations did not realize that such data would be important, and the other is that they realized the data would be important but were not capable of measuring the needed data, or they did not even know the data existed.

An example of this phenomenon will be explained by going back to the 1940s to a gentleman by the name of Fred Hoyle, who was a well-known scientist in the field of cosmology. Cosmology is the scientific study of the nature or creation of the universe. Fred Hoyle championed a theory called the "steady state theory," which was competing with the "big bang" theory. Fred actually coined the term "big bang" in what I suspect was an effort to belittle the theory that he so detested. The "big bang" theory suggested that the universe had a beginning that took place from an extremely high-density premortal atom, which created a huge explosion that then created the universe.

Fred Hoyle found the logic behind the big bang theory extremely troubling, as it suggested that the universe had a beginning, which meant, to many, that there was a creator. Fred Hoyle did not like this, as he was, at the time, a passionate atheist. So Fred Hoyle went to the airwaves and promoted his steady state theory. Fred Hoyle and his followers did an excellent job of promoting the steady state theory to the general public, as it was the most accepted theory of its day. Then one day Fred Hoyle mentioned that if the big bang theory was correct, then where was all the background radiation from this supposed big bang? You have to realize that if there was such an explosion, there would still be a lot of cosmic radiation in the universe.

Before moving on with the story, you have to understand what is going on here. Fred Hoyle and his steady state theory were arguing against the big bang theory, and he was not losing credibility. In other words, they were attempting to solve the problem with subjective problem-solving techniques. Why? Because they could not measure the critical variables such as cosmic radiation that should have resulted from such an explosion. And the result of this inability to measure the cosmic radiation caused subjectivity to rule the day. They could argue without losing credibility. Subjectivity was incapable of moving the discovery of truth forward.

There were many diverse parties participating in this argument, including scientists and theologians. You have to understand that theologians were hoping for the big bang theory, as it would suggest a beginning of the universe, which would in turn suggest the creation, which then in turn would suggest a creator. When Fred Hoyle asked, "Where is all the radiation from this 'big bang'?" the champions of the big bang theory knew what they needed to do. They needed to learn how to measure cosmic microwave background radiation. Bob Dickie, from Princeton, realized the importance of measuring background radiation and formed a team of students that began the research with the objective of learning how to measure something that had not been measurable in the past. If they could make their argument objective, through measurement and data analysis, then the competing idea would lose credibility.

One of the students who provided leadership on this project was a twenty-eight-year-old by the name of David Wilkinson. David Wilkinson, with direction from his instructor, Bob Dickie, began building what was called a directional horn antenna, which they felt had a chance of measuring cosmic radiation. In the meantime, just up the street from Princeton University, Bell Laboratories recruited a talented graduate from Caltech whose name was Dr. Robert Woodrow Wilson.

Robert Wilson was an expert at radio astronomy and was hired by Bell Laboratories to help them work on a horn antenna that was designed to receive signals from satellites. To their dissatisfaction at Bell Laboratories, once this horn antenna had been put up, it had a constant "hiss" sound. They could not figure out what it was. No matter where they aimed the antenna, the hissing sound continued. It was driving them crazy. At one point in time they felt it may be the fault of pigeons. So they sent the pigeons away and cleaned up after them; however, the pigeons were homing pigeons, so before they knew it, the pigeons were back. Eventually they shot the pigeons and cleaned up after them one last time. I refer to this as pigeon PBP. It didn't matter—the hissing sound persisted. Eventually Bell Labs called Princeton, and the call was forwarded to Bob Dickie.

As soon as Bob Dickie heard of the problem, he knew what was happening. Bell Labs was the first to measure the cosmic radiation. As soon as Bob got off the phone he told his team, "Well boys, we've been scooped." Eventually Bob Wilson won the Nobel Prize for being the first to measure cosmic microwave background radiation.

As soon as the scientists were capable of measuring cosmic radiation, the popular steady state theory quickly lost credibility, and, with additional advances in measurement and the accompanying logical discoveries, the steady state theory died. Fred Hoyle continued to argue against the big bang theory even though objective evidence continued to mount.

Per our previous discussions, we would suspect that Fred Hoyle lost credibility by arguing against a properly solved objective problem. You can investigate the Fred Hoyle story for yourself, but in my opinion, he did ultimately lose credibility for arguing against a properly solved objective problem. Later on, one of Fred Hoyle's associates won the Nobel Prize based on earlier formative work performed by Fred Hoyle. Fred Hoyle never received credit for his earlier contribution, even though his associate, the one who won the Nobel Prize, attempted to give credit where credit was due. Truly, Fred Hoyle lost credibility by arguing against a properly solved objective problem.

Remember that, as discussed earlier, the acid test of objective problem solving is that if you argue about a properly solved objective problem, you will lose credibility among your peers. There are many examples throughout scientific history to back up the argument that the constraint to objective problem solving is indeed measurement.

Albert Einstein's theories were passionately argued in the scientific community until they ultimately learned how to measure the bending of light as predicted by his equations. Only after these measurements were effectively taken and the observations matched Einstein's theory did the arguments stop and scientific theory moved forward. Remember that objectivity creates the power to move forward, and subjectivity harnesses the power. Subjectivity does not create the power to move organizations forward.

Many organizations try to move forward or transform with subjectivity without significant success. In my opinion, measurement should be found in the strategic elements of an organization; however, it seldom if ever is, which suggests the Dark Ages' mentality of many modern-day organizations. Remember that subjectivity is largely incapable of moving organizations forward in competitive environments. In some cases, subjective problem solvers try to get enough political power to subdue the objective problem solvers. Should they be successful, then the ability to transform the organization would be lost. In a perfect world, the various problem solvers will understand their role in the transformation and respect others' roles, and only then can transformation be realized.

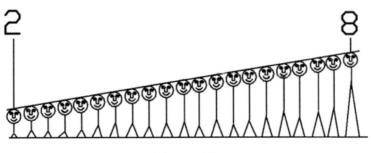

Figure 78

Now we will review an earlier lesson in an effort to prepare you for the next level of our discussion. Perhaps you will recall that we had an example where we had a million people line up according to their height. We had a two-foot-tall line to the far left and an eight-foot-tall line to the far right. Then we had all these people, physically mature adults, stand up in a line according to their height. Once we had all these people lined up according to their height, we looked at the top view—so in this example, we got in our helicopter and we hovered over this mass of a million people, and what did we find? Something we call the "normal distribution."

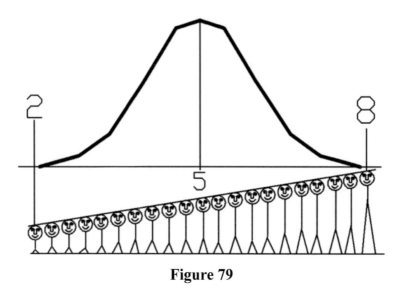

Figure 79

As you may recall, we then took this normal distribution, or the majority of it—actually, we took 99.73 percent of this normal distribution—and we divided it up into six equal lengths. We call that equal length the standard deviation, or a sigma. Remember that sigma was used for nothing more than a unit of length. So in some places where we work, we may measure length in inches or millimeters or centimeters. In the world of statistics, we measure distance in units of standard deviation. So remember that a standard deviation is a unit of length.

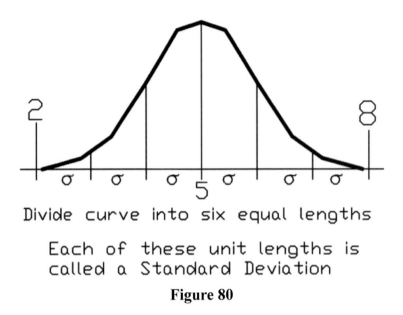

Divide curve into six equal lengths

Each of these unit lengths is
called a Standard Deviation

Figure 80

The average on the normal distribution is a point of reference for measurement. We could call it the "datum of the normal distribution." We always measure from the average. The standard deviation is a unit of length, and we always measure from the average.

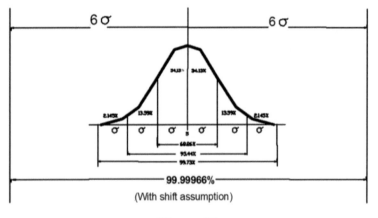

Figure 81

On the normal distribution, if we go out ± one sigma, it will always equal 68.26 percent of the population. If we go out ± two sigma, it will equal 95.44 percent of the population. And if we go out ± three sigma, it equals 99.73 percent of the population. If we go out

± six sigma, then it equals 99.99966 percent of the population. When we talk about that percentage with six sigma, there are also some assumptions involved that we're not going to delve into in this study. I want you to understand at this point that the number of sigma and percentages go hand in hand. In fact, in industries that don't have a lot of "and" statements, you may call up the supplier and say, "Hey, what are you capable of on meeting my spec limits?" And they may tell you, "Yeah, there is a 99 percent chance that we can meet those."

It's pretty easy to communicate that 99 percent, but let's say you move over to an industry that has a lot of "and" statements, and it has standards. So you call up your supplier and say, "What are you capable of?" And let's say the supplier is Six Sigma. And when you ask the question, "What are you capable of?" he says, "We're capable of meeting your specs 99.99966 percent of the time." And what you'll hear is people saying, "What was that again?" And you'll say it was 99.99966 percent, and they won't get it, so they'll ask you several times, and then ultimately they will write it down incorrectly anyway. So once you get a lot of nines, there becomes a difficulty with communication. To solve this problem, many in high "and" statement competitive industries have stopped speaking in percentages and started communicating in sigma. But remember that they mean the same thing. So if they say, "How capable are you?" and you say one sigma, this means 68.26 percent. Those numbers of sigma equal percentages. Remember, in high "and" statement industries, they communicate in sigma, not percentages. Why? Because it's easier to communicate sigmas than it is to communicate in percentages, at least when you are working with a lot of nines.

The Z Statistic

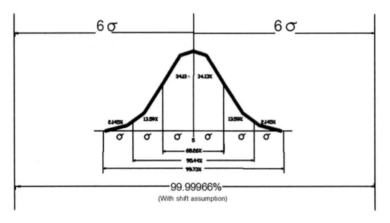

Figure 82

Since the number of sigmas out from the average is such an important number in the calculation of "and" statement probabilities, we gave it a name. We call the number of sigmas to a point of interest (in this case, spec limits) the "Z statistic." If you are six sigmas from your average to your upper spec limits, it's Z = 6. That's called Z upper. If the distance from your average to your lower spec limit is six sigmas, then the Z lower = 6. If you ever want to know what the Z statistic is, just cover up the sigma symbol and what's left over is the Z statistic. For example, let's say your upper spec limit is 4.22 sigmas above your average. Remember that the sigma or standard deviation is nothing more than a unit of length. So you may feel more comfortable saying, "Hey, it's 4.22 inches." But in statistics we do not use inches as a unit of length; we use sigma. So it's 4.22 sigmas.

The Z Statistic

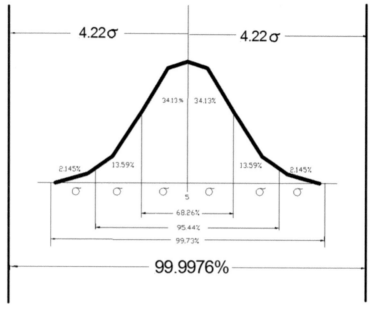

Figure 83

What is the Z statistic in the above figure? Obviously, the Z will equal 4.22. And of course then we have the lower spec limit as 4.22 sigmas away from the average. Therefore, Z lower will equal 4.22. It's very simple. Remember that Z is how many sigmas you are away from a point of interest or the distance from the average.

Z	0	0.01	0.02	0.03	0.04	0.05	0.06	0.07
4	3.17E-05	3.04E-05	2.91E-05	2.79E-05	2.67E-05	2.56E-05	2.45E-05	2.35E-05
4.1	2.07E-05	1.98E-05	1.90E-05	1.81E-05	1.74E-05	1.66E-05	1.59E-05	1.52E-05
4.2	1.34E-05	1.28E-05	1.22E-05	1.17E-05	1.12E-05	1.07E-05	1.02E-05	9.78E-06
4.3	8.55E-06	8.17E-06	7.81E-06	7.46E-06	7.13E-06	6.81E-06	6.51E-06	6.22E-06
4.4	5.42E-06	5.17E-06	4.94E-06				4.10E-06	3.91E-06
4.5	3.40E-06	3.24E-06	3.0					2.44E-06
4.6	2.11E-06	2.02E-0						1.51E-06
4.7	1.30E-06	1.24						E-07
4.8	7.94E-07	7						07
4.9	4.80E-07							7
5	2.87E-07							7
5.1	1.70E-07							7
5.2	9.98E-08	9.						08
5.3	5.80E-08	5.49						E-08
5.4	3.34E-08	3.16E-0						2.26E-08
5.5	1.90E-08	1.80E-08	1.7				E-08	1.28E-08
5.6	1.07E-08	1.01E-08	9.57E-09	9.			E-09	7.59E-09	7.16E-09

Find 4.2 on the Z column. Then go along the top row until you find the 0.02 column. Where the 4.2 row and the 0.02 column intercect is where the % under the curve is found. In this case it is 1.22 X 10^-5 or .00122%.

Figure 84

In statistics there is a table called a "Z table." The objective of the Z table is to convert the distance from the average in sigmas into the proportion of the population that will lie beyond that distance. Refer to figure 84 for an understanding on how to use the Z table. You can see there's one column called the "Z column" (that's the first column); then there are the 0 and the 0.01 columns, the 0.02 column, etc. We're going to look up 4.22 sigmas in the Z table. So first find 4.2 on the Z column. You'll notice that we went down the Z column to the 4.2. Then go along the top row until you find the 0.02 column. If you add 4.2 and 0.02 together, you get 4.22, which we're looking for. So where the 4.2 row and the 0.02 column intersect is where the proportion that lies beyond the upper spec limit is found. In this case it is 1.22×10^{-5} or, in other words, it's .0000122 as the proportion. To convert the proportion to a percentage you multiply the proportion by one hundred to get .00122 percent. That percentage is the percent of the population that lies beyond 4.22 sigmas. In other words, that's the percentage that will fall above the upper spec limit, or the scrap rate you would expect to violate the upper spec limit.

Alpha Quality Consulting   (801)-942-9274   e-mail: info@alphaqc.com
www.alphaqc.com

Single - Upper Tail z-Table

z	0	0.01	0.02	0.03	0.04	0.05	0.06	0.07	0.08	0.09
0	0.5	0.496	0.492	0.488	0.484	0.4801	0.4761	0.4721	0.4681	0.4641
0.1	0.4602	0.4562	0.4522	0.4483	0.4443	0.4404	0.4364	0.4325	0.4286	0.4247
0.2	0.4207	0.4168	0.4129	0.409	0.4052	0.4013	0.3974	0.3936	0.3897	0.3859
0.3	0.3821	0.3783	0.3745	0.3707	0.3669	0.3632	0.3594	0.3557	0.352	0.3483
0.4	0.3446	0.3409	0.3372	0.3336	0.33	0.3264	0.3228	0.3192	0.3156	0.3121
0.5	0.3085	0.305	0.3015	0.2981	0.2946	0.2912	0.2877	0.2843	0.281	0.2776
0.6	0.2743	0.2709	0.2676	0.2643	0.2611	0.2578	0.2546	0.2514	0.2483	0.2451
0.7	0.242	0.2389	0.2358	0.2327	0.2296	0.2266	0.2236	0.2206	0.2177	0.2148
0.8	0.2119	0.209	0.2061	0.2033	0.2005	0.1977	0.1949	0.1922	0.1894	0.1867
0.9	0.1841	0.1814	0.1788	0.1762	0.1736	0.1711	0.1685	0.166	0.1635	0.1611
1	0.1587	0.1562	0.1539	0.1515	0.1492	0.1469	0.1446	0.1423	0.1401	0.1379
1.1	0.1357	0.1335	0.1314	0.1292	0.1271	0.1251	0.123	0.121	0.119	0.117
1.2	0.1151	0.1131	0.1112	0.1093	0.1075	0.1056	0.1038	0.102	0.1003	0.0985
1.3	0.0968	0.0951	0.0934	0.0918	0.0901	0.0885	0.0869	0.0853	0.0838	0.0823
1.4	0.0808	0.0793	0.0778	0.0764	0.0749	0.0735	0.0721	0.0708	0.0694	0.0681
1.5	0.0668	0.0655	0.0643	0.063	0.0618	0.0606	0.0594	0.0582	0.0571	0.0559
1.6	0.0548	0.0537	0.0526	0.0516	0.0505	0.0495	0.0485	0.0475	0.0465	0.0455
1.7	0.0446	0.0436	0.0427	0.0418	0.0409	0.0401	0.0392	0.0384	0.0375	0.0367
1.8	0.0359	0.0351	0.0344	0.0336	0.0329	0.0322	0.0314	0.0307	0.0301	0.0294
1.9	0.0287	0.0281	0.0274	0.0268	0.0262	0.0256	0.025	0.0244	0.0239	0.0233
2	0.0228	0.0222	0.0217	0.0212	0.0207	0.0202	0.0197	0.0192	0.0188	0.0183
2.1	0.0179	0.0174	0.017	0.0166	0.0162	0.0158	0.0154	0.015	0.0146	0.0143
2.2	0.0139	0.0136	0.0132	0.0129	0.0125	0.0122	0.0119	0.0116	0.0113	0.011
2.3	0.01072	0.01044	0.01017	0.0099	0.00964	0.00939	0.00914	0.00889	0.00866	0.00842
2.4	0.0082	0.00798	0.00776	0.00755	0.00734	0.00714	0.00695	0.00676	0.00657	0.00639
2.5	0.00621	0.00604	0.00587	0.0057	0.00554	0.00539	0.00523	0.00508	0.00494	0.0048
2.6	0.00466	0.00453	0.0044	0.00427	0.00415	0.00402	0.00391	0.00379	0.00368	0.00357
2.7	0.00347	0.00336	0.00326	0.00317	0.00307	0.00298	0.00289	0.0028	0.00272	0.00264
2.8	0.00256	0.00248	0.0024	0.00233	0.00226	0.00219	0.00212	0.00205	0.00199	0.00193
2.9	0.00187	0.00181	0.00175	0.00169	0.00164	0.00159	0.00154	0.00149	0.00144	0.00139
3	0.00135	0.00131	0.00126	0.00122	0.00118	0.00114	0.00111	0.00107	0.00104	0.001
3.1	0.000968	0.000936	0.000904	0.000874	0.000845	0.000816	0.000789	0.000762	0.000736	0.000711
3.2	0.000687	0.000664	0.000641	0.000619	0.000598	0.000577	0.000557	0.000538	0.000519	0.000501
3.3	0.000483	0.000467	0.000450	0.000434	0.000419	0.000404	0.00039	0.000376	0.000362	0.00035
3.4	0.000337	0.000325	0.000313	0.000302	0.000291	0.00028	0.00027	0.00026	0.000251	0.000242
3.5	0.000233	0.000224	0.000216	0.000208	0.0002	0.000193	0.000185	0.000179	0.000172	0.000165
3.6	0.000159	0.000153	0.000147	0.000142	0.000136	0.000131	0.000126	0.000121	0.000117	0.000112
3.7	1.08E-04	1.04E-04	9.96E-05	9.58E-05	9.20E-05	8.84E-05	8.50E-05	8.16E-05	7.84E-05	7.53E-05
3.8	7.24E-05	6.95E-05	6.67E-05	6.41E-05	6.15E-05	5.91E-05	5.67E-05	5.44E-05	5.22E-05	5.01E-05
3.9	4.81E-05	4.62E-05	4.43E-05	4.25E-05	4.08E-05	3.91E-05	3.75E-05	3.60E-05	3.45E-05	3.31E-05

Figure 85

I have also shown you part of a Z table here just for reference. Notice that this Z table goes to 3.99. There are many different Z tables. They should all have the same answers, obviously, as far as percentages go, but this is the first page of a two-page table. The first page goes to 3.99 sigmas, and if I were to put the second page there, it would go to 7.99 sigmas. That's considered quite a few sigmas out, so that's a rather large Z table.

In summary there's a relationship between how many sigmas you are away from a distribution average to a given point of interest, such as an upper and lower specification limit, and a percentage of the population that lies beyond that point of interest, such as scrap rates.

Z	0	0.01	0.02	0.03	0.04	0.05	0.06	0.07	0.08	0.09
4	3.17E-05	3.04E-05	2.91E-05	2.79E-05	2.67E-05	2.56E-05	2.45E-05	2.35E-05	2.25E-05	2.16E-05
4.1	2.07E-05	1.98E-05	1.90E-05	1.81E-05	1.74E-05	1.66E-05	1.59E-05	1.52E-05	1.46E-05	1.40E-05
4.2	1.34E-05	1.28E-05	1.22E-05	1.17E-05	1.12E-05	1.07E-05	1.02E-05	9.78E-06	9.35E-06	8.94E-06
4.3	8.55E-06	8.17E-06	7.81E-06	7.46E-06	7.13E-06	6.81E-06	6.51E-06	6.22E-06	5.94E-06	5.67E-06
4.4	5.42E-06	5.17E-06	4.94E-06	4.72E-06	4.50E-06	4.30E-06	4.10E-06	3.91E-06	3.74E-06	3.56E-06
4.5	3.40E-06	3.24E-06	3.09E-06	2.95E-06	2.82E-06	2.68E-06	2.56E-06	2.44E-06	2.33E-06	2.22E-06
4.6	2.11E-06	2.02E-06	1.92E-06	1.83E-06	1.74E-06	1.66E-06	1.58E-06	1.51E-06	1.44E-06	1.37E-06
4.7	1.30E-06	1.24E-06	1.18E-06	1.12E-06	1.07E-06	1.02E-06	9.69E-07	9.22E-07	8.78E-07	8.35E-07
4.8	7.94E-07	7.56E-07	7.19E-07	6.84E-07	6.50E-07	6.18E-07	5.88E-07	5.59E-07	5.31E-07	5.05E-07
4.9	4.80E-07	4.56E-07	4.33E-07	4.12E-07	3.91E-07	3.72E-07	3.53E-07	3.35E-07	3.18E-07	3.02E-07
5	2.87E-07	2.73E-07	2.59E-07	2.46E-07	2.33E-07	2.21E-07	2.10E-07	1.99E-07	1.89E-07	1.79E-07
5.1	1.70E-07	1.61E-07	1.53E-07	1.45E-07	1.38E-07	1.30E-07	1.24E-07	1.17E-07	1.11E-07	1.05E-07
5.2	9.98E-08	9.46E-08	8.96E-08	8.49E-08	8.04E-08	7.62E-08	7.22E-08	6.84E-08	6.47E-08	6.13E-08
5.3	5.80E-08	5.49E-08	5.20E-08	4.92E-08	4.66E-08	4.41E-08	4.17E-08	3.95E-08	3.73E-08	3.53E-08
5.4	3.34E-08	3.16E-08	2.99E-08	2.82E-08	2.67E-08	2.52E-08	2.39E-08	2.26E-08	2.13E-08	2.01E-08
5.5	1.90E-08	1.80E-08	1.70E-08	1.61E-08	1.52E-08	1.43E-08	1.35E-08	1.28E-08	1.21E-08	1.14E-08
5.6	1.07E-08	1.01E-08	9.57E-09	9.04E-09	8.53E-09	8.04E-09	7.59E-09	7.16E-09	6.75E-09	6.37E-09
5.7	6.01E-09	5.67E-09	5.34E-09	5.04E-09	4.75E-09	4.48E-09	4.22E-09	3.98E-09	3.75E-09	3.53E-09
5.8	3.33E-09	3.13E-09	2.95E-09	2.78E-09	2.62E-09	2.47E-09	2.32E-09	2.19E-09	2.06E-09	1.94E-09
5.9	1.82E-09	1.72E-09	1.62E-09	1.52E-09	1.43E-09	1.35E-09	1.27E-09	1.19E-09	1.12E-09	1.05E-09
6	9.90E-10	9.31E-10	8.75E-10	8.23E-10	7.73E-10	7.27E-10	6.83E-10	6.42E-10	6.03E-10	5.67E-10
6.1	5.32E-10	5.00E-10	4.70E-10	4.41E-10	4.14E-10	3.89E-10	3.65E-10	3.43E-10	3.22E-10	3.02E-10
6.2	2.83E-10	2.66E-10	2.50E-10	2.34E-10	2.20E-10	2.06E-10	1.93E-10	1.81E-10	1.70E-10	1.59E-10
6.3	1.49E-10	1.40E-10	1.31E-10	1.23E-10	1.15E-10	1.08E-10	1.01E-10	9.49E-11	8.89E-11	8.33E-11
6.4	7.80E-11	7.31E-11	6.85E-11	6.41E-11	6.00E-11	5.62E-11	5.26E-11	4.92E-11	4.61E-11	4.31E-11
6.5	4.04E-11	3.78E-11	3.53E-11	3.30E-11	3.09E-11	2.89E-11	2.70E-11	2.53E-11	2.36E-11	2.21E-11
6.6	2.07E-11	1.93E-11	1.81E-11	1.69E-11	1.58E-11	1.47E-11	1.38E-11	1.29E-11	1.20E-11	1.12E-11
6.7	1.05E-11	9.79E-12	9.14E-12	8.53E-12	7.96E-12	7.43E-12	6.94E-12	6.48E-12	6.04E-12	5.64E-12
6.8	5.26E-12	4.91E-12	4.58E-12	4.27E-12	3.98E-12	3.71E-12	3.46E-12	3.23E-12	3.01E-12	2.81E-12
6.9	2.62E-12	2.44E-12	2.27E-12	2.12E-12	1.97E-12	1.84E-12	1.71E-12	1.59E-12	1.49E-12	1.38E-12
7	1.29E-12	1.20E-12	1.12E-12	1.04E-12	9.68E-13	9.01E-13	8.38E-13	7.80E-13	7.26E-13	6.75E-13
7.1	6.28E-13	5.84E-13	5.43E-13	5.05E-13	4.70E-13	4.37E-13	4.06E-13	3.78E-13	3.51E-13	3.26E-13
7.2	3.03E-13	2.82E-13	2.62E-13	2.43E-13	2.26E-13	2.10E-13	1.95E-13	1.81E-13	1.68E-13	1.56E-13
7.3	1.45E-13	1.35E-13	1.25E-13	1.16E-13	1.08E-13	9.99E-14	9.27E-14	8.60E-14	7.98E-14	7.40E-14
7.4	6.86E-14	6.37E-14	5.90E-14	5.47E-14	5.07E-14	4.70E-14	4.36E-14	4.04E-14	3.75E-14	3.47E-14
7.5	3.22E-14	2.98E-14	2.76E-14	2.56E-14	2.37E-14	2.19E-14	2.03E-14	1.88E-14	1.74E-14	1.61E-14
7.6	1.49E-14	1.38E-14	1.28E-14	1.18E-14	1.10E-14	1.01E-14	9.38E-15	8.68E-15	8.03E-15	7.42E-15
7.7	6.86E-15	6.35E-15	5.87E-15	5.43E-15	5.02E-15	4.64E-15	4.29E-15	3.96E-15	3.66E-15	3.38E-15
7.8	3.12E-15	2.89E-15	2.67E-15	2.46E-15	2.27E-15	2.10E-15	1.94E-15	1.79E-15	1.65E-15	1.53E-15
7.9	1.41E-15	1.30E-15	1.20E-15	1.11E-15	1.02E-15	9.42E-16	8.69E-16	8.01E-16	7.39E-16	6.82E-16

Figure 86

This is the second page of the Z table. Notice that it goes from 4.00 to 7.99. Also notice that when you get to 7.99 sigmas out it's fifteen zeros and a 682. Imagine trying to communicate that to someone when they say, "What would you expect your scrap rate to be above your upper spec limit?" And you'd say,"000000000000000682." Is that hard to communicate? Yes, it is; it's very difficult, and if you read that off they wouldn't write it down correctly anyway. So you're much better off to communicate in sigmas, and when they say, "What are you capable of on your upper spec limits?" you say, "7.99 sigmas." It's much easier to write that down, and if they want it in a percentage, they can look it up in the Z table. That is how people in high-and statement competitive industries, such as the automotive or electronic industries, communicate.

Statistics is a necessary and potentially powerful analytical tool in the element of tools transformation. From my experience, I would suggest that 80 percent of all statistics are designed to answer one important question: Did something change? Organizations must be capable of answering this question in an objective manner if they are to be capable of transformation. To answer why this question is so important, let me tell a simple story.

Once upon a time there was a perverted king who had decided he wanted a shorter population because they did not use as much clothing. The king hypothesized that the people would grow shorter if they ate more fish. So the king calls you up and tells you that you will be helping him as his project statistician. He then decides to run an experiment. You arrive at work, and the king tells you that the first thing he wants you to do is go out among the population and select a sample of the height of the people before they are fed fish. So you go out and collect this sample to see what the average height is. Then of course the king is going to have you feed them fish and then go out and get another sample to see if anything changed.

You leave the king's presence and do what you are told by selecting your sample of twenty people from the population of one million residents. Let's assume that the true population average is five feet tall and the average height of the sample you collected was four feet eleven inches. Now I ask you, is this common? When you go out and collect a sample of data, does it usually equal the population value? The answer to this question is no. The sample will never equal the population value. We call this phenomenon "sampling error." The population may be five feet in height, but your sample may be four feet eleven, or it may be five feet one. Or it may be many different values. Sampling error is the phenomenon that takes place when the sample value does not equal the population value—which is always.

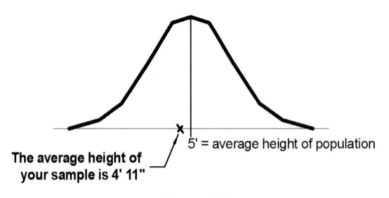

5' = average height of population

**The average height of
your sample is 4' 11"**

Figure 87

Now that we understand the current sampling error, let's return to our story. You return to the king and let him know that the average height of the people is four feet eleven inches, according to your sample. The king is very pleased with your work and gives you the next assignment, which is to go out and feed the population fish and directly after they have finished eating the fish to collect another sample to see the impact of the fish on the height of the general populace. Now obviously, eating fish is not going to make people shorter. Even if it did, you would definitely not be able to tell if you measured the people right after they ate the fish.

As instructed by the king, the complete population eats the fish, and directly after they finish their meal, you go out and select another sample of twenty from the population of a million residents.

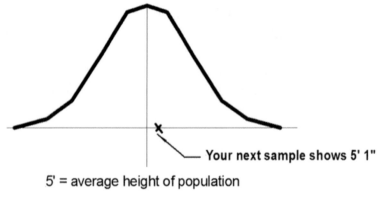

Your next sample shows 5' 1"

5' = average height of population

Figure 88

Your next sample shows an average height of five feet one inch. You become very upset when you realize that the numbers are different. The four feet eleven and the five feet one are obviously different numbers. Numerically, there's a difference between the before and after, and you're concerned that the fish actually made the people taller. You become very upset, as the king beheads all people who disprove his hypotheses. So what are you to do? Well, you understand that there is this phenomenon called "sampling error," and perhaps you can use this sampling error to your advantage. You can possibly use this to save your very life. So you collect more samples, because you know that if you collect enough samples, eventually you'll get a smaller number. After multiple efforts, you finally select a sample with an average height of four feet ten inches.

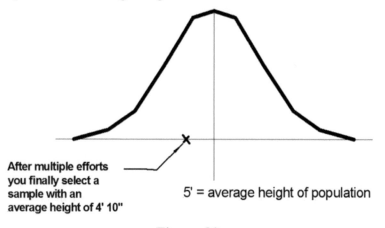

After multiple efforts you finally select a sample with an average height of 4' 10"

5' = average height of population

Figure 89

As a result, you ultimately go back to the king and say, "Dear wise king, as always you are correct. Eating fish made the population shorter." This may seem crazy to you, but with a culture of fear and one's inability to answer the question "Did something change?" in an objective manner, the scenario could be a reflection of reality in your own organization.

This becomes especially important when you consider that the most common way of improving "and" statement probabilities is by reducing variability. However, if you cannot objectively answer the question "Did something change?" and people are telling you things are getting better (lower variability) when they are just making such statements based on sampling error, then you obviously have a problem.

Eventually everyone is telling you that things are getting better, but you are unable to see it on your accounting sheets, and eventually no one trusts the statement "We are getting better." Therefore, the organization falls into subjectivity, and the ability to transform becomes an unachievable pipe dream.

Before moving on, we need to understand the methodologies used in reducing sampling error. There are two general things you need to remember in your attempts to reduce this problem. First, you can reduce sampling error by increasing the size of the sample. In our example of the height of the people, the average height was five feet—that was the correct answer. As our sample approaches the population size, sampling error will approach zero, and if the sample size equals the population size, the sampling error will, in fact, be zero. Obviously, if there are no numbers out there that you haven't entered into the calculation, there cannot be sampling error. Remember that you can reduce sampling error by increasing sample size.

The other way to reduce sampling error is to select your samples randomly. By "randomly," I mean that everyone in the population must have an equal opportunity of being selected. For example, let's say we take all of the people in the population and put them in a Bingo roller. We then roll them around, turn our head to minimize bias, and select our samples. Let's say we're going to use a sample size of ten. So we look the other way and select ten people out of the Bingo roller. Will this Bingo roller methodology create a random sample? In other words, will this methodology give all members of the population an equal opportunity of being selected? The answer to this question is no. Why? Because the larger people will have a higher probability of being selected, because there is more surface area on the larger people; thus the sample will not be random. In reality your sample average is likely to be taller than the true population average.

Instead of having the people get in the Bingo roller, what if we had them put their social security cards into the Bingo roller? Assuming that the cards were the same dimensions and densities, then this approach would create a much more random sample. In other words, there would be less sampling error. However, even if you drive sampling error to zero, it is still difficult (without statistics), due to inherent variability or the normal curve, to answer the question "Did something change?"

Let's go over what we've just learned. First of all, when you're trying to change something, such as reducing variability or changing the average of the normal distribution, there are two things that can happen. First of all it is a given that you will have a numerical difference. Now that numerical difference could be from random variation or sampling error. In other words, there is a numerical difference, but in reality nothing changed. We refer to that as Scenario 1 in the figure below.

Let's summarize what was just taught

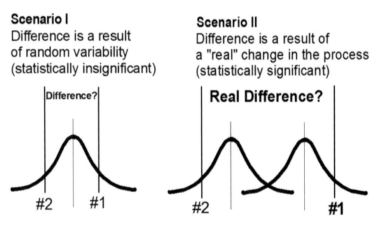

Scenario I
Difference is a result
of random variability
(statistically insignificant)

Difference?

#2   #1

Scenario II
Difference is a result of
a "real" change in the process
(statistically significant)

Real Difference?

#2   #1

Figure 90

In Scenario 2, you find that there is a "real" difference—something really changed. Whatever you did had a serious impact on the process output, and therefore, in your experiment, you know whether it's good or bad and you can start manipulating the situation to make it better, improving your "and" statements' probability or whatever you are trying to improve. In Scenario 1, there is a numerical difference, but there is no change in the process; it is only due to sampling error or random variability. In Scenario 2, there's a real difference, so not

only is there a numerical difference, but a real difference as well—
something indeed did make a change in that phenomenon.

Now we will discuss an example of using the analytical tools to improve a situation. The problem we desire to solve is to reduce inventory by 25 percent without increasing the risk of running out of product. Conceptually, this is not a difficult problem to solve, so let's get started. Implementing this concept into the organization's culture is not easy. As you can see in the figure below, we have a demand for this product of 100 pieces per day with a standard deviation of 10 pieces per day.

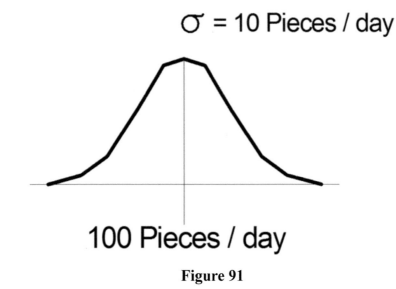

$\sigma = 10$ Pieces / day

100 Pieces / day

Figure 91

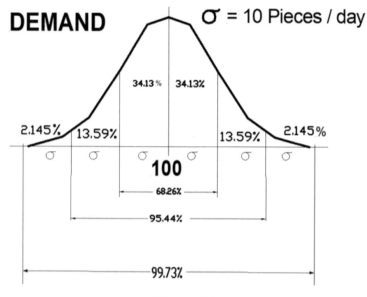

Figure 92

The next figure shows more detail concerning the situation. We're just going back to remind you of the nature of normal distribution. Remember that if you go out ± one sigma that equals 68.26 percent of the population. If you go out ± two sigma from the average, you have 95.44 percent of the population, and if you go out ± three sigma from the average, you end up with 99.73 percent of the population. Now let's take this figure and start adding more information to it.

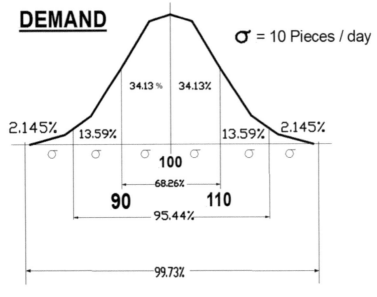

Figure 93

As you'll recall, on demand we had 100 pieces per day, and sigma equals 10 pieces per day. Notice that on the average we put the value of 100. Well, if the average is 100 and the standard deviation, or sigma, is 10 pieces per day, then what will the value be at one sigma above the average? We take 100 and add the standard deviation to it, which gives us 110. Now we go the other way; we go out one sigma below 100, since sigma is 10, and 100 minus 10 is 90; then we put the value there.

So what do we know about the process so far? Well, we know that 68.26 percent of the time the demand will lie between 90 and 110 pieces per day. In other words, there's uncertainty, just as there is about everything else. Uncertainty means sigma. If someone asked you, "What will the demand be tomorrow on this project?" you can't say 100. You could say on average it's 100, but you can't give an exact estimate. You have to come up with what we call "confidence intervals," and that's what we have just done. If someone asked you, "What is the demand going to be today?" you would say, "Well, I don't know for sure, but I do know that 68.26 percent of the time the demand will be between 90 pieces per day and 110 pieces per day."

And, of course, this would be a correct statement assuming we have a normal distribution.

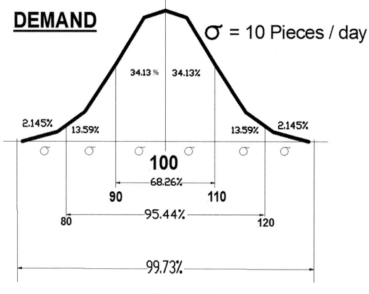

Figure 94

Let's move on and fill out the figure with greater detail. This time we're going to add another sigma. So remember that we went to 100, which is the average plus one sigma, and it gave us 110 as we go toward the top of the curve (to the right), so 100 plus 10 gives us 110. Then we take 110 and add another sigma to it—remember that sigma equals 10—so one sigma out from 110 gives us a value of 120. Notice we've put that in the figure above. Then we go to the other side of the curve (left side). Remember that we had 100 and we subtracted one sigma, which gave us 90, so from 90 we subtract another sigma, and this gives us 80. So this is another true statement that you can say about demand: 95.44 percent of the time, the daily demand will be between 80 and 120. Again, you don't know for sure what it's going to be, and therefore you just have to give a range of values and a confidence interval.

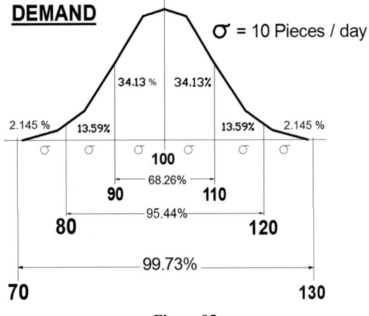

DEMAND

σ = 10 Pieces / day

34.13 % 34.13%

2.145 % 13.59% 13.59% 2.145 %

σ σ σ **100** σ σ σ

68.26%

90 **110**

95.44%

80 **120**

99.73%

70 **130**

Figure 95

In this figure we carry it out another sigma again. So now we take our 100, and remember we added the sigma of 10, which gave us 110. Another sigma out gave us 120, and now we're going to go three sigmas out, which is 120 plus the sigma of 10, giving us 130. Notice that on the left side of the curve, we went from 100 to 90 to 80; 80 minus 10 gives us 70. So now we know the values for the ± three sigma, and we can say, assuming a normal distribution, then 99.73 percent of the time our daily demand will be between 70 and 130 pieces. So, as you can see, there is uncertainty in demand. By the way, if you look up "uncertainty" in a statistics book, guess what you'll find? You'll find that uncertainty is equal to the standard deviation. So we use those terms of uncertainty and standard deviation interchangeably. Now we have three names for the same phenomena: "standard deviation," "sigma," and "uncertainty."

Now that we understand the span of uncertainty let's move on to the next step of reducing inventory by 25 percent. Again, there's a 99.73 percent chance that the demand will be between 70 pieces per day and 130 pieces per day. When you perform these types of problems, you have to come up with a level of risk that you're willing to take. In this example I'm going to say, "We're willing to take a 2.28 percent chance that when we need a part, it will not be there." That's called the "standard risk" or "alpha risk"—2.28 percent. In actual practice the alpha risk on inventory should be a strategic decision coming from upper management. Publishing a rule and backing it up with authority will make it functionally objective, assuming you have a functional organization.

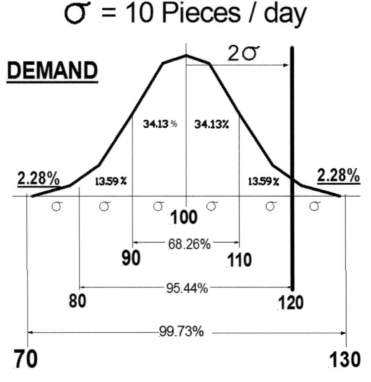

Figure 96

The only problem with the figure above is that it doesn't show how many sigmas I have to go out to experience the 2.28 percent risk. I cannot successfully solve the problem without knowing this value. By definition how many sigmas you are away from something is called the "Z statistic." The figure below shows the Z table, and you may notice that I have to go out two sigmas above the average to obtain my 2.28 percent risk level.

Here is how I found out how many sigmas (Z) out I needed to go to get the standard risk that I'm willing to take. Remember that it was 2.28 percent. So I go to my Z table and find that standard risk in the main body of the table. Notice I have bolded the 0.0228, which is the proportion, and the percentage would be 2.28 percent. To get my 2.28 percent, I find it in the main body of the Z table. I then go over to the Z column where it says 2.0; then I go up to see what the top row says, and it's 0, and that tells me if I want a 2.28 percent risk, standard or alpha risk, then I go out two sigmas. That's how I came up with the Z statistic.

z	0	0.01	0.02	0.03	0.04	0.05	0.06	0.07	0.08	0.09
0	0.5	0.496	0.492	0.488	0.484	0.4801	0.4761	0.4721	0.4681	0.4641
0.1	0.4602	0.4562	0.4522	0.4483	0.4443	0.4404	0.4364	0.4325	0.4286	0.4247
0.2	0.4207	0.4168	0.4129	0.409	0.4052	0.4013	0.3974	0.3936	0.3897	0.3859
0.3	0.3821	0.3783	0.3745	0.3707	0.3669	0.3632	0.3594	0.3557	0.352	0.3483
0.4	0.3446	0.3409	0.3372	0.3336	0.33	0.3264	0.3228	0.3192	0.3156	0.3121
0.5	0.3085	0.305	0.3015	0.2981	0.2946	0.2912	0.2877	0.2843	0.281	0.2776
0.6	0.2743	0.2709	0.2676	0.2643	0.2611	0.2578	0.2546	0.2514	0.2483	0.2451
0.7	0.242	0.2389	0.2358	0.2327	0.2296	0.2266	0.2236	0.2206	0.2177	0.2148
0.8	0.2119	0.209	0.2061	0.2033	0.2005	0.1977	0.1949	0.1922	0.1894	0.1867
0.9	0.1841	0.1814	0.1788	0.1762	0.1736	0.1711	0.1685	0.166	0.1635	0.1611
1.0	0.1587	0.1562	0.1539	0.1515	0.1492	0.1469	0.1446	0.1423	0.1401	0.1379
1.1	0.1357	0.1335	0.1314	0.1292	0.1271	0.1251	0.123	0.121	0.119	0.117
1.2	0.1151	0.1131	0.1112	0.1093	0.1075	0.1056	0.1038	0.102	0.1003	0.0985
1.3	0.0968	0.0951	0.0934	0.0918	0.0901	0.0885	0.0869	0.0853	0.0838	0.0823
1.4	0.0808	0.0793	0.0778	0.0764	0.0749	0.0735	0.0721	0.0708	0.0694	0.0681
1.5	0.0668	0.0655	0.0643	0.063	0.0618	0.0606	0.0594	0.0582	0.0571	0.0559
1.6	0.0548	0.0537	0.0526	0.0516	0.0505	0.0495	0.0485	0.0475	0.0465	0.0455
1.7	0.0446	0.0436	0.0427	0.0418	0.0409	0.0401	0.0392	0.0384	0.0375	0.0367
1.8	0.0359	0.0351	0.0344	0.0336	0.0329	0.0322	0.0314	0.0307	0.0301	0.0294
1.9	0.0287	0.0281	0.0274	0.0268	0.0262	0.0256	0.025	0.0244	0.0239	0.0233
2.0	**0.0228**	0.0222	0.0217	0.0212	0.0207	0.0202	0.0197	0.0192	0.0188	0.0183
2.1	0.0179	0.0174	0.017	0.0166	0.0162	0.0158	0.0154	0.015	0.0146	0.0143

Figure 97

Another assumption I'm going to make is that we have a forecast. Most organizations forecast on the average. Since our average pieces per day are 100, I have created a contract with our suppliers to give me 100 pieces per day. And I'm going to assume that they can do that without problems. I know that every day, when I go to the dock in the morning, there will be 100 pieces waiting there for my production or whatever I'm doing. And that's fine, but the problem is that 100 may not be enough, because 99.73 percent of the time it will be between 70 and 130 pieces per day. So it could be greater than 100. And, of course, the 95.44 percent confidence interval says that it will be between 80 and 120 pieces per day. Remember that outside the two sigmas is our targeted 2.28 percent risk. So that means that if I want to take a 2.28 percent risk, I need to have 20 in inventory (two sigmas) to cover the uncertainty of the 2.28 percent risk. Thus, if I go out two sigmas, that means I need 120 parts; I have 100 coming in on forecasting contracts, so I must have an additional 20 pieces in inventory. This will allow me to have a 2.28 percent risk for a given day of production. The only reason we need inventory is because of uncertainty (sigma).

So we forecasted 100 pieces per day. Let's assume the first day I have fewer than 100 pieces. Let's say, on day one, I had demand for 90 pieces, so I had 10 pieces left over. The next day I had demand for 110 pieces, so I used up my 10 additional, which drove my inventory back to zero; the next day I get delivery of 100 and I get demand of 90 again. So I have an additional 10 pieces. And then it just goes in the same cycle—I use up those 10 pieces the next day, then I get to save additional because demand's down, and so on and so forth. If this scenario was a reflection of reality, I would be all right with just my forecast—I would not have to have any inventory. The problem is, this is not the way nature works. It's not quite that predictable.

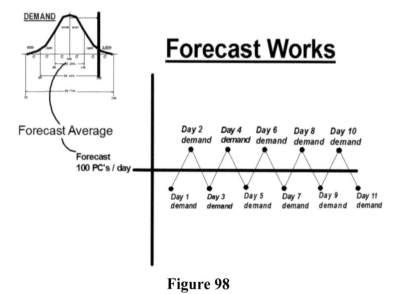

Figure 98

Reality tends to look more like the next figure. Let's continue the assumption that I get 100 pieces per day from the forecast. The first day, the demand is 110, so I'm already in trouble. I'm missing shipments and I'm going to be losing market share. So day one I'm down 10. The next day I get five more than the day before, so now I'm up to 115 for day-two demand, which gives me a total, from the two days of deficit, of 25 short (10 + 15 = 25). Notice I have four days in a row that are above my forecast. This creates more and more missed ship dates, missed opportunities, and eventually a shrinkage in market share. So we have to prepare for this type of scenario.

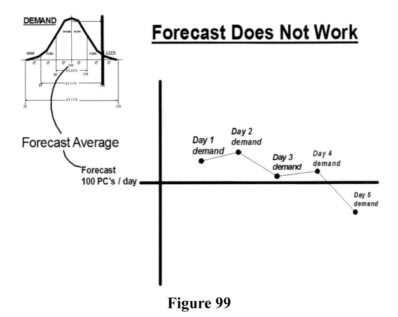

Figure 99

Forecast Does Not Work
Sigma = Uncertainty

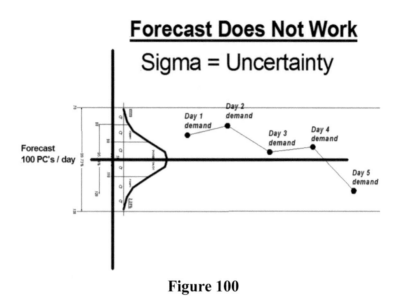

Figure 100

Figure 100 shows something we call "uncertainty." Let's say the forecast is normally distributed—often forecasts are, at least the residuals from the forecast. If you don't understand this, don't worry about it at this time. In this problem we're going to assume that demand is normally distributed, so we forecast a demand for 100 pieces per day (the average). With the normal distribution and the nature of processes it is reasonable that we could get four consecutive points above average. It's just natural that the above scenario could take place. I could make this assumption more objective, but it would be outside the scope of what I am trying to accomplish here. The objective of this discussion is to give you some basic conceptual information concerning the relationship between uncertainty and inventory and how Solution #3 can help you run your businesses more effectively and efficiently. In our problem-solving exercise, we're going to assume that we could get four days in a row with above-average demand. Not only four days above average—four days that are at the two-sigma level. In other words, we're going to assume that for four days we'll get demand for 120 pieces per day. Now that's rather unlikely, but that's the assumption we're going to use in this exercise. Our whole inventory system is going to be set up for handling this scenario.

233

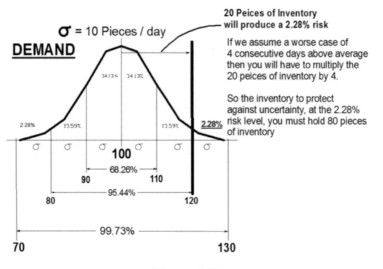

Figure 101

As the figure above shows, we have a forecast of 100, so we need 20 additional pieces every day to cover the additional risk of uncertainty. If we assume the worst-case scenario, or four consecutive days of above-average demand, at that 95 percent level, which is 120 pieces per day, then we will have to multiply the 20 pieces of required inventory per day by four for the four days above average. So for the inventory to protect against uncertainty at the 2.28 percent risk level, you must hold 80 pieces of inventory. The cost of covering uncertainty and demand is going to cost us 80 pieces of inventory. We must remember, however, that these 80 pieces of inventory are only for demand variability in the supply chain (variability from forecast). This is not the only unknown or uncertainty in the supply chain. There are other forms of uncertainty, including administrative lead time and production lead time. These are the forms of uncertainty that we're going to assume in this exercise.

So we know there are other forms of variability. Maybe another form of variability is that your supplier can't deliver 100 pieces per day, even though he has a contract to do so. What I am trying to say is that there could be other forms of variability that have to be taken into account. In this exercise we're going to assume that the only three elements of uncertainty are administrative lead time, production lead time, and, as already mentioned, demand uncertainty.

Administrative lead time, in this discussion, means the time it takes purchasing to order a part from a supplier after the part has been requested internally. Production lead time, in this discussion, means the time it takes from the time the order from purchasing is received by the supplier to the time the order is delivered to the purchasing organization from the supplier. Of course, both production lead time and administrative lead time have uncertainty. Remember that we also call uncertainty "standard deviation," "sigma," or "variability" (variability is actually sigma squared). I know it's unfortunate that we have so many words meaning the same things, but I'm just preparing you for what you will see in the real world.

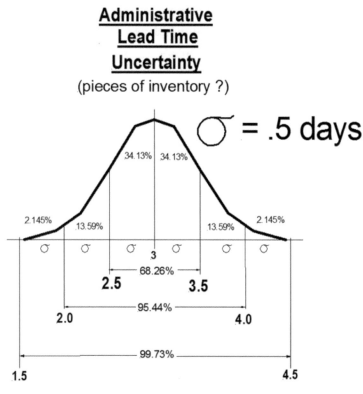

Figure 102

In the figure below, you'll see that I have added up all the uncertainties in the study.

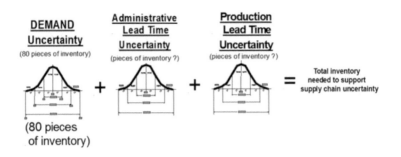

Figure 103

We have demand uncertainty, which we've already decided would require 80 pieces of inventory, to meet our standard risk of 2.28 percent. Now we have administrative lead time uncertainty. We don't know how many pieces of inventory are needed to get the 2.28 percent risk for that uncertainty, but we'll show you how to determine that in the following pages.

Now we will move forward to the next step and discuss the concepts used for calculating required inventory levels for administrative lead time and production lead time. First we will look at administrative lead time uncertainty.

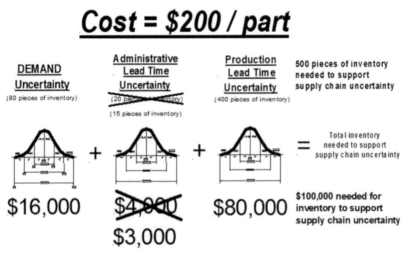

Figure 104

Figure 102 is the normal curve for administrative lead time. So on average, when the production line says, "We need more parts," purchasing will take an average of three days before it has that PO or purchasing order sent off to the supplier. We will assume that production realizes that on average it takes three days for purchasing to purchase their parts and as a result production will always place the order three days before it is actually needed. The standard deviation is .5, so if we take 3± on sigma, we will get 3.5 and 2.5. So we know that 68.26 percent of the time, administrative lead time will be between 2.5 days and 3.5 days. Now we go out another sigma, and we go from 3.5 out one other sigma, and sigma is equal to .5, and therefore, our next sigma out will be equal to 4. And we do the same thing on the lower side of the curve. We go from 2.5 to 2. So we are 95.44 percent confident that the administrative lead time will take between two and four days.

If we go out one more sigma to make it ± three sigma and we end up with 4.5 on the upper side of the curve and 1.5 on the lower side of the curve (see the above figure). Now we can say that we are 99.73 percent confident that the administrative lead time will take between 1.5 days and 4.5 days. Next we look at our standard risk, which we know to be 2.28 percent for this problem. We know that to get to the 2.28 percent risk, we need to go out two sigmas.

Notice the average is three days, and if I go out two sigmas, it is equal to four days. So the actual distance for two sigmas is equal to one day. And since I know that per our demand analysis, one day of uncertainty requires 20 pieces of inventory, then the needed inventory to support administrative lead time is 20 pieces.

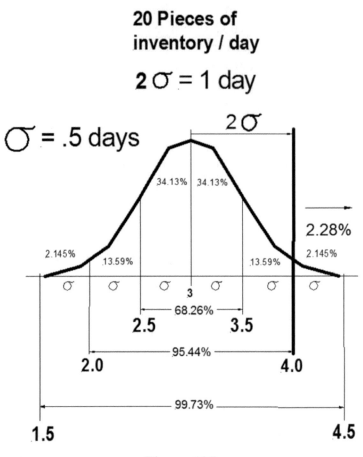

**20 Pieces of
inventory / day**

2σ = 1 day

σ = .5 days

Figure 105

Now we will do the same calculation for production lead time. Notice on the figure below that the average production lead time is 40 days and the standard deviation is 10 days. So 40 plus the sigma of 10 gives us 50 for the next one-sigma distance out. So we know that 68.26 percent of the time production lead time will take between 30 and 50 days.

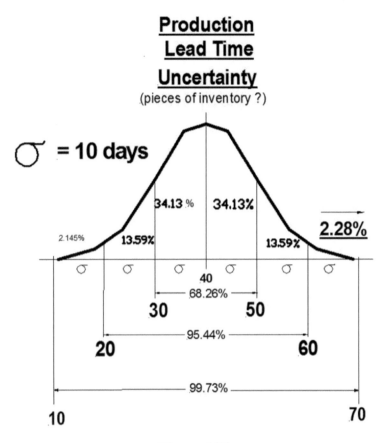

Figure 106

Now let's go out two sigma. That takes us out to a range of 20 and 60, so we know that 95.44 percent of the time production lead time will fall between 20 days and 60 days. And, of course, down to the 99.73 percent range, we know that 99.73 percent of the time production lead time will take between 10 and 70 days. So there's quite a bit more uncertainty in this production lead time than there was in administrative lead time. It is going to cost us more money to maintain our 2.28 percent risk on this one.

Note we do not have to worry about the 40-day average because we are assuming that purchasing knows that it usually takes 40 days, on average, to get parts so they will order the parts 40 days before they are needed. If this is not the case, then we would also have to consider the average days as well. Two sigmas out from average gives us 60, so the difference between the average and two sigma is 20 days. So we need 20 pieces per day for 20 days, the 20 x 20 equates to 400 pieces of inventory to cover the uncertainty from production lead time.

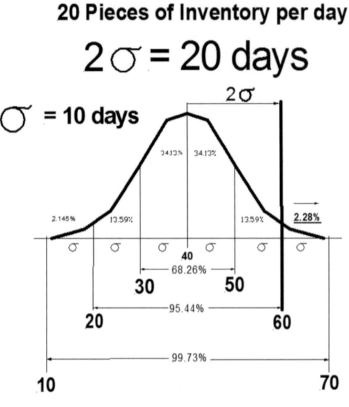

Figure 107

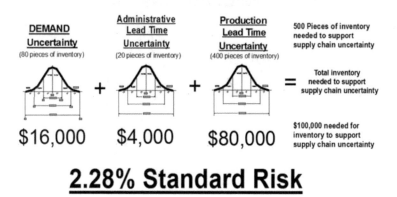

Cost = $200 / part

2.28% Standard Risk

Figure 108

This figure shows a summary of all of our calculations, plus some cost calculations that we will be performing shortly. Now I'm going to assume that each part in inventory costs $200, so it's $200 per part. Notice in demand uncertainty that we have 80 pieces of inventory, which equates to $16,000. So it's going to cost us $16,000 to support the uncertainty of demand. Administrative lead time, as you'll recall, demanded 20 pieces of inventory at the 2.28 percent risk level, which equates to $4,000. Then, for production lead time uncertainty, we needed 400 pieces of inventory. This equates to $80,000—so the total cost to support our standard risk is $100,000. This $100,000 is needed for inventory to support supply-chain uncertainty, which also equates to 500 pieces of inventory.

Now that we understand our current state, how do we reduce inventory costs without violating our standard risk? Remember that the problem we're trying to solve is to reduce inventory by 25 percent while maintaining our standard risk. The answer to this question is to reduce supply-chain variability.

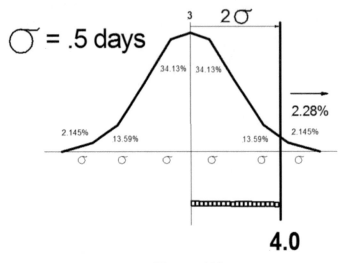

**20 Pieces of inventory to support
Administrative Lead Time uncertainty**

Figure 109

Remember that 20 pieces of inventory were needed to support the administrative lead time uncertainty. I have drawn the number of inventories to scale to the bell curve, so notice that two sigmas equals 20 pieces of inventory. Therefore, I have put 20 pieces of inventory at the bottom of that sketch.

Notice that I have, in the figure below, reduced uncertainty (Solution #3). I went out in the supply chain and worked with purchasing to improve the process and reduce the variability. The top bell curve, in the figure below, shows the current state, and after the project, it shows the improved lower bell curve.

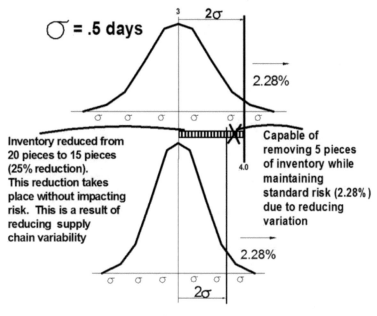

Figure 110

As a result of this reduction in variability uncertainty, inventory can be reduced from 20 pieces to 15 pieces, which is a 25 percent reduction. This reduction takes place without impacting risk. This is a result of reducing supply-chain variability. That's the beauty of reducing variability. When we reduce variability, we can reduce inventory without increasing risk.

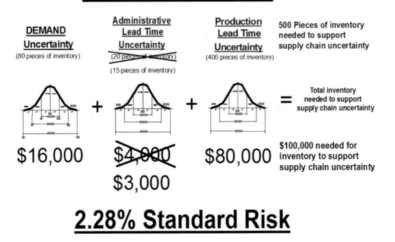

Cost = $200 / part

2.28% Standard Risk

Figure 111

Now we've updated our figure. Notice that administrative lead time for uncertainty was 20 pieces; now, due to the reduction in variability (Solution #3), it is 15 pieces. This reduces the cost of inventory from $4,000 to $3,000. The important question to ask is: "How do we reduce variability?" There are many different methods that can be used to reduce variability. Which method is used depends on the type of variability.

One methodology that could be used to reduce variability in time, such as administrative lead time and production lead time, is Lean. Lean methodology has its roots in the Toyota production system. Lean's main objective is to improve processes through the removal of waste. This is an important concept in the world of process-improvement. When you take waste out of processes, variability in time goes down.

In summary, if you want to reduce time variation or time uncertainty in administrative lead time or production lead time, you take waste out of the process as suggested by Lean methodology.

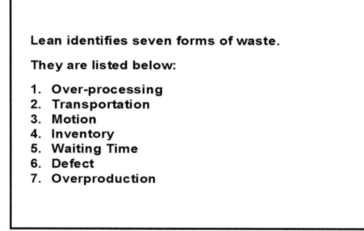

Lean identifies seven forms of waste.

They are listed below:

1. **Over-processing**
2. **Transportation**
3. **Motion**
4. **Inventory**
5. **Waiting Time**
6. **Defect**
7. **Overproduction**

Figure 112

We're going to use transportation and motion in an example: Transportation is how far you have to transport material. Motion is bodily movement. As an example of how we can reduce both of these items and also, as a result, reduce variation or uncertainty, let's tell a little story. Let's say you are an engineer, you are at your desk, and you get thirsty. You may have to travel, let's say, one hundred yards to get to the nearest water cooler. So you get up and start your journey, and on your way, you notice that your shoelaces are untied, so you bend over and tie them. Then as you approach the cooler you see an old buddy, so you stop and talk. Sometimes these situations happen and sometimes they won't, but they could happen and do happen from time to time. You finally make it to the water cooler and realize that it's empty, so you have to travel another three hundred yards to get a new container for the water cooler. You take the water container back, get it set up, and then get your drink. Next you start walking back to your desk. What I'm trying to tell you is through this transportation and motion, things take place. The problem is that sometimes they take place and sometimes they don't, so that makes it difficult to estimate the time it takes to get a drink. In summary, increased travel and motion creates uncertainty (sigma) in the time it takes you to go get a drink.

For the sake of argument, let's say we take this water cooler and put it right next to your desk. Now when you feel thirsty you just reach over and get a cup of water and drink. You have very little transportation and just a little bit of motion. By doing this, you take the risk out of seeing the buddy, recognizing your shoelaces are untied, and on and on. There are all kinds of things that could happen while walking to the water cooler that's a hundred yards away. By reducing transportation and motion, we reduce time variability. This is, again, a very important concept: when we reduce waste out of the process, we reduce variation, and when we reduce variation, we can reduce inventory levels.

Now we will spend a little bit of time defining each of the forms of waste: number one is overprocessing. Overprocessing takes place when you perform more work on a product or service than the customer is willing to pay for. One of the reasons for overprocessing is not being aware of customer wants and needs. For example: Let's say we have a factory that produces threaded hex nuts. One day we decide to start painting them green. However, the customer couldn't care less if they are green, or any other color for that matter, and definitely is not willing to pay for a green hex nut. You have also just added another set of "and" statements, and additional "and" statements tend to add more variability in time. Therefore, painting the hex nuts green is considered overprocessing. When you do something to the process, product, or service that the customer really couldn't care less about and is totally unwilling to pay for, that is called overprocessing. And in the end, it will create uncertainty in time. So if you do not know your customer's wants, you'll probably add more value than the customer is willing to pay for. There are several ways to identify customer wants. These include surveys, focus groups, customer interviews, and tools such as quality function deployment (QFD).

Another cause of overprocessing is letting known nonvalue-added activities creep into the process. This often consists of hand offs and sign-offs. You have to ask yourself if the customer cares about these additional hand offs and sign-offs or if the customer would prefer to receive the product sooner and more consistently (less inventory). Again, communication with the customer is key to reducing overprocessing.

The next form of waste that we'll talk about is transportation. Transportation is the unnecessary movement of materials, products, or information. Transportation is important because it takes time, and time equates to money. Lean thinkers desire to reduce time in an effort to create wealth more efficiently. Ultimately, transportation manifests itself in people wandering around. We can often reduce transportation by combining steps or rearranging processes to match the process flow of products or services.

There is a well-documented case study about a bank that recently performed a transportation study on loan documents. They discovered that the documents traveled 1½ miles before service completion. The bank's "Lean Team" redesigned the bank's floor layout to match the process flow and, as a result, reduced travel to 386 steps. That's an 80 percent reduction. So not only did they reduce the cost of wandering around, but they also reduced the inherent variability in the process and thus reduced inventory levels accordingly—which made the bank more efficient with its cash output to run their business activities.

The next form of waste in "Lean thinking" is referred to as motion. Motion in Lean thinking, is defined as the unnecessary movement of people. Transportation is the unnecessary movement of product, and motion is the unnecessary movement of people. Motion may manifest itself in moving between different computer domains or unnecessary keystrokes in accomplishing a task. If you can reduce motion, you will reduce uncertainty or variability in the supply chain.

The fourth form of waste that we will study is referred to as inventory. Inventory, in Lean thinking, is defined as any work in process that's in excess of what is required by the customer. Work in process, or WIP, may manifest itself in stockpiled work in process at a given step in the process. Work in process is often the result of overproduction.

The next form of waste that we will discuss is waiting time. Waiting time in Lean thinking is defined as any delay between when one process ends and the next step begins. The process value maps or flowcharts should include waiting time between process steps. The value map should define the actual waiting time for both baseline studies and improved processes. Reducing waiting time will also reduce variability in the supply chain, thus resulting in lower levels of inventory needed to support the uncertainty.

The next form of waste on our list is defect. A defect in Lean thinking is defined as any attribute of a service or product that does not conform to customer needs. The process value maps (flowcharts) should include this process in dealing with defects. The value map should define the actual time needed for reworking the service or product. In my experience, nothing will create more devastating variation in time in the supply chain than producing in lots. The second most severe is defects. You must get quality under control in order to improve your supply-chain performance. I suspect if your process created single piece flow and you did not create defectives, thus eliminating rework, then you could reduce your need for inventory by approximately 70%. Do the math and then you can decide if it is worth it.

The last form of waste that we will discuss is overproduction. Overproduction, in Lean thinking, is defined as the production service or product outputs that are larger than those needed for immediate use. In other words, you are building more product than the customer is willing to pay for, which means someone is going to have to store inventory. Reducing overproduction will inherently reduce the need for inventory. A good concept to follow in reaching your inventory reduction goals would be to calculate what the standard deviation needs to be, (which I call "critical sigma") in order to realize the goal and then perform Lean events until the actual sigma, or standard deviation, is equal to or less than the critical sigma, or critical standard deviation. Most organizations that perform Lean events don't understand the relationship between waste reduction and inventory reduction and as a result leave "money on the table." After these improvements have been achieved, you will need to sustain your gains through various activities, which will most likely include an effective auditing program.

Theory of Constraints (TOC) is another important methodology to understand. TOC's objective is to find the single constraint that is holding back organizational transformation. Once you find the actual constraint you can use the proper set of process-improvement tools and improve the constraint, thus getting the best return on investment. My experience suggests that the biggest constraint to most organizations is its organizational culture.

One of the most embarrassing things in the process-improvement world is when you see grownups treat these different methodologies like they are a religion. They bicker back and forth trying to determine which methodology is best. I would suggest to all to "get over it all ready"—these are methodologies to improve processes. If you can't use all of them to get the final result, then something is wrong with the way you're looking at the world. For example, some people who consider themselves "Lean" people would get very upset if I used Lean to reduce variability in the process but then used math to determine inventory levels. Because the math comes from Six Sigma! "TOC people" would feel the same way if you used Lean or Six Sigma to help remove the constraint. My suggestion to all is get over it. The methodology I prefer is to use TOC to determine the constraint and then use the proper tools that are necessary to overcome the constraint, whether these tools come from the Lean tool box or the Six Sigma tool box or some other place makes no difference to me. The point is this: "Don't become the slave of tools; make the tools a slave to you." Sometimes I even make up tools that are needed to solve a problem (that will tick some people off). As mentioned earlier I feel that a lot of this problem finds its roots in the rule already discussed: "You stop becoming greater the instant you think you're great." For example, if you become "great" at Six Sigma you can't become "great" at anything else, because accepting other knowledge would suggest that you currently don't know it all, and that is evidently hard to swallow sometimes. This needed to be said, but now it is time to move on.

Now back to the inventory problem. We will assume that we went out to perform process-improvement to the supplier's production, sent a Lean team, and performed a reduction in time variability through Lean events. As a result we went from 400 pieces of inventory to 320 pieces, while maintaining our 2.28% risk.

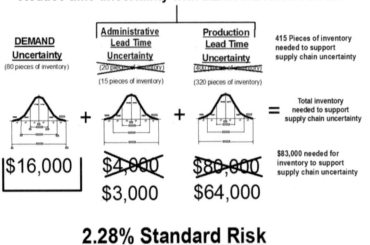

Reduce time uncertainty with LEAN METHODOLOGY

2.28% Standard Risk

Figure 113

We have now discussed how to reduce variability in administrative lead time and production lead time, and really it's the same way with all-time uncertainty. If you want to reduce time variation or time uncertainty, you can simply take waste out of the process. It will also reduce average times, which is an added benefit. We didn't discuss the change in averages in this study because I felt it was complicated enough already; but know that we left quite a bit on the table by not taking averages into account. So Lean reduces averages and variability, and both of these reduce inventory.

Now we need to say to ourselves, *That's fine; we understand how to reduce variability in time elements, but what about demand?* How can we reduce variability in demand? This is very difficult. You're dealing with customers, and they're going to purchase things when they decide to purchase them, and you probably don't have a lot of control over that. I suspect you could make some changes in advertising and what have you. Another way to reduce variability in demand is by improving, or I should say diversifying, your market— maybe serving other diverse needs in the market that you're not currently in, perhaps in different parts of the country, different parts of the world, maybe different demographics, those types of things.

As you more thoroughly diversify and grow your market, demand variability tends to go down.

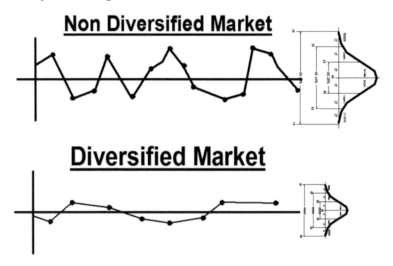

Figure 114

Another way to improve demand variability is to improve forecasting methodologies. For example, look at the figure 115 and look at that top line, which shows variability in demand. If we take the variability of that whole sector, it creates a fairly wide normal distribution. But let's say we can use those sectors to predict when the market goes up and down. Now I'm going to take that sector that I have outlined and put it down on the lower part of the figure. Notice that I found that I could predict that upswing. I couldn't predict it perfectly, so I still have variability about that forecasting line, but the variability is way less than just trying to produce the whole demand without looking at the sectors. As a result of forecasting that sector, my variability goes way down. So if you can predict those changes in direction, then your variability will go way down in your forecast— and this allows you to hold less inventory.

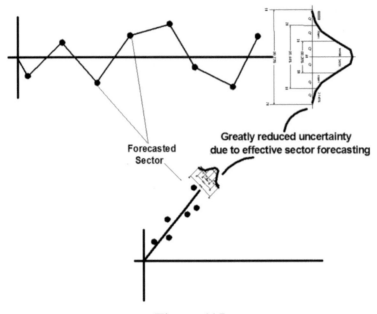

Figure 115

Now, through improved forecasting and diversification of the market, we have reduced uncertainty on demand and have reduced it to our goal of 25 percent reduction. We went from 80 pieces needed to support the demand uncertainty at our standard risk to 60 pieces, or a 25 percent reduction, which takes us from $16,000 to $12,000. So now we have solved the problem. How did we solve the problem? We identified the uncertainty in the supply chain and reduced it to the level needed to reach our goal of a 25 percent reduction. And the cost of inventory went from $100,000 to $75,000, which equates to an original 500 pieces of inventory down to 395 pieces of inventory. Of course, if we wanted to reduce inventory even further, we could continue to reduce variability in the supply chain. As mentioned earlier, you should create a culture of continuous process-improvement in your organization, so these improvement events continue reducing the need for inventory. If you ever achieve zero uncertainty in the supply chain, then you can have zero inventory to run the supply chain, which is known as Just in Time (JIT). If you demand Just in Time delivery from your supply chain without driving uncertainty to zero, then the result will be just reshuffling where inventory is located in the supply chain, which from a big picture perspective is a big waste of time. In essence the most politically powerful element of the supply chain will hold less inventory and the relatively politically weak part of the supply chain will hold more inventory. In the end as a whole you are not creating more widgets per person, which makes society at large the big loser.

Reduce time uncertainty with LEAN METHODOLOGY

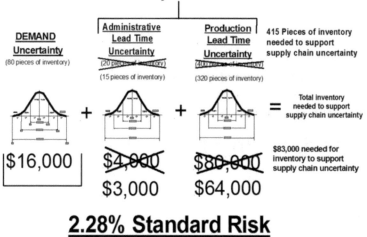

2.28% Standard Risk

Figure 116

In summary, the problem of reducing inventory levels by 25 percent while maintaining standard risk has been achieved through the reduction of variation or uncertainty or standard deviation. This problem was solved in an objective manner, albeit with some assumptions (assumptions are subjective). Sometimes you see companies demand a 25 percent reduction in inventory, which happens, but with an increase in risk. The increased risk is suddenly realized when the organization runs out of critical parts. What happens next is that the stress level goes up and the sacrifice demanded by the organization will exceed the organizational character and everyone slides down to Phase I behavior. The problem is then solved by punishing the people who were asked to reduce inventory. This type of methodology, of course, does not allow transformation to take place, because this is a subjective way of reducing inventory, which results in personifying, blaming, and punishing.

CHAPTER SEVEN

SYSTEMATIC PROBLEM-SOLVING

The purposes of this chapter are to define the basic model for systematic problem solving, to discuss the benefits of systematic problem solving, and to discuss the DMAIC model for systematic problem solving in the Six Sigma methodology.

Standard Problem Solving Model

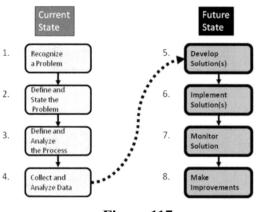

Figure 117

The figure above shows a standard problem-solving model. Notice that it's broken into two standard categories: current state and future state. I can also tell you this: there are many standard problem-solving models out there. Every company or organization tends to have its own, but when you really look at them and break them down, they all consist of the same types of things. And again, we have two standard breakups here—a current state and a future state in our standard problem-solving model. And by the way, this is the one they use to teach the students in the Air Force during continuous process-improvement—and it's a good one. It covers all the steps.

Later on in this chapter, we're going to discuss in detail the DMAIC model. It's just another form of a systematic problem-solving model and is probably one of the more commonly used ones out there. But for right now, let's look at the standard problem-solving model.

Step #1: *Recognize that a problem exists.* That's pretty important when you're going to solve a problem.

Step #2: *Define and state the problem.* In other words, document it. Make sure you understand the problem and that it is documented in such a way that all the stakeholders can understand it. Albert Einstein was once asked, "If you had one hour to solve a problem to save the world, how would you do it?" He said, "Well, I can tell you this, I would spend fifty-five minutes identifying the problem." And so a very important step in problem solving is to just get a good definition of exactly what the problem is.

Step #3: *Define and analyze the process.* This is usually where you create a flowchart to help the team understand all the steps in the process.

Step #4: *Collect and analyze data.* This is in the current state of the process. After you collect data that represents the current performance of the process you analyze the data so you can document current state. One reason you need to understand and document current state is so when the project is over you can determine if the process was improved and by how much (how much money was saved). At this point in the process you should understand the problem you are trying to improve to such an extent that you can turn it on and off. You can't improve a situation without fully understanding it first.

Step #5: *Develop solutions.* This is the most analytically challenging portion of the problem-solving model. Often the phenomena under investigation will be mathematically modeled. Once you have the mathematical model it is reasonably easy to optimize the solution. Of course not all solutions demand a mathematical model, but all solutions must be optimized for best results.

Step #6: *Implement these solutions.* That's an art form all its own. This is where Phase III behavior must take over. You can't shove solutions down people's throats and expect them to support these solutions. You should involve all the applicable stakeholders in the problem, solution, and solution implementation. If people don't feel ownership they will not take ownership. Let everyone else take credit for the success.

Step #7: *Monitor the solution.* If you fail here you will not be capable of sustaining gains from the process-improvement over time.

Step #8: *Make improvements.* In other words start another project and keep improving the process.

This is an example of a systematic problem-solving model. What do I mean by "systematic"? It means that most organizations have systematic problem-solving models and follow them step by step. If this was your company's systematic problem-solving model, you would start with Step 1, then Step 2, and work your way all the way through to Step 8. And as you're going through, many people may ask you, "Where are you at on that particular problem?" And you can say, "Oh, we're on Step 6." And of course everyone understands it's the systematic problem-solving model, and it gives them a good idea of where you are. Systematic problem solving helps us to optimize our problem-solving skills, and it also helps in communication. Now we're going to move on and discuss in greater detail another systematic problem-solving model, referred to as the DMAIC model.

The following figure shows the DMAIC model. DMAIC, again, is a systematic problem-solving model used in the world of Six Sigma. The *D* in the DMAIC model stands for *Define*, *M* stands for *Measure*, *A* stands for *Analyze*, *I* stands for *Improve*, and *C* stands for *Control*. There are many versions of the DMAIC model. If you read books on this subject, they will all have a little bit of their own unique flavor to the DMAIC model, which is to be expected. The next figure shows you a model that's taught by the US Air Force in its transformation courses. Later I'll share with you a more simplistic example, and that will help you understand at least how to go about defining Six Sigma projects. It's an important model to understand if you are working in the world of process-improvement. So let's move forward and look at the next figure.

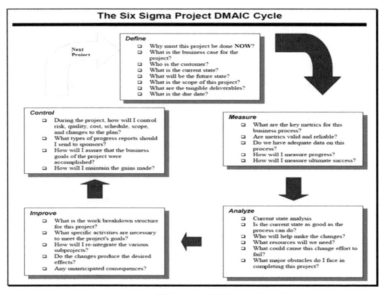

Figure 118

This is an example of the DMAIC model. You'll notice that each of the boxes stands for the various elements of the DMAIC model: "Define" is the first box, and then you go around clockwise and you see "Measure," "Analyze," "Improve," and "Control." Feel free to read all of the elements in each of those boxes. We will go over some of the bullets, but not all. In the Define step it says: "Why must this project be done NOW?" Why is it so important that it needs to be completed? And let's skip down a little bit, to where it says, "What is the current state?" That's a part of every systematic problem-solving model—how well is the current process performing? It's very important to define that upfront. And, of course, "What is the scope of this project?" is another important part of defining a project. You can read through those other bullets if you'd like.

Now let's move on to Measure and read a couple of those bullets: "What are the key metrics for this business process?" In other words, what's important? What should we be looking at? What kind of data should we be gathering to improve this process? And, of course, the third bullet down, "Do we have adequate data on this process?" If you already have data that you can start analyzing, that's going to speed up this process a lot. When you are performing Six Sigma projects, most of your time is spent in Define and Measure. I would say 60 percent to 70 percent of the project is spent on these two steps. Part of that is because measuring also includes collecting data in most DMAIC models and data is very time consuming to gather, at least in most situations.

Now let's look at the Analyze box. Notice where it says "current state analysis." You gather data and then crunch that data and do capability studies and the like to perform analysis on the current state to see how it's performing ("and" statement probabilities). Then, "Who will help make the changes?" That's a good thing to ask at this point when you're analyzing. And last, but not least, in that Analyze box, "What major obstacles do I face in completing this project?" Again, all good questions.

Now let's look at the Improve box. Under improvement in the DMAIC model it says, "What is the work breakdown structure for this project?" So now you're starting to define how you're going to implement this a little bit more. You're getting a little more specific. And then it goes on and says, "How will I reintegrate the various subprojects?" So you may have subprojects, and you have to tie all those together.

Now let's look at the Control box. Under control in the DMAIC model it says, "During this project, how will I control risk, quality, cost, schedule, and scope?" And it also says, "How will I assure that the business goals of the project were accomplished?" You want to do that, obviously, in a very objective manner so people won't argue about whether your project was a success or not. This is just a quick comb through of the DMAIC model. Remember this: the more complex the project, the more specificity you need when you define and work your way through that project. The DMAIC shown is one of the more sophisticated ones I have seen. So this would be a good model to follow for extra-large projects.

Now I'm going to use a more simplistic DMAIC model that I think is still very effective. However, if you have a really complicated problem that you're solving, with many people involved, and it crosses the entire organization, then you may want to use the earlier DMAIC model. But let's move on and we'll discuss the Define element of the simplified DMAIC model.

Define

– **Upper management responsibility**

– **Output = Charter**

Figure 119

Remember that this is a more simplistic model than the one I showed you on the earlier figure. I think it's very functional though. In the Define step, we must remember that upper management is usually the one responsible. This is where we define the project, and the output of the Define step is a project charter. We will go into great detail on the project charter later.

Define:

– **Upper management responsibility**

– **8 to 12 hours of Champion Training (not project based)**

– **Teaches high level management how to Champion 6 Sigma projects**

Figure 120

Let's move on to the next figure. As mentioned earlier, during this Define step it is management's responsibility to define these projects. This is important because it allows management to take ownership of the project, which means that they are more likely to remove barriers when they appear. In order to make this more effective, upper management usually attends a class that lasts from eight to twelve hours of lecture time called "champion training." It is not a project-based class. They don't go in and complete a project in most cases; they just listen and ask questions about their responsibilities in the business strategy of process-improvement. Basically, champion training teaches high-level management how to champion process-improvement projects. It is a well-known fact in the world of successful projects that one of the ingredients is upper-management support. If you go to an organization that is highly effective, one that's identifying, working through, and successfully completing projects, there is one element you'll always find—it is supported by top management. If you go into an organization that can't seem to complete a project, it's usually because they do not have upper-management support. So in champion training, upper management learns that their role is extremely important in project success.

The basic model for the creation of the charter in this presentation was used from the Six Sigma project planner authored by Thomas Pyzdek. He is one of the leading authorities on Six Sigma, and you can purchase the planner from www.qualityamerica.com. It's a very reasonably priced book, and you can just fill it out as you go along. It's a great book to have if you feel that it's necessary for your project.

Six Sigma Project Charter

Project Name / Number					
Sponsoring Organization					
Project Sponsor	Name:			Phone:	
	Office Location:			Mail Stop:	
Project Black Belt	Name:			Phone:	
	Office Location:			Mail Stop:	
Project Green Belt	Name:			Phone:	
	Office Location:			Mail Stop:	
Team Members (Name)	Title / Role	Phone	Office Location	Mail Stop
Principal Stakeholders	Title / Role	Phone	Office Location	Mail Stop
Date Charted:		Project Start Date:		Target Completion Date:	
Revision:		Date:			DMAIC
Sponsor Approval Signature:					

Figure 121

The figure above shows an example of the project charter that we will be discussing. We will go through every element of the project charter to make sure you understand how to use it. This is a two-page document. The figure above represents page 1. In the next figure, we'll talk about page 2. You'll notice on page 1 that some of the elements in this project charter are "Project Name and Number," "Sponsoring Organization," "Project Sponsor," "Project Black Belt," "Project Green Belt," "Team Member" (names and how to contact them), "Principal Stakeholders," "Date Charted," "Project Start Date," "Target Completion Date," "Revision Date," and "Sponsor Approval Signatures."

That's all on page 1. We'll go through each one of those elements in enough detail that you will be able to fill out a charter.

Six Sigma Project Charter	
Project Name / Number	
Project Mission Statement	
Problem Statement	
Project Scope	
Business Need Addressed by This Project	
Deliverables	
Resources Authorized for This Project	DMAIC

Figure 122

Now let's look at page 2 of the project charter.

The second page has "Project Mission Statement," "Problem Statement," "Project Scope," "Business Need Addressed by This Project," "Deliverables," and "Resources Authorized for This Project." Those are all the elements of the project charter that we will be teaching you.

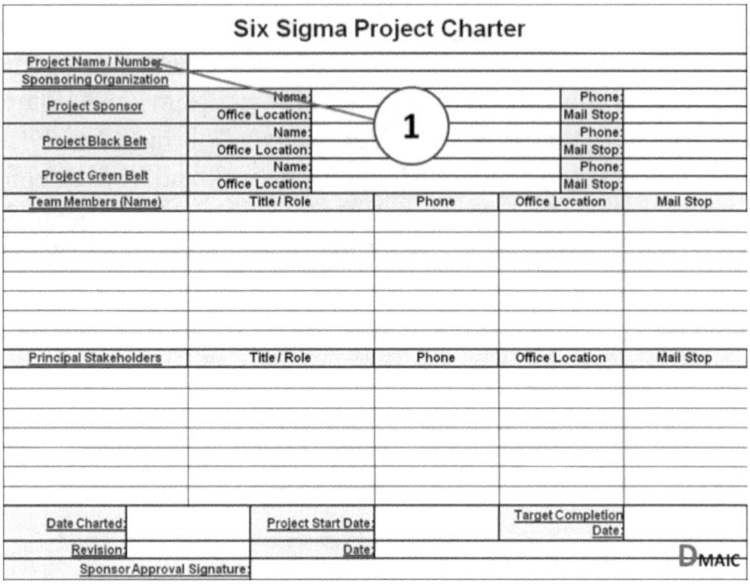

Six Sigma Project Charter

Project Name / Number						
Sponsoring Organization						
Project Sponsor	Name			Phone		
	Office Location			Mail Stop		
Project Black Belt	Name			Phone		
	Office Location			Mail Stop		
Project Green Belt	Name			Phone		
	Office Location			Mail Stop		
Team Members (Name)	Title / Role	Phone	Office Location	Mail Stop		
Principal Stakeholders	Title / Role	Phone	Office Location	Mail Stop		
Date Charted		Project Start Date		Target Completion Date		
Revision		Date				
Sponsor Approval Signature				DMAIC		

Figure 123

Now let's move on to the next figure and look at all of these elements in greater detail. The first element of the project charter that we'll talk about is "Project Name and Number." Remember that this is indicated on both page 1 and page 2 of the charter. In the project name and number section, just enter a short title for the project. If your organization has a project-numbering system, include that assigned number in that element of the project charter. The reason for numbering a project is so it can be tracked and given visibility.

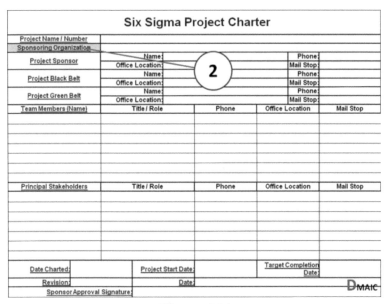

Figure 124

The second element of the Six Sigma project charter is the "Sponsoring Organization." In the sponsoring organization element of the project charter, enter the name of the lowest-level organization that includes all processes changed by the project. This organizational unit must agree to sponsor the project. It is very important that you get agreement that this part of the organization will sponsor the project. If there are going to be problems in that area, this is the time to find out what they are and resolve them, and perhaps, if you don't get the sponsorship, never move forward on the project beyond this point. You are better off killing projects earlier vs. later. Later project kills tend to be more expensive. You need this group's support.

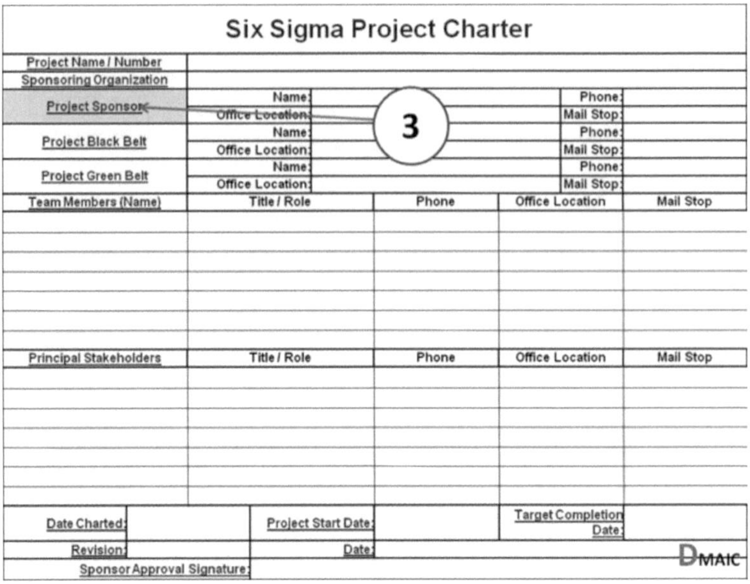

Six Sigma Project Charter					
Project Name / Number					
Sponsoring Organization					
Project Sponsor	Name:		**3**	Phone:	
	Office Location:			Mail Stop:	
Project Black Belt	Name:			Phone:	
	Office Location:			Mail Stop:	
Project Green Belt	Name:			Phone:	
	Office Location:			Mail Stop:	
Team Members (Name)	Title / Role	Phone		Office Location	Mail Stop
Principal Stakeholders	Title / Role	Phone		Office Location	Mail Stop
Date Charted:		Project Start Date:		Target Completion Date:	
Revision:		Date:		DMAIC	
Sponsor Approval Signature:					

Figure 125

The third element of the project charter is entitled "Project Sponsor." The sponsor of the project should be the process owner or line management at a level that can allocate resources for the project. Process owners are often trained as "green belts." Training includes thirty to forty hours of lecture time and is project based. This thirty to forty hours is usually just lecture time, but there also needs to be time allocated for the green belts to finish their project. Of course, part of that project will be to have a completed project charter.

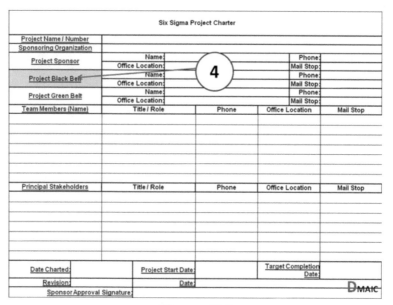

Six Sigma Project Charter					
Project Name / Number					
Sponsoring Organization					
Project Sponsor	Name:	**4**		Phone:	
	Office Location:			Mail Stop:	
Project Black Belt	Name:			Phone:	
	Office Location:			Mail Stop:	
Project Green Belt	Name:			Phone:	
	Office Location:			Mail Stop:	
Team Members (Name)	Title / Role	Phone	Office Location	Mail Stop	
Principal Stakeholders	Title / Role	Phone	Office Location	Mail Stop	
Date Charted:		Project Start Date:		Target Completion Date:	
Revision:		Date:		DMAIC	
Sponsor Approval Signature:					

Figure 126

The fourth element of the project charter is to select a "Project Black Belt." In this element of the project charter, you are to enter the name and contact information of the Six Sigma black belt assigned to this project. Black belts are usually recruited from the engineering department or are people who like mathematically modeling processes. If the project is being worked on by a team of black belts, enter the name of the lead black belt responsible for the project. Many organizations use black belts as project consultants, so a black belt may be assigned to two or as many as five teams. The black belts will spend most of their time on the Improve step. You'll find out later that in the Improve step there is a big demand for a lot of math and statistics.

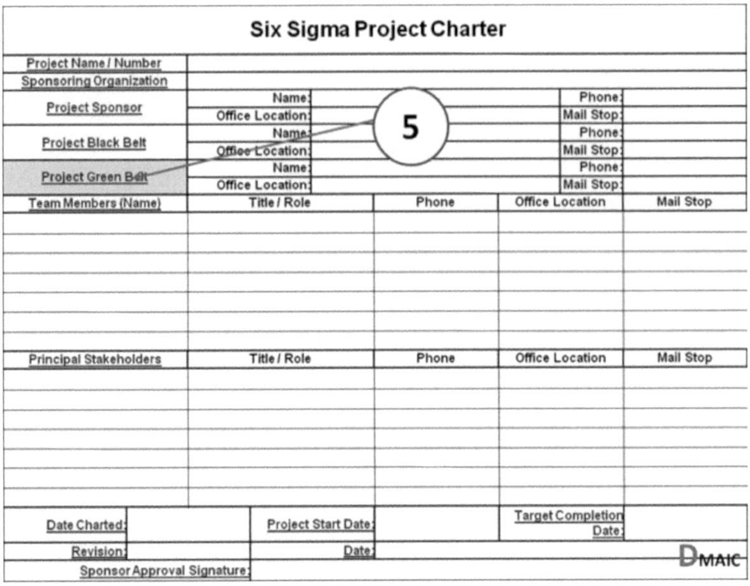

Figure 127

The fifth element of the Six Sigma project charter is "Project Green Belt." In the project green belt category of the charter, enter the name and contact information of the "green belt" project leader whose area is most directly impacted by the project.

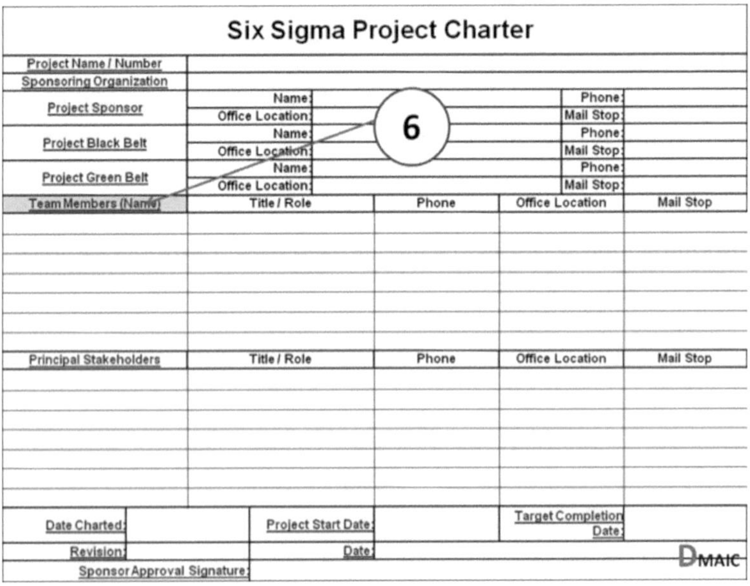

Figure 128

The sixth element of the Six Sigma project charter includes "Team Members." This is where we list all the team members with their contact information. Core team members usually receive "yellow-belt" training, which lasts around sixteen to twenty-four hours. In that training we teach the yellow belts the basics of team dynamics. In other words, what to expect when you join a team—you may have heard of the model "form, storm, norm, perform." We teach them the form, storm, norm, perform model so once they join a team they will not be surprised by what it takes to create a functional team and what it means to be a functional member of a team. So "form, storm, and norm," is where you get used to each other and learn to work together, which includes dealing with each other's idiosyncrasies. And then, of course, "perform," which means you're pretty much a self-functioning team—you understand the team really well, what motivates them, which buttons not to push, those types of things, and you're just a great team at that point. Perform is Phase III behavior, which means the team members are more about lifting up the team and finishing projects than they are about self-glorification (Phase II). Phase III teams do not need a lot of direction because you just need to teach them correct principles and they will govern themselves. We teach these principles to all employees in the target organization.

We also teach them about problem-solving techniques—especially tools used for brainstorming. Value stream charting is also a common lesson taught to the yellow belts. The yellow belts will definitely be involved in the brainstorming element and value stream mapping of projects. We also teach them data-collection techniques. Often organizations have the yellow belts collect data. This makes sense because data collection is the most time-consuming element in a project, so why not fulfill the need with the lower cost; perhaps even more important is that it gets them involved in the projects. Remember that employees are more likely to support a project when they feel that it is their project.

Now let's review. In the process-improvement team, every organization will be slightly different, but the standard in especially bigger companies is that a green belt will lead the team and the team will be made up of yellow belts. Then, of course, we have black belts, who are the highly analytical people who love to do math and statistics, and most projects include some analytical studies. So the black belts are there to be consultants for the teams and may support up to six or more teams.

Then we have the champions. The champions are extremely important members of the process-improvement organization. The champions will champion projects, and they'll sign off on the project charter, saying, "We agree with this and we will support this project." When there are barriers in the way of the team, and there will be, then the project sponsor will come out and help remove those barriers.

Those are the key figures thus far in the process-improvement organization. But again, the sixth element in the project charter is identifying who these core team members are. Often they are people from the shop floor who understand the process very well; they work with it every day, so they're great people to have on the team. Another good reason to put them on the team is that they help you come up with good ideas; if you involve them early on in solving the problem, then the problem is theirs. If you do not get their involvement, the problem is yours and implementing the solution is your problem, not theirs. So pick the right people to get the buy-in necessary to make this project a success.

Six Sigma Project Charter

Project Name / Number					
Sponsoring Organization					
Project Sponsor	Name:			Phone:	
	Office Location:			Mail Stop:	
Project Black Belt	Name:	7		Phone:	
	Office Location:			Mail Stop:	
Project Green Belt	Name:			Phone:	
	Office Location:			Mail Stop:	
Team Members (Name)	Title / Role	Phone	Office Location	Mail Stop	
Principal Stakeholders	Title / Role	Phone	Office Location	Mail Stop	
Date Charted:		Project Start Date:		Target Completion Date:	
Revision:		Date:		DMAIC	
Sponsor Approval Signature:					

Figure 129

The seventh element of the project charter includes the identification of "Principal Stakeholders." In this element of the project charter, we enter the names and contact information of people other than the sponsor, who has already been listed in another element of the project charter.

We enter the names and contact information of the people who have a direct interest in the outcome of the project. For example, it may be a customer, a supplier, a functional area manager, a supervisor, a responsible engineering authority, etc. An extremely important element at the very front of the project is to identify who these stakeholders are. Who is going to be impacted by this project? Why do we need to know this? Because you need to communicate with them. Imagine if you went home tonight to the neighborhood where you live and someone had totally wiped out all the roads; all the infrastructure is gone, they've ripped the lights out, and there is no way to get to your house except to walk. You would probably be a little bit upset because no one told you about it. So you go home and talk to your family and say, "Hey, what's going on here?" and they say, "We have no idea," and you say, "Well, how long is this going to be messed up?" No one has any idea. It tends to create great frustration. If the city officials had identified the stakeholders upfront, they would have communicated with you maybe a month or so before the project to see if you had any concerns. They would let you know how long it would be shut down and contact you if anything changed. So identifying stakeholders is an extremely important element of the project charter.

Now, of course, it will do you no good if all you do is write down their names. Remember that you must communicate! Notice also that we have, under "Principal Stakeholders," their titles, role in the organization, phone numbers, office locations, and e-mail addresses. So we get all the information we need to effectively communicate.

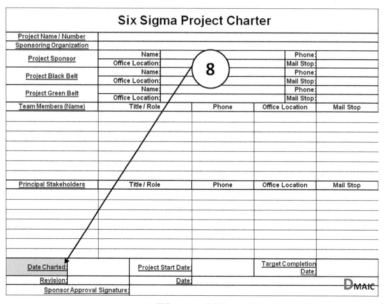

Figure 130

The eighth element of the Six Sigma project charter is "Date Charted." In the date-charted box, enter the date that the charter was accepted and signed by the sponsor or champion. Sometimes we use the word "sponsor," sometimes "champion"—same individual. Management support is extremely important. Without support from leadership, the project will fail. One of the biggest causes for project failure is lack of management support, so you should never work on a project until you get that date-charted section filled in. First you put in the date, and later you'll make sure to get a signature as well. This is an extremely important part of the project charter.

Six Sigma Project Charter

Project Name / Number					
Sponsoring Organization					
Project Sponsor	Name:		Phone:		
	Office Location:		Mail Stop:		
Project Black Belt	Name:		Phone:		
	Office Location:		Mail Stop:		
Project Green Belt	Name:		Phone:		
	Office Location:		Mail Stop:		
Team Members (Name)	Title / Role	Phone	Office Location	Mail Stop	
Principal Stakeholders	Title / Role	Phone	Office Location	Mail Stop	
Date Charted:		Project Start Date:		Target Completion Date:	
Revision:		Date:			
Sponsor Approval Signature:					DMAIC

Figure 131

The ninth element of the Six Sigma project charter is the "Project Start Date." In the project start date box, enter the date that the project is scheduled to begin. Update when the actual start date is known. When you first start this, you may have an initial start date that's your best guess, but as time goes along, that may change. As it does change, update the project charter so that you have documentation showing when you actually started working on this project.

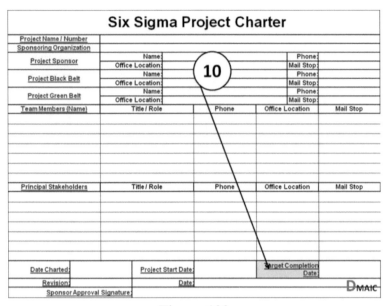

Figure 132

The tenth element of the Six Sigma project charter is "Target Completion Date." In the target completion date section of the charter, enter the date when the project's deliverables are expected to be completed. Most Six Sigma projects' target completion dates are four to seven months out from the projected start date.

Your company should have a portfolio of projects. Some may take hours, others may take weeks, and others, as mentioned here, may take months. The projects that take hours are often referred to as a "kaizen blitz." The project charter we are studying was designed for projects that will take months. Shorter projects do not need as much documentation because they are less complex.

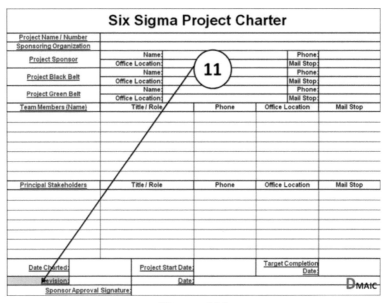

Figure 133

The eleventh element of the Six Sigma project charter is the "Revision" section. In this section of the charter, enter the charter revision tracking information. Change the revision as changes are made to the charter. You may also want to record what was actually changed during that revision. In other words, make a revision history for the project.

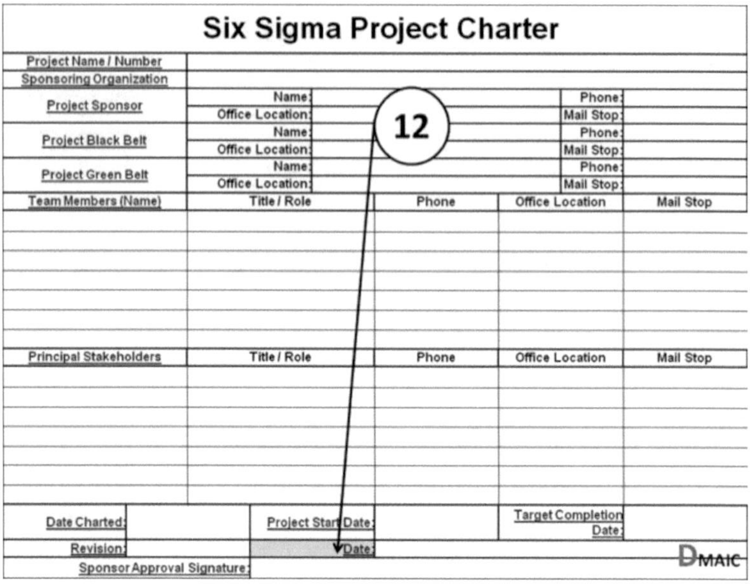

Figure 134

The twelfth element of the Six Sigma project charter consists of the "Date." In the date section of the charter, you should enter the date the sponsor signed the charter.

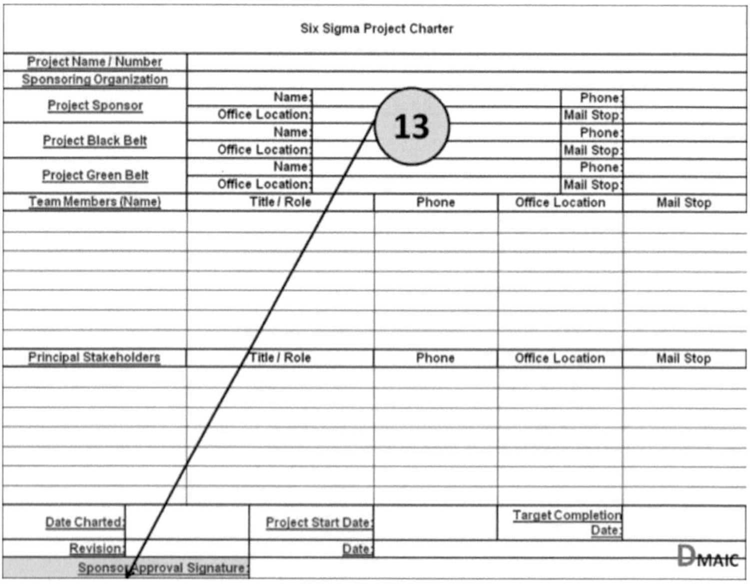

Figure 135

In the thirteenth element of the Six Sigma project charter, you will see a place for the "Sponsor Approval Signature." You *must* obtain the signature of the sponsor. Before signing, the sponsor should enter all project-related meetings into his or her schedule. This signature symbolizes upper-management support, and it shouldn't be given unless the sponsor is committed to supporting the project.

Now we are on page 2 of the project charter. Notice that the first element there gives a place to put the project name and number. We have already discussed this. We put it on the second page just for clarity issues.

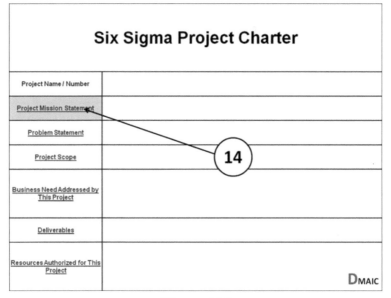

Figure 136

In the fourteenth element of the project charter is the "Project Mission Statement." In this section, a brief statement in clear and concise terms on what this project will accomplish for the organization or its customers must be documented. Do not begin until every member of the project team and the sponsor are in agreement with the mission. An example of a project mission statement may be as simple as "Decrease purchase order cycle times by 50 percent related to vendor approvals."

The fifteenth element of the project charter is the "Problem Statement." In this section you need to describe the "burning platform" for this project. In other words, why is this project necessary?

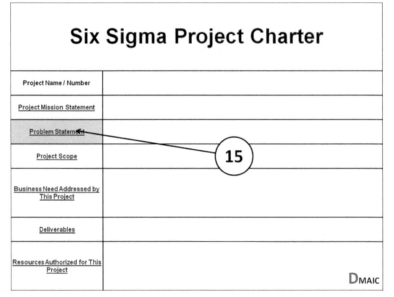

Figure 137

An example of a problem statement would be: "Field cycle time is defined as the time from receipt of purchase request until the PO is sent to the supplier. This PO cycle time for unapproved vendors currently averages twenty-seven days, with 95 percent of orders sent within eleven days. The incidence of overtime pay in quality and procurement, which shares responsibility for vendor approval, increases as the time goes beyond thirty days."

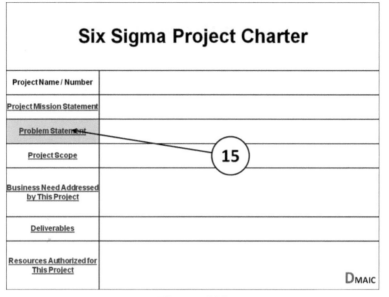

Figure 138

The sixteenth element of the project charter is entitled "Project Scope." In the project scope element of the project charter, we are to define the boundaries for the project. This is extremely important. Boundaries constrain the project. If you do not constrain or put boundaries on the project, the project will grow until you no longer have enough resources to finish it. That may sound crazy, but you'd be surprised how many times it happens. It's very important that you define the scope of the project. In other words, what will be addressed by this project and what will not be addressed by this project—it may include things like geographical locations or time boundaries; it could be many different things, but you need to put boundaries on your project if you ever hope to finish it. Not finishing projects can become a costly and destructive habit. You should be careful expanding the scope of your project. You are better off finishing the project with the smaller scope and then creating a new project with additional tasks. This allows you to create the habit of finishing projects.

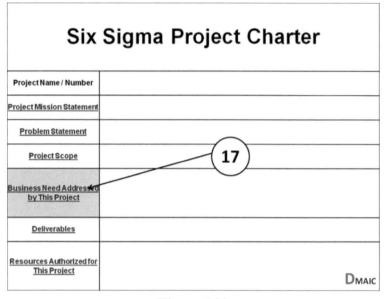

Figure 139

The seventeenth element of the project charter is the "Business Need Addressed by This Project." In the business-need section, you need to explain why the problems described in the problem statement should be solved. How will the business or its customers benefit from this project? How will this project improve quality, cycle time, cost, customer satisfaction, or competitiveness? For example: "Late orders constituted the number-one complaint from customers for fiscal year 2009. Awaiting vendor materials was identified as a significant cause of the late orders. When orders are late from the vendor, the traditional response has been an increase in overtime pay for production areas to meet the scheduling demands. By decreasing PO cycle time, we can cut overtime expenses and improve customer satisfaction by decreasing delivery times."

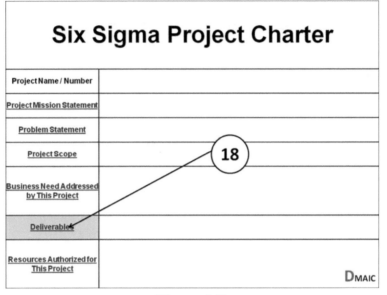

Figure 140

In the eighteenth element of the project charter you need to define the "Deliverables." In the deliverables section, you need to specifically document what will be created by this project—for example, increased sales, reduced warranty expenses, lower costs, shorter cycle time, etc. It must include dollars. An example of deliverables would be: "Revised procedures resulting in PO cycle time decrease. Projected savings of approximately $110,000 based on decreased overtime pay and an additional savings of $50,000 based on work-in-process stoppage."

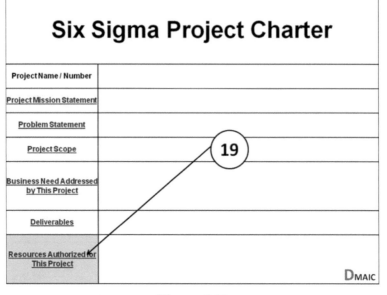

Figure 141

The nineteenth and last element of the project charter covers "Resources Authorized for This Project." In this section you need to list significant resources that must be made available and those that will be consumed to support this project. Examples would include raw materials, machine time, overtime pay, operations personnel, etc. Remember that you are better off to under-promise and over-deliver, so make sure you have plenty of resources to fulfill the needs of the project. This is what the sponsor will be signing off on, and it's obviously better if you can perform this project within the budget requested.

Now we have finished describing the Define step of the DMAIC model. Next we're going to talk about the Measure step. I'm attempting to describe the DMAIC model in its simplest form, so you may need more clarity for larger projects; however, in most cases the one described will suffice. I feel that it's important for you to understand the simplest form of this model; then you can custom build one that meets the specific needs of your organization.

Now let's discuss the Measure step. The Measure step is usually the green belts' responsibility, but they can assign other people to do these duties, such as the yellow belts. So every green belt will have five to seven yellow belts under him or her on a traditional Six Sigma team. The green belt traditionally leads the project. One of the first things the green belt does is validate the measurement system, which in most cases is an analytical exercise. Depending on the objective of the exercise some math and statistics may be necessary to validate this measurement system. We call them "gauge R & R studies," or the more complex ones are called "uncertainty studies." So green belts will need to understand how to perform these gauge R & R studies. It's probably the most analytical part of their job and involves the most math. They will perform these studies to determine whether the measurement system is effective or not. They will probably enlist the participation of the yellow belts to accomplish this task. Once the measurement system is validated and effective at measuring the important variables within the project scope, it's the job of the yellow belts to go out and collect the data. The green belts, of course, can also go out and collect the data themselves, but usually the green belt is the leader of the project and he or she will assign the yellow belts to do this part of the job, after which the green belt will look at the collected information to ensure that it is good data.

I'd say that the Measure step tends to take more time than any other step, except for perhaps the Define step. Why? Because collecting data is a time-consuming element of a Six Sigma project. To me, it is the *most* time-consuming element of the Six Sigma project. Once we have good data, we analyze it and improve processes. This is often rather simple with the modern-day computer software that's available. We can go through those steps very quickly if we have good data.

Now let's move on and discuss the Analyze section of the DMAIC model. As we said before, the green belts are responsible for this step as well. Now remember that the green belts also have yellow belts to help them. Yellow belts will usually collect the data, but ultimately the Analyze step is the green belts' responsibility. The green belts are to analyze baseline data, which includes performing capability studies—maybe Cpk or Z statistic studies, which are simply a way of saying "to calculate the 'and' statement probabilities." Why do we "analyze the baseline" "and" statement probabilities? Why is this important? Well, how are you going to know if you have improvement if you didn't record baseline data? So don't make the mistake of skipping the Analyze step—it could get you into a lot of trouble. It will make the results of the project very subjective, and subjective people will argue whether you really made a difference or not. But if you collect the baseline data, you can argue with mathematics and statistics to prove that you did indeed create a significant amount of improvement in the project. So the Analyze step is extremely important, but it's not nearly as time consuming as the Define and Measure steps in most cases. Baseline analysis is only one objective of the Analyze stage. The Analyze stage is also the step where you discover the root cause of the problem.

After analyzing the baseline by calculating "and" statement probabilities, it is time to perform root-cause analysis. During the Analyze step you need to ultimately understand the problem so well that you can turn it off and on. There are many different books, and the way they describe the DMAIC model will be slightly different, but in our discussion we're going to say that in the Analyze section you should understand the problem so well that you can turn it off and on. This is a good acid test to show that you truly understand problem location. You may need some help from a black belt on this step of the project. However, the goal is to develop the green belts enough that they can effectively lead the team through the root-cause analysis stage of the DMAIC model.

Now let's move on to the Improve step of the DMAIC model. I'll warn you that the Improve step is the most analytically challenging section of this model. In other words, it takes a lot of math and engineering skill to effectively implement or perform the Improve step in the DMAIC model. As a result, usually black belts are responsible for this element of the project. However, sometimes—it depends on the project—the team may not even need a black belt. It just depends on how complicated the problem is from an analytical perspective. It is usually rather complex, so most organizations tend to use black belts in the Improve stage.

During the Improve stage you should be able to mathematically model the solutions, and after performing this mathematical modeling, you should be able to select the optimum solution from all the options available. At this point you need to have buy-in from the all applicable stakeholders. With the help of the stakeholders, you can implement the solution. Why do you want buy-in during the Improve stage? Because this is where you decide the ultimate solution that will be implemented into the process. If you do not have stakeholder input, you will not get buy-in, and it will be very difficult to have a successful project if you do not have stakeholder buy-in. We have green belts and yellow belts responsible for much of the work in the DMAIC model because, for one thing, it creates buy-in, and the problem becomes their problem and the solution becomes their solution. This naturally improves morale and it also allows the improvements from the project to be sustained over time. Nothing makes up for the lack of employee involvement in continuous process-improvement.

Throughout this whole DMAIC process up to this point, you should have been communicating on a weekly or possibly even a daily basis concerning how well this project is progressing. Let the stakeholders know what you're doing, what you have found, the challenges, etc. When you get down to the Improve step, you're identifying solutions and being able to present solution options in a way that the stakeholders can understand them. Once you provide all the options, you should get the stakeholders' input on what they feel the best solution is, and you should attempt to sell them on the solution you feel is best.

Now we're at the Control section of the DMAIC model, which is the last element. Control is usually the green belts' responsibility, with heavy involvement from the yellow belts. The objective of the Control step is to maintain project benefits over time. The yellow belts should have been the people who worked on this process, because they will be responsible for controlling the gains from this project, so they should feel ownership. But ultimately it is the green belts' responsibility, since they are usually the supervisors. It's the green belts' responsibility to make sure the gains are maintained over time. Control mechanisms must be capable of maintaining the gains, so the green belts and the yellow belts should come up with a control plan and exercise it. You know the control plan is successful if you're capable of maintaining the gains over long periods of time. I would recommend frequent and effective audits planned before I ever started my Six Sigma program, and I would have that auditing team audit a project very frequently and in depth to make sure that the green belts are living up to their end of the deal in controlling the process or maintaining the gains. If you do not do this, you will probably not be able to maintain those gains. Auditing is a very important element in the Six Sigma organization (system).

Successful control will change habits of the organization. I would say this is the most challenging part of the control element of the DMAIC model, because you have to change the culture.

Now we will perform a quick review of the DMAIC model. Remember that in the Define step we are to create the project charter with full management support. Champions and sponsors, or management, are responsible for this step in the model. This is true in most organizations. Every organization uses the DMAIC model a little bit differently, and that's good. You should customize the DMAIC model to fit the needs of *your* organization.

Next let's look at the Measure step. In the Measure step we identify what we are going to measure and how we are going to measure it, ensure that the measurement system is effective, and then collect the baseline data. This is the green belts' responsibility. However, usually the green belts get the yellow belts involved in collecting the data, as they should. Make sure the yellow belts have been effectively trained at data collection before assigning them to perform such an important task. As my experience would suggest, collecting data is the most time-consuming element of all of the steps of the DMAIC model. Many people would suggest that the Define-Measure steps of the process takes up to 70 percent of the Six Sigma project time.

Now let's summarize the Analyze step. During the Analyze step we use the data collected to perform a baseline analysis. In other words, we perform capability studies or similar studies designed to show what the baseline performance is ("and" statement probabilities). What I mean by "baseline performance" is that before we change the process we determine how well the unchanged process performs,

Also in the Analyze stage we must understand the problem so well that we can turn it off and on. You have to be able to understand a problem *very* well to be able to shut it off and on—and that's the goal in the Analyze stage. This is referred to as root-cause analysis. Also in the Analyze stage, there are usually two parties involved—a green belt and black belt. If the green belt can handle it all, that's good, but sometimes he or she needs the help of a black belt.

In summary, the Improve step is to identify multiple solutions for a given problem. Have stakeholders help choose the optimum solution. Traditionally Six Sigma black belts perform this Improve step in the DMAIC model. Why? Because it's highly analytical, and that's what Six Sigma black belts are trained to do—to perform very challenging analysis using a lot of math and statistics.

The objective of the Control step of the DMAIC model is to maintain the gains of this project over time. You must have audits scheduled as well as a control plan well documented and followed. Green belts are responsible for making this happen.

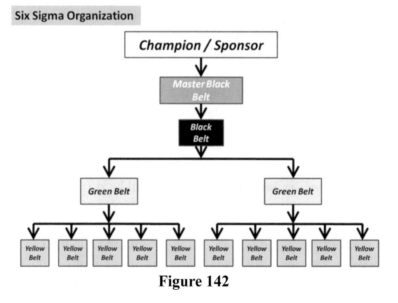

Figure 142

This figure shows one possibility for a Six Sigma organization's organizational chart. Notice that the champion or sponsor is located at the top of the organization. This usually consists of upper management, which utilizes master black belts. The master black belt is a consultant to the champions and sponsors and makes sure management understands how to select effective projects. The master black belt will also monitor performance on how well deployed projects are moving through the DMAIC process. A master black belt will also provide training to the other black belts, green belts, and yellow belts. That's a big part of a master black belt's job, and keeping the training up-to-date in the Six Sigma organization is no small task. The master black belts must be good at analytical techniques—they're usually ex-black belts—and they must also be able to communicate the difficult parts of Six Sigma in a way that management understands so that management can make well-informed decisions.

Traditionally, master black belts will have black belts reporting to them. I didn't have enough room on this figure to put a work chart that shows multiple black belts answering to the master black belt, but depending on the size of the organization, you could have eight or ten black belts answering to a master black belt.

Also, the black belt may have many green belts answering to him or her. I've seen as many as seven green belts answering to one black belt. This is an example of an organizational chart for a Six Sigma organization. It is a very functional one. As the organization grows, it will expand. You'll add more black belts, and often the people who come in to be black belts are old green belts who show great talent—and the same with yellow belts being promoted to green belts. You may find some yellow belts who are just naturals and desire to learn and excel in hopes of becoming green belts. As your organization grows, so should your Six Sigma organization.

The perfect Six Sigma organization will be different depending on the specific needs of the organization. The model I presented is fairly typical of larger organizations, but you should look upon it as a starting point and not an ending point for your final decision. Customize the program to best fit the culture of your organization.

You may not even decide to use the DMAIC at all, and this may very well be what is best for your organization. My background was heavily focused on Six Sigma, but you may need to implement Lean before you get into the more rigorous Six Sigma. This will probably be best for your organization, so don't feel constrained by our discussion—it was only meant to get you thinking.

The most crippling element in the world of process-improvement is people learning one methodology (Lean, Theory of Constraints, Six Sigma, etc.) and thinking that all other methodologies are stupid, ridiculous, and of no value. I see this quite often and find it to be embarrassing.

CHAPTER EIGHT

PROBABILITY STATISTICS

The purposes of this chapter are to understand the value of probability statistics, to understand which formulas to use for a given problem, to understand the definition of "mutually exclusive," and to understand how to calculate expected scrap rates in a multiple-step process due to normal variation.

Probability statistics define the odds of a given event taking place under a given set of circumstances. For example, if you had three cars that are used to get you to work and back, you may be interested in how likely it would be for all three cars to start without problems.

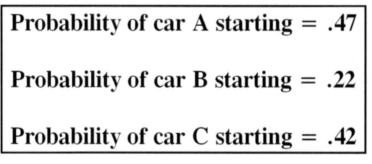

Probability of car A starting = .47

Probability of car B starting = .22

Probability of car C starting = .42

Figure 143

Or you may be interested in your chances of getting a six on your next roll of the die. You may be interested in the odds of getting a good part off the end of a multiple-step production line. The solution to these problems demands an analytical tool referred to as "probability statistics." In probability statistics you can break most problems into two general formats by determining if the problem is an "and" or an "or" statement. The first problem we will address is the "and" statement.

Say you have a problem that is stated as such: What is the probability of event A "and" event B taking place? For this type of problem, you only need to multiply the two probabilities. Remember that the "and" statement = (multiply) in probability statistics.

- We will assume that P(a) = .50 and P(b) = .50

– SO –

- The probability of both a and b occurring equals:

P(a) and P(b) = (.5)(.5) = .25 or 25%

Figure 144

For example, we will assume the probability of event A = .50 and the probability of event B is also .50, or 50 percent. So the probability of both A *and* B occurring equals the product of A times B. Remember that we multiply the probabilities when it's an "and" statement, so it's .5 times .5 equals .25, or 25 percent. So the probability of both A "and" B occurring equals 25 percent, and the key to this problem is the "and" statement. When you see both A "and" B, you know to multiply the probabilities. Now if it was A "or" B, we would use a different mathematical model. Let's move onto the next figure.

- So the probability of "a" and "b" taking place is 25%.

- With this type of problem, we assume independence between "a" and "b."

- By independence we mean that if "a" takes place, or does not take place, it will not affect the probability of "b" taking place.

Figure 145

In summary, the probability of A "and" B taking place, from the previous figure, is 25 percent. With this type of problem, we assume independence between A and B. By "independence," we mean that whether A takes place or does not take place, it will not affect the probability of B taking place.

Now we will perform one more example. In this illustration we will use the data offered in the introduction:

Probability of car A starting = .47
Probability of car B starting = .22
Probability of car C starting = .42

We will assume that all three cars must start in order to achieve the objective. We will also assume independence. So, under the assumption that all three cars must start in order to achieve the objective, what is the probability of success in meeting the objective? Assume independence between the cars. Is this an "and" statement? It *is* an "and" statement. We're asking what the probability is of car A "and" car B "and" car C starting. Therefore, we just need to multiply their probabilities, so the probability of all three cars starting equals .47 (the probability of car A starting), times .22 (the probability of car B starting), times .42 (the probability of car C starting). We multiply these three together and the product becomes .043. So the probability of A, B, and C starting equates to .043, or 4.3 percent.

- We will assume that all three cars must start in order to achieve the objective.

- What is the probability of success in meeting the objective? Assume independence between cars.

  Probability of car A starting = .47

  Probability of car B starting = .22

  Probability of car C starting = .42

P(a) and P(b) and P(c) = (.47)(.22)(.42) = .043

Figure 146

As you see, your probabilities can be reduced quite quickly with "and" statements. With these three cars, you would have a very difficult time getting all three to start at once. Of course, these are very unreliable cars.

Concerning the statements "and" or "or," which statement would you consider to give the greatest odds of success, the "and" or the "or" statement? For example, which of the following examples would be most likely to happen?

Example #1: In order to arrive at work, car A "and" car B must start.

Example #2: In order to arrive at work, car A "or" car B must start.

Which one is most likely to take place? Which one has the greatest probability of success? In Example #2, only one of the cars must start to arrive at work (A "or" B). In Example #1, both cars must start for you to arrive at work (A "and" B). If you said Example #2 is more likely, car A "or" B must start to arrive at work, then you are correct. A "or" B is more likely to happen than A "and" B.

In probability statistics, the "or" statement will give higher probabilities than the "and" statement. So, if "and" means multiply, what mathematical manipulator will we use for the "or" statement?

To answer this question, we must first define the term "mutually exclusive." A mutually exclusive event means that two events cannot take place at the same time. For example, a coin is flipped to determine if the output will be heads or tails. This is a mutually exclusive event because you cannot get heads and tails during a single event. It's impossible—therefore, this is a mutually exclusive event. Let's read that again.

> - **Mutually exclusive events mean that two events cannot take place at the same time.**
>
> - **For example, a coin is flipped to determine if the output will be heads or tails. This is a *mutually exclusive event because you cannot get heads and tails during a single event.***

Figure 147

A mutually exclusive event means that two events cannot take place at the same time. If you can get that definition down, then probability statistics is going to be fairly easy for you. Of all the topics in probability statistics, the one that students seem to struggle with the most is the concept of mutual exclusivity. Remember, mutually exclusive events means that two events cannot take place at the same time.

I recommend that students write down the words "mutually exclusive events" and then draw a picture of a coin. This may be helpful for you in remembering the definition of mutually exclusive events.

> - **The mathematical formula for the *"or"* statement is *addition* if the events are mutually exclusive.**
>
> - **For example, if you are to flip a coin, a mutually exclusive event, what are the odds of a heads "or" tails event?**
>
> **P (heads) = .50**
> **P (tails) = .50**

Figure 148

The mathematical manipulator for the "or" statement is addition if the events are mutually exclusive. For example, if you are to flip a coin, a mutually exclusive event, what are the odds of a heads "or" tails event? The probability of heads = .50, or 50 percent. And the probability of tails is also = .50, or 50 percent. So what are the odds of getting a heads "or" tails? The odds are 50 percent for heads and 50 percent for tails. Since it's a mutually exclusive event and it's an "or" statement, we simply add the probabilities. So the probability of getting a heads "or" tails equals .5 + .5 = 1, or 100 percent. This is an obvious solution to a commonsense problem. The example does show how simple the "or" statement is if the two probabilities in consideration are mutually exclusive; in other words, the two events cannot happen simultaneously.

- The odds are 50% for heads and 50% for tails.

– SO –

.5 + .5 = 1 – or – 100%

- So the odds of a heads "or" tails are equal to 100%. This is an obvious solution to a common sense problem.

- However, the example does show how simple the "or" statement is if the two probabilities in consideration are mutually exclusive (the two events cannot happen simultaneously).

Figure 149

But what happens if the probability problem is stated as an "or" type problem but is not mutually exclusive? For example, assume you have two cars—car A and car B. In order to get to work, car A "or" car B must start. What are the odds of making it to work on time? Well, the first thing we ask ourselves is whether it is an "or" or an "and" statement. Well, it is an "or" statement. The next question we ask is whether it is mutually exclusive. Can both car A "or" car B start simultaneously? Is it physically possible? In this case, we'd have to say yes. Therefore, we have an "or" statement that is not mutually exclusive. So how do we calculate this probability?

Car A starting or car B starting is not a mutually exclusive event because it is possible for both cars to start. In other words, events A or B can happen simultaneously, which is another way of saying the two events are not mutually exclusive. The formula shown below is used to calculate probabilities in "or" statement problems that are not mutually exclusive.

- The formula shown below is used to calculate probabilities in "or" statement problems that *are not mutually exclusive.*

P(A) or P(B) <u>*not*</u> Mutually Exclusive =

$$P(A) + P(B) - (P(A)(B))$$

Figure 150

So the probability of A "or" B, which are not mutually exclusive events, equals the probability of A plus the probability of B minus the probability of A times the probability of B.

Let's use the "or" not mutually exclusive formula to solve this problem. The problem is to calculate the odds of making it to work if car A "or" car B must start. These are not mutually exclusive events. The probability of car A starting = .47, and the probability of car B starting = .22. Can you calculate the probability of car A or car B starting? Give it your best attempt, and then we'll go to the next figure and see how the problem is solved.

- This problem is not mutually exclusive because both events *can* take place simultaneously.

So we will use the formula:

P(A) or P(B) = P(A) + P(B) - (P(A)P(B))

P(A) or P(B) = .47 + .22 - (.47)(.22)

P(A) or P(B) = .5866 or 58.66%

Figure 151

This problem is not mutually exclusive, because both events can take place simultaneously. So we will use this formula: probability of A or probability of B not being mutually exclusive equals the probability of A plus the probability of B minus the probability of A times the probability of B. So we put in .47, which is the probability of A plus .22, which is the probability of B minus the probability of A times the probability of B, which is .47 times .22. That should equate to .5866, which is equivalent to 58.66 percent. So the probability of car A or car B starting is 58.66 percent.

Now we will explain the probability formulas in a more graphical manner. First we will discuss the probability for the "or" statement for mutually exclusive events. You may recall that if you have mutually exclusive events, you just simply add the two probabilities. If we were to describe this graphically, we would draw two circles representing the probability of B in one circle and the probability of A in the other circle. Note that there is no overlap between the two probabilities. This is another way of showing that the two events are mutually exclusive. If they were not mutually exclusive, they would have an intersection between the circles where A and B could take place. Remember, mutually exclusive events are separate from one another with no intersections. The math for this is simple—you simply add the two probabilities together.

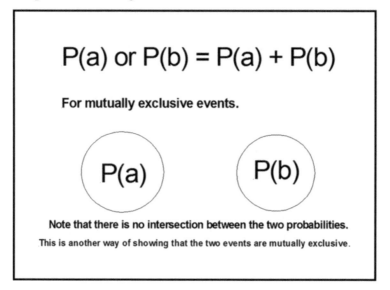

$$P(a) \text{ or } P(b) = P(a) + P(b)$$

For mutually exclusive events.

P(a)   P(b)

Note that there is no intersection between the two probabilities.
This is another way of showing that the two events are mutually exclusive.

Figure 152

Now we will discuss the situation for the probability of A "or" the probability of B for not mutually exclusive events. Remember that the formula for finding the probability is to add the two probabilities and then multiply the two probabilities. After the addition and multiplication you simply subtract the product (the numbers that were multiplied) from the sum (the numbers that were added) to get the probability of such an event taking place. In this particular situation since they are not mutually exclusive, you would expect to see an intersection between the circles, just like you do on the circles in the figure below.

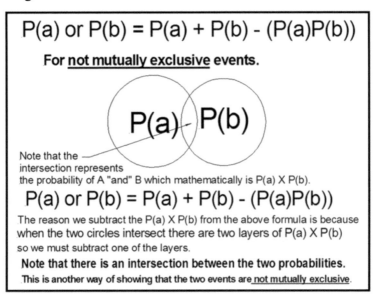

Figure 153

This represents two events and an "or" statement that are not mutually exclusive. Now notice that intersection. We had two circles that we brought together. Remember that the intersection represents the "and" statement. That's the area where the probability of A "and" B takes place. But notice that that intersection has two layers of circles. Because of this, we have to strip off one of the layers; otherwise we have the potential of getting something greater than 100 percent, which shows there would be erroneous results (you cannot get over 100 percent in probability statistics). And again, how do we calculate A "and" B taking place, which is represented by that intersection? Of course, per our previous conversation, this is where we would multiply the probabilities (assuming independence).

Let's look at the formula again. We have the probability of A plus the probability of B minus the probability of A times the probability of B. That subtraction of the probability of A times the probability of B simply means we're stripping off one of the layers, leaving one layer behind like it should be. (You don't want to calculate the "and" statement probability twice.) This makes for a correct equation that will predict the probabilities correctly.

We have discussed the "and" and "or" statements for probability and discussed their mathematical models. The next probability model we will discuss is for conditional probabilities. Conditional probabilities means that the two variables are dependent on one another. In other words, whether event A takes place or does not take place will have an impact on whether event B takes place. A classic example of this is that event A (rain) is dependent upon event B (a cloudy day). You can see how those two are dependent. We must have clouds before we can have rain. This is a conditional relationship. Another example would be if a given part will crack before it breaks, and the probability of a crack is .35 and the probability of a part breaking is .15, then what are the odds of a cracked part breaking? For this type of dependent probability problem, we use the mathematical model shown below.

- For example, if a given part will crack before it breaks and the probability of a crack is .35 and the probability of a part breaking is .15 then what are the odds of a cracked part breaking?

- For these types of dependent probability problems we use the mathematical model shown below:

$$P(A\ B) = \frac{P(A \cap B)}{P(B)} = \frac{.15}{.35} = .4286$$

Figure 154

Students often have a terrible time trying to figure out which number goes in the numerator and which number goes in the denominator. There's an easy way of doing this. Remember that the odds cannot be over 100 percent. Therefore, you put the smaller probability in the numerator and the larger probability in the denominator. In this case .15 goes in the numerator, which is the probability of a cracked part breaking. That's where we say, "Okay, what's the probability of a part breaking given that it is already cracked?" For this example, it equates to .4286. So the probability of one of the cracked parts breaking is 42.86 percent.

I hope you feel comfortable with the concepts taught thus far. If not, put the process on hold, go back, perform the calculations until you feel comfortable with the principles taught, and then continue reading. Before we move on, let's take all the information we've gathered thus far in this chapter and put it on one page in the form of a flowchart.

Probability Flowchart

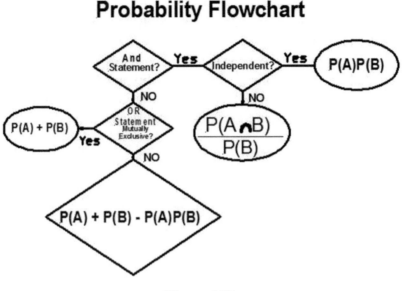

Figure 155

This flowchart should help you with your probability principles. Let's read our way through it. We'll start up in the left-hand corner with the "and" statement where it says, "And Statement." If it is an "and" statement and you say, "Yes." This leads you to the diamond that says, "Independent?" If you say, "Yes," then you use the formula probability of A times the probability of B. If, back at the independent diamond, you say, "No, it is not an independent relationship," then you use the probability of B, given that A has already taken place, divided by the probability of B (remember that B is the probability of the earlier event). Going back to the "and" statement, if you answer "No," then you ask yourself, *Is it an "or" statement that is mutually exclusive?* If you say, "Yes, it is an 'or' statement and it is mutually exclusive," then you go to the formula probability of A + the probability of B. If you answer the question to the "or" statement mutually exclusive and you say, "No, it is not mutually exclusive," then you end up with the following formula: probability of A plus the probability of B minus the probability of A times the probability of B. That pretty much sums up the probability statistics module to this point in time. In fact, these are all the formulas I'm going to deal with in probability statistics. You can solve many various problems with these formulas. For the rest of the chapter we will take a practical problem and attempt to solve it using the probability statistic formulas.

Let's move on to the next figure and apply our knowledge of Cpk studies, the Z statistic, and probability statistics to determine expected scrap rates due to normal variation on a multiple-step process using the assumptions of probability statistics.

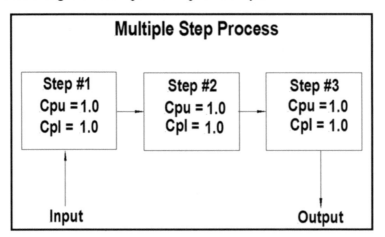

Figure 156

The first step in solving this problem is to identify the process. Notice that we have a three-step process here, and we have also added the Cp upper and Cp lower for each of the steps in the process. We are going to make it easy on ourselves by using 1 for both the upper and lower Cp values for all three steps.

The next step is to convert the Cp upper and Cp lower values into the Z statistic. Remember that the relationship between Cp upper and Z upper is just a factor of three, and the same way with Cp lower and Z lower. So here we convert all our Cp statistics into Z statistics, so they go from the Cp value of 1.0 to a Z statistic of 3.0 (specification limits three sigmas away from the average). With the Z statistics we can now calculate the probability of success for each of the steps in this operation or this process.

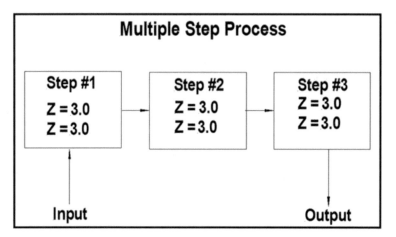

Figure 157

We will now calculate the probability of creating a good part for each of the steps. Remember that the probability of creating a good part is only under the assumption of normal variability. To perform this calculation we will first calculate the probability of creating a bad part. We simplify the problem by making all of the Z statistics equal to 3.0.

Z	0	0.01	0.02	0.03	0.04	0.05	0.06
2.9	0.00187	0.00181	0.00175	0.00169	0.00164	0.00159	0.00154
3	0.00135	0.00131					0.00111
3.1	0.000968	0.00	The Z statistic shows that				00789
3.2	0.000687		.135% of the population will lie				57
3.3	0.000483		above the UCL and below the				
3.4	0.000337		LCL since the Z upper and Z				
3.5	0.000233		lower are equal to 3.				
3.6	0.000159						126
3.7	1.08E-04	1.04E					3.50E-05
3.8	7.24E-05	6.95E-05	6.0			1E-05	5.67E-05
3.9	4.81E-05	4.62E-05	4.43E-05	4.25E-05	4.08E-05	3.91E-05	3.75E-05

Figure 158

Next we will go to the Z statistic table to determine what the probability is of getting a part outside those values. To do this, we simply go to the Z table and look up the Z value of 3.0. Notice that 3.0 tells us that .00135 or .135 percent of the population will lie above the upper spec limit or below the lower spec limit. Remember that both the Z upper and Z lower are equal to 3.0. Therefore, we can take this value and multiply it by 2 for each step in the process. So the probability of getting a bad part with the spec limits being three standard deviations above the average and the lower spec limit being three standard deviations below the average is .00135 times 2, or .0027 (.27 percent).

The probability of getting a bad part with a Z statistic equaling 3.0 is equal to .0027. So the probability of getting a good part will be the complement of the probability of getting a bad part. By "complement," we mean we take the .0027 and subtract it from 1.

- ## So the probability of getting a bad part is equal to:

   ## (2)(.00135) = .0027

- ## So the probability of getting a good part will be the complement of the probability of getting a bad part.

   1 - .0027 = .9973

   or

   99.73%

Figure 159

Now we need to calculate the probability of getting a good part. To do that, we just calculate 1 minus .0027, which equals 99.73 percent, and you already knew this. You already knew that the probability of getting a good part with a ± three sigma operation equals 99.73 percent. As you'll remember, the distance between the upper and lower control limit is three sigma, and the probability of lying between the upper and lower control limit is 99.73 percent.

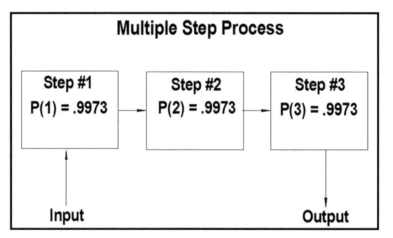

Figure 160

Now we can move on to the next step of applying the probability of getting a good part.

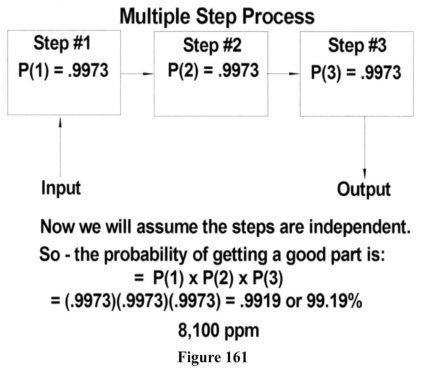

Now we will assume the steps are independent.
So - the probability of getting a good part is:
= P(1) x P(2) x P(3)
= (.9973)(.9973)(.9973) = .9919 or 99.19%
8,100 ppm

Figure 161

The figures above show the new process flowchart with the probabilities of getting a good part in each of the steps. Now we're ready to use probability statistics to determine how likely it is for us to get a good part coming off the end of the multiple-step production line.

The next step in solving this problem is to ask yourself, "Is this an 'and' statement or an 'or' statement?" Notice in this problem that to get a good part, we must have a good part out of Step #1 "and" out of Step #2 "and" out of Step #3. So it's an "and" statement. If you'll recall, for "and" statements we multiply the probabilities. We are assuming that each of these steps is independent of one another. Based upon these assumptions, we can now multiply the three probabilities to get the ultimate probability. So the probability of getting a good part off of this line equals .9973 times .9973 times .9973 equals .9919, or 99.19 percent. If we take this 99.19 percent and subtract it from 100 percent, it will be the probability of getting a bad part off the line. If you take that and multiply it by one million, you'll end up with a quality rating of 8,100 parts per million.

When performing capability studies it is important to focus on the complete process and not just the single steps in the process. With traditional Cpk or Z studies, we work with one piece of a large puzzle. This is a weakness in the analysis, but using the Cpk values and probability statistics we can perform capability studies on multiple-step processes.

CHAPTER NINE

CONTROLLING PROCESSES

In this chapter we will discuss two types of variation: normal-cause variation and special-cause variation. Remember that normal variation creates a normal curve. It's very predictable. If you'll recall, ± one sigma was 68.26 percent of the population, ± two was 95.44, and ± three sigma was ± 99.73 percent. In other words, normal-cause variation is very, very predictable.

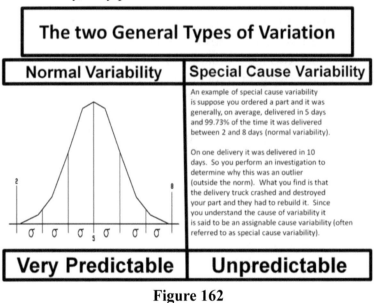

Figure 162

We have already talked about normal-cause variation (normal distribution), so now we will spend some time describing special-cause variation. For example, let's suppose you ordered a part and it is generally, or on average, delivered in five days, and 99.73 percent of the time it is delivered in between two and eight days. When you plot this data out, you find that this is just normal variability—again, very predictable.

Let's continue on with our example. Let assume that one delivery was delivered in ten days. Remember that 99.73 percent is between two and eight days, so to have one at ten days is rather unusual (an outlier). You perform an investigation to determine why this was an outlier—it was outside the norm, outside three sigma. You find that the delivery truck crashed and destroyed your part, and the supplier had to rebuild it. Since you understand the cause of variability, it is said to be an assignable-cause variability, often referred to as "special cause" variability. An important thing to remember is that special cause or assignable-cause variability is considered to be unpredictable. This suggests that the two forms of variability are inherently different. Remember that normal variability is very predictable, and special cause or assignable-cause variability is considered to be unpredictable.

In the world of continuous process-improvement, we must first get our processes under control and then improve them. Generally speaking, it's a two-step situation. First we get the process under control, and after we get it under control, then we can start improving it. "Getting the process under control" means making it predictable. So what is the first step to making our processes predictable? The answer to this question is to first get rid of all Special-Cause Variability so that the only variability left is the normal distribution, which is predictable.

- **In the world of Continuous Process (CPI) Improvement we must first get our processes under control and then improve the process**

- **Getting the process under control means to make it predictable**

- **In other words we must first get special cause variability under control and then start reducing (improving) normal cause variability**

Figure 163

We must first get Special-Cause Variability under control before we can start reducing or improving normal-cause variability (Solution #3). Getting Special-Cause Variability under control makes the process predictable. It also allows you to objectively determine if you have truly improved the process. It is very difficult to objectively show improvement when a process is unpredictable. Processes that are said to be "out of control" are unpredictable.

In this section of the book we will concentrate on reducing Special-Cause Variability. The proposed methodology for continuous process-improvement of special-cause variation is shown in the next figure. Take note that this model was designed to be proactive. In other words, we're going to look at our processes before they are ever implemented to try to understand the risks of the process and how to control those risks (special causes) before we ever push the "on" button of the process. That doesn't mean that you can't perform this process with already existing processes, but ideally you would do this as part of the design portion of the process.

Proposed Methodology for CPI of Special Cause Variation

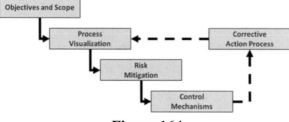

Figure 164

This is a rather simple five-step process. First we define the objective and scope of the process. We perform process visualization, risk mitigation, and control mechanisms, and should our control mechanisms fail (and they will), we have a corrective-action process to back everything up and allow us to keep improving process control over time, making it more and more predictable.

Now we'll discuss the first step—the objective and scope of the process. The objective of the process is what you hope to accomplish with this process.

The proposed objective of a project may be to reduce quality and regulatory defects by 50 percent per year in an effort to achieve and exceed the industry's current best practices.

Objective

- **The proposed objective of a project may be to reduce Quality and Regulatory defects by 50% per year in an effort to achieve and exceed current industry best practices**

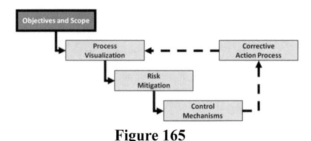

Figure 165

The key word for scope is to set boundaries. Identification of project scope is important so that everyone understands the project boundaries in an effort to eliminate "scope creep." If an effective scope or boundary is not defined and followed, the project or design of the process will naturally grow outside its original vision. The project will grow to the point that you will no longer have enough resources to finish it, and the project will ultimately fail. My neighbors are always remodeling their house, and the other day, after returning from a business trip, I went outside my home and noticed that their house was stripped down to the studs. Now I hope that they have enough resources to finish that project, but the point is that often, if we don't identify a scope, the project will just grow and grow and grow until ultimately we will not have enough resources available to finish it.

Scope

- Identification of project scope is important so everyone understands the project boundaries in an effort to eliminate "Scope Creep"

Figure 166

Scope

- If an effective scope is not defined and followed the project will naturally grow outside its original vision
- The project will grow to the point you will no longer have enough resources to finish it and the project will ultimately fail

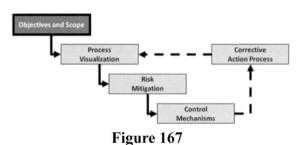

Figure 167

Scope

- **Part of project scope may include time, criteria, and geographical boundaries**

Figure 168

Not finishing projects is a very bad habit to get into, so the way we avoid creating projects that we cannot finish is by creating an effective scope or boundary on the project. Habitually not finishing projects shows a lack of organizational character. There are many potential elements of project scope; some of the more common ones for project scope may include time, criteria, and geographical boundaries.

Process Visualization

- **The objective of process visualization is to understand, define and help standardize our processes**

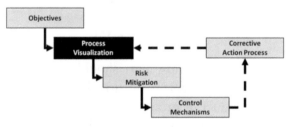

Figure 169

Now that we have discussed objectives and scopes of the process or project, we will perform the process-visualization step, which is the second step. The objective of process visualization is to help you and the team that's designing the process understand what the process is going to look like. Process visualization is traditionally performed with a tool referred to as a flowchart. The flowchart is designed to help the group see what the ultimate proposed process will look like. If the process has already been designed and you're just trying to improve the existing process, then you can go down to the process area and watch the process and start creating your flowchart through actual observation. If this is the case, you should go through the process multiple times to make sure your flowchart matches reality. Don't miss out on any steps—if you do, it could create problems later on, because it is hard to identify risk in a process when you haven't clearly identified the complete process.

Process Visualization

- **Process Visualization is traditionally performed with a tool referred to as a Flowchart**

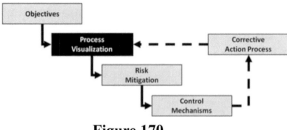

Figure 170

Remember that the flowchart should be created with a cross-functional team in an effort to accurately define the current process and to create product or process buy-in. The cross-functional team should be from, for example, engineering, production, and quality. You should have the people who are actually going to run the process there as well. I'd say the biggest reason for processes not being successful after we design them is that we did not get stakeholder buy-in. In other words, the people who are impacted by this process were not called in to help design the process. And people don't like it when you come up with a process and then go out and tell them how to do it. Most people like to feel a little bit of freedom, a little bit of independence, so that's one of the reasons we create these cross-functional teams to help us create the processes.

Process Visualization

- **The flowcharts should be created with a cross functional team in an effort to accurately define the current process and to create product / process buy in**

- **The flowchart must have enough detail to meet project objectives**

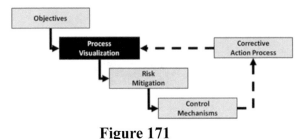

Figure 171

The flowchart must have enough detail to meet the project objectives. Remember that more documentation is better at this point in the game. I would recommend that you document team members and meeting minutes. This is especially important if you are working in a regulated industry such as pharmaceutical, medical devise, aviation, etc. It is important to regulators to see that you used cross-functional teams. Cross-functional teams are important because of the buy-in aspect but also to get multiple perspectives on process design and improvement. Many people ask, "What size cross-functional team should we form?" Every organization will be slightly different, but I'd say between five and eight people is most common. If you get too many, it's hard to move forward, and if you don't get enough people, then you don't see the problems from the various different viewpoints. So I'd say five is the minimum and eight the maximum; but that could be different depending upon your situation.

We have now covered objectives, scope, and project visualization in the process or product design and effectively documented all of our work.

Risk Mitigation

- **Risk Mitigation is a methodology used to identify the higher risk elements of a process**

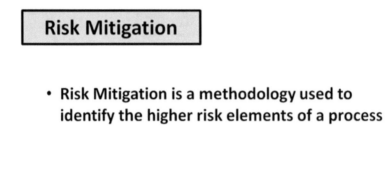

Figure 172

Now we will investigate the third step, risk mitigation. Risk mitigation is a methodology used to identify and minimize or mitigate the higher-risk elements of our proposed process. We're going to look at every step in this process and try to identify the risk elements of it. One of the more common tools used in performing risk mitigation is the FMEA. FMEA stands for "failure mode effects analysis." The FMEA looks at every step in our process and is designed to discover all the risks in every step of the process. The FMEA has the cross-functional team ask three questions concerning each of the process steps.

Risk Mitigation

- **The most common tool used in performing Risk Mitigation is a FMEA**

- **FMEA stands for Failure Mode Effects Analysis**

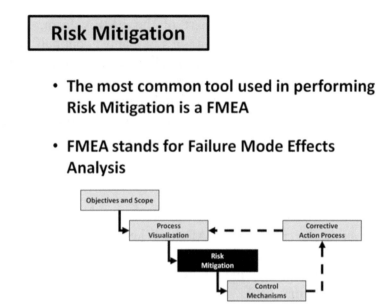

Figure 173

The three questions consist of, first, "What could possibly go wrong while performing this step?" The answers to this question are referred to as "failure modes." The second question asks, "If the failure mode is realized, how will it impact the process or customer?" The third question is "What is the potential cause or causes of the failure?"

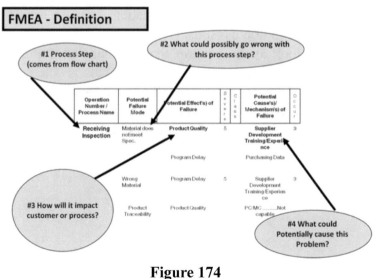

Figure 174

This figure actually shows part of the FMEA form. Now remember that this is only part of it—it's probably about half of it, maybe not even half, but if I put the whole chart here, it would be hard to visualize and to read, so I broke it up into sections. But notice the first column, where it says: Operation Number/Process Name. That's where you take information from the flowchart and feed it into the FMEA form. In other words, the first column of the FMEA form has a description of the process step under investigation. When the FMEA is completed all the steps from the process flowchart will be in the first column of the FMEA form.

The second column, labeled in the bubble as number two, is identified as the Potential Failure Mode. When you ask the cross-functional team, "What could possibly go wrong in this step of the process?" they will identify the failure mode. Notice that you could have many things that could go wrong, so you have the operation number or process step name (first column), and then you may have multiple elements underneath that in the second column because you can have more than one failure mode for a given process step. So the FMEA can sometimes be pretty long. I have seen FMEA forms as long as 20-plus pages.

The third column in the FMEA form is defined as Potential Effects of Failure, so to fill in third column the cross-functional team will be asked: "How will it impact the customer or process?" You may have multiple answers to this question, because each failure mode could have multiple results.

Now let's look at the column that I've labeled number four: Potential Causes or Mechanisms of Failure. This is where you ask the questions: "What could potentially cause this problem? What is the cause of the problem that creates that failure mode?" And so far, that's what we have—those are the first four steps in creating an FMEA.

> ## FMEA
> ## (Risk Mitigation)

- **After asking and documenting the results from the 3 questions the team will perform 3 ratings of every failure mode, which include:**

  −Severity

  −Occurrence

  −Detection

Figure 175

Now let's go to the next figure and go over the other columns. After asking and documenting the results from the three questions—"What could possibly go wrong?" "If it does go wrong, how will it impact the process or the customer?" and "What caused that failure mode?"—the team will perform three ratings of every failure mode, including severity, occurrence, and detection.

Each one of these elements will receive a rating. The automotive industry usually uses a scale from 1 to 10. Many other organizations use a scale from 1 to 5, assuming this gives them enough clarity, but you'll have to choose what you prefer depending upon your organization. You can either rate them from 1 to 5 or 1 to 10. For example, on severity, if the failure mode is not very severe, such as not even causing the customer to notice it if it fails, then severity would be a lower number. If severity would result in a fatality without warning, then that would obviously be a 10. So in all these ratings, the higher the number, the worse the situation, or the higher the risk. And the lower numbers are less risk. Keep that in mind.

Now we're going to go through some figures to show you how the Society of Automotive Engineers ranks these three categories of severity, occurrence, and detection.

Process FMEA Severity Criteria

Effect	Severity Criteria	Ranking
Hazardous without warning	May endanger machine or assembly operator. Very high severity ranking when a potential failure mode affects safe operation and/or involves noncompliance with regulation. Failure will occur without warning.	10
Hazardous with warning	May endanger machine or assembly operator. Very high severity ranking when a potential failure mode affects safe operation and/or involves noncompliance with regulation. Failure will occur with warning.	9
Very high	Major disruption to production line. 100% of product may have to be scrapped. Item inoperable, loss of primary function. Customer very dissatisfied.	8
High	Minor disruption to production line. A portion of product may have to be sorted and scrapped. Item operable, but at reduced level. Customer dissatisfied.	7
Moderate	Minor disruption to production line. A portion of product may have to be scrapped (no sorting). Item operable, but some comfort items inoperable. Customer experiences discomfort.	6
Low	Minor disruption to production line. 100% of product may have to be reworked. Item operable, but some comfort items operable at reduced level of performance. Customer experiences some dissatisfaction.	5

Derived from Technical Standard SAE J 1739

Reprinted by permission of The Society of Automotive Engineers (SAE).

Figure 176

Another thing I should mention is that in FMEAs, there are two general types that we usually look at. One is called the process FMEA and the other is called the design FMEA. The big difference is that in the design FMEA you use a schematic that shows all the parts of the machine, and in the process FMEA you use a flowchart that shows all the steps in the process. So let's continue on and discuss those different criteria ratings from the Society of Automotive Engineers.

The table shown above is helpful for grading severity criteria. Let's look at a couple of the ratings just to give you an idea. Again, this is for the process FMEA, not the design FMEA—each FMEA has its own table. We'll go over the design FMEA also, but notice number 10, which says, "Hazardous without warning." If the severity criterion gets a number 10, it says: "May endanger machine or assembly operator." We give it a very high severity rating when a potential failure mode affects safe operation and/or involves noncompliance with regulation. Failure will occur without warning. So that's what they define a number 10 to be. Now let's skip down to number 5 and look at the difference between a 5 and a 10.

Five is considered to be low severity, a minor disruption in the production line; 100 percent of the product may have to be reworked.

The item is operable, but some comfort items are operable at a reduced level of performance. The customer experiences some dissatisfaction. So that's where you get the number 5.

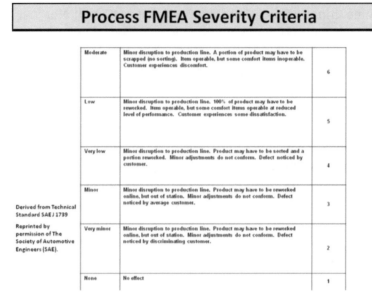

Process FMEA Severity Criteria

Moderate	Minor disruption to production line. A portion of product may have to be scrapped (no sorting). Item operable, but some comfort items inoperable. Customer experiences discomfort.	6
Low	Minor disruption to production line. 100% of product may have to be reworked. Item operable, but some comfort items operable at reduced level of performance. Customer experiences some dissatisfaction.	5
Very low	Minor disruption to production line. Product may have to be sorted and a portion reworked. Minor adjustments do not conform. Defect noticed by customer.	4
Minor	Minor disruption to production line. Product may have to be reworked online, but out of station. Minor adjustments do not conform. Defect noticed by average customer.	3
Very minor	Minor disruption to production line. Product may have to be reworked online, but out of station. Minor adjustments do not conform. Defect noticed by discriminating customer.	2
None	No effect	1

Derived from Technical Standard SAE J 1739

Reprinted by permission of The Society of Automotive Engineers (SAE).

Figure 177

Notice that number 6 is considered moderate: "Minor disruption to production line. A portion of product may have to be scrapped (no sorting). Item operable, but some comfort items inoperable. Customer experiences discomfort." Let's drop down to number 3. This is considered minor severity: "Minor disruption in production line. Product may have to be reworked online, but out of station. Minor adjustments do not conform. Defect noticed by average customer." That gives you a 3, which again is minor severity. Notice that number 1 is just no effect—there's no severity. So that is the 1 through 10 criteria for severity ratings, and notice that a lot of the items mention production line, so if you're not in manufacturing, you probably don't want to use the SAE criteria. Often companies will just use 1 through 5, with 5 being the worst and 1 being best, and just kind of calibrate from 1 to 5 as they go along.

If you're the facilitator of one of these risk-mitigation teams, or FMEA teams, remember that the facilitator's main goal in life is to make sure everyone's involved. In other words, facilitators are interested in group dynamics. Their job is to get everyone's ideas out of their heads and document them on the FMEA forms. Now you don't have to document everything, because you may realize that some things are not that important, but as a facilitator you have to decide, because if you don't use people's ideas, they may not give you any more. I would suggest that you put everything down there—if they get a low rating, they won't be looked at anyway. That way you're not shutting anyone off.

Another thing that you need to be aware of as a facilitator is that people will start arguing back and forth as to whether it's a 4 or a 5 or a 6 or an 8, or whatever the case may be. Do not let them argue for long periods of time. You are the authority figure and must listen to all the arguments and just make a decision about whether it's a 5 or a 4. If someone says, "I think it's a 4," and someone else says, "I think it's an 8," then I'll say, "Okay, I'll put it down as a 6." Make sure everyone knows upfront that you're the authority figure so that you're not arguing all day about these things. People will get quickly burned out in doing FMEAs; it's a rather long, boring job, and usually a couple of hours will pretty much be as long as most people can work on it. So I would target two hours a day as a pretty aggressive goal to put on a daily FMEA exercise. If it's an emergency and you have deadlines to meet, you may have to do more than two hours a day, and that's just the way life is—you have to go with your priorities.

Another thing you'll notice is that the tools used to control Special-Cause Variability are usually more subjective—that's why we can argue about these things without losing credibility. Tools that are designed to deal with special or assignable causes tend to be more subjective than the tools used to deal with normal cause. So keep all that in mind as you go through this. Don't let things stall—keep the process moving the best you can; being an effective authority figure is key.

Process FMEA Occurrence Criteria

Process FMEA occurrence criteria

Probability of Failure	Possible Failure Rates	Ranking
Very High: Failure almost inevitable	>1 in 2 1 in 3	10 9
High: Generally associated with processes similar to previous processes that have often failed.	1 in 8 1 in 20	8 7
Moderate: Generally associated with processes similar to previous processes that have experienced occasional failures.	1 in 80 1 in 400 1 in 2000	6 5 4
Low: Isolated failures associated with similar processes.	1 in 15,000	3
Very Low: Only isolated failures associated with almost identical processes.	1 in 150,000	2
Remote: Failure is unlikely. No failures associated with almost identical processes.	< 1 in 1,500,000	1

Derived from Technical Standard SAE J 1739

Reprinted by permission of The Society of Automotive Engineers (SAE).

Figure 178

Let's review the Process FMEA Occurrence Criteria. In other words, how often are things likely to fail? Notice the number 10 here—I was able to put the whole ranking here in one figure, which makes it nice. Notice that a ranking of 10 means the event will take place more than 50% of the time. Let's scoot down a little bit to number 6. Number 6 is moderate, generally associated with processes similar to previous processes that have experienced occasional failures. If 1 in 80 opportunity experiences failure, we will give it a rating, for occurrence, of a 6. Go down to a number 2 rating, which is 1 in 150,000, and if it's less than 1 in 1.5 million, you give it a 1. So that's how that criteria rating works for occurrence.

If you're designing a new process, you may not have these numbers, so as the occurrence criteria suggested, you go to processes that are similar to the one you are designing and get numbers from there. This can be an objective exercise if you have enough data because you can use the Z calculation to determine the actual expected numbers. If you're creating a new process and you don't have a "similar to" process, then you just have to give it your best guess. Again, these tools tend to be rather subjective, especially when you're creating a new process and you don't have data.

Process FMEA Detection Criteria

Process FMEA detection criteria

Effect	Detection Criteria	Ranking
Absolutely Impossible	No known controls to detect failure mode.	10
Very remote	Very remote likelihood current controls will detect failure mode.	9
Remote	Remote likelihood current controls will detect failure mode.	8
Very low	Very low likelihood current controls will detect failure mode.	7
Low	Low likelihood current controls will detect failure mode.	6
Moderate	Moderate likelihood current controls will detect failure mode.	5
Moderately high	Moderately high likelihood current controls will detect failure mode.	4
High	High likelihood current controls will detect failure mode.	3
Very high	Very high likelihood current controls will detect failure mode.	2
Almost Certain	Current controls will almost certainly detect a failure mode. Reliable detection controls are known with similar processes.	1

Derived from Technical Standard SAE J 1739

Reprinted by permission of The Society of Automotive Engineers (SAE).

Figure 179

Now, here we are at the Process FMEA Detection Criteria. This is how likely you are to detect a failure before it creates an impact on the customer. Notice that I have 1 through 10 on the same figure again; let's begin by looking at number 10: "Absolutely impossible—no known controls to detect failure mode." So if the failure takes place, there's no way you can detect it and it's going to impact the customer.

Let's look at number 6. This is considered a low-detection criteria: low likelihood that current controls will detect failure mode. Let's look at number 2; this is considered a very high detection, so it's highly likely. As the numbers go lower, it means that you're more likely to detect and find the problem and fix the problem before it reaches the consumers or customer. So number 2 is a very high likelihood that current controls will detect failure mode. Number 1 is almost certain: "Current controls will almost certainly detect a failure mode. Reliable detection controls are known with similar processes."

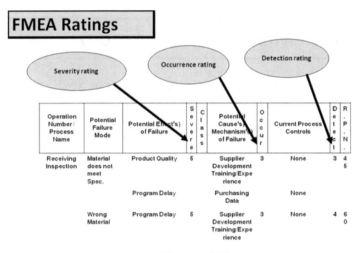

FMEA Ratings

Operation Number / Process Name	Potential Failure Mode	Potential Effect's) of Failure	S e v e r e	C l a s s	Potential Cause's) Mechanism's) of Failure	O c c u r	Current Process Controls	D e t e c t	R P N
Receiving Inspection	Material does not meet Spec.	Product Quality	5		Supplier Development Training/Experience	3	None	3	45
		Program Delay			Purchasing Data		None		
	Wrong Material	Program Delay	5		Supplier Development Training/Experience	3	None	4	60

Figure 180

This figure shows where we document those ratings. Notice the severity rating—we gave it a 5, occurrence was given a 3, and detection was given a 3. It's common practice to use the highest severity rating for all of the ratings on your potential failure modes.

The next column is called the RPN column, standing for "risk priority number." We'll go over this formally on the next figure, but just informally know that you multiply the severity rating times the occurrence rating times the detection rating to get your RPN. You can weight them also; that is what the Class column is for. I have not had experience with that column, so we won't spend time discussing it.

FMEA (Risk Mitigation)

- After you rate severity, occurrence, and detection you multiply the three ratings together to create what is called the risk priority number (RPN)
    - Severity = 6
    - Occurrence = 3
    - Detection = 2

$$RPN = 6 \times 3 \times 2 = 36$$

Figure 181

In this example, we have a severity of 6, an occurrence of 3, and a detection of 2. To find the RPN, multiply your severity rating of 6 times the occurrence rating of 3 times the detection rating of 2. So 6 times 3 is 18; 18 times 2 is 36.

FMEA (Risk Mitigation)

- By ranking the R.P.N numbers we can prioritize process concerns

- We can use the FMEA to select current and future process projects based off the higher R.P.N values

Figure 182

By ranking the RPN or risk priority number, we can prioritize process concerns from higher risk (high RPNs) to low risk (low RPNs). We can use the FMEA to select current and future process projects based off these higher RPN values.

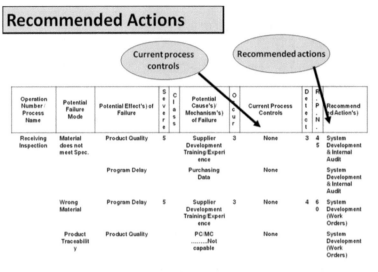

Recommended Actions

Operation Number/ Process Name	Potential Failure Mode	Potential Effect('s) of Failure	Sev	Cls	Potential Cause's)/ Mechanism's) of Failure	Ocur	Current Process Controls	Det	RPN	Recommend ed Action's)
Receiving Inspection	Material does not meet Spec.	Product Quality	5		Supplier Development Training/Experi ence	3	None	3	45	System Development & Internal Audit
		Program Delay			Purchasing Data		None			System Development & Internal Audit
	Wrong Material	Program Delay	5		Supplier Development Training/Experi ence	3	None	4	60	System Development (Work Orders)
	Product Traceabilit y	Product Quality			PC/MC ....Not capable		None			System Development (Work Orders)

Figure 183

Now let's add another column to the FMEA and discuss that. Notice that we've added the Recommended Actions column and also notice the Current Process Controls column. In the Current Process Controls column put current process controls that are being used for the existing process or what you're currently considering for the future process.

If it's a preexisting situation, then lots of times you'll just have nothing there. You'll put "None." We don't currently have process controls, and hopefully that's where the RPNs are real low. If you have a real high RPN and you don't have current process controls, this would be looked at as an oversight, I suspect.

Let's go to the next column that we just added—Recommended Actions. This is reserved for the high RPNs, so for the higher RPNs you may put in a recommended action. What are these recommended actions for? They are actions that would reduce the value of the RPNs (reduce risk), and the team gives input on how we may be able to reduce those high RPN items.

Recommended Actions (FMEA)

- The intent of recommended actions is to institute preventative action on the higher R.P.N failure modes

- If the FMEA does not result in projects that reduce the severity, occurrence, and / or detection ratings, then the FMEA is most likely a waste of resources

Figure 184

Remember that the intent of recommended actions is to institute preventative action on the higher RPN failure modes. If the FMEA does not result in projects that reduce the severity, occurrence, and/or detection ratings, then the FMEA is most likely a waste of resources. This is supposed to be a living document, and if I'm an auditor and I come into your company and look at your risk mitigation and it hasn't been revised for the last twenty years, I'm going to raise my eyebrows, because you're not using it to continuously improve the process. And if you are doing it, you're not documenting it. So it's extremely important that you use these recommended actions to create projects and ultimately reduce the RPNs on the more critical areas of your process. I'd say it's a waste of time if this doesn't happen, but that isn't completely true. When you work with a cross-functional team, you'll find that it's a great learning exercise. People learn about parts of the process and risks in the process that they had never considered before. And the knowledge level of the process tends to go up significantly when people participate in a risk mitigation activity or an FMEA activity.

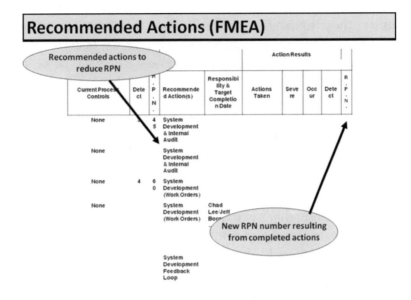

Figure 185

So here it is—the rest of the FMEA form. Remember that this isn't the full form; this is the last portion. Notice the recommended actions. If you're going to start a project on those recommended actions, you should have individuals responsible for the improvement process and a completion date. If you don't put estimated completion dates on projects, the projects will never get done. That doesn't mean that they'll always get them finished on time, but at least people will have a date to shoot toward and eventually will finish them, assuming the organizational culture and character are capable. Depending on the organization, some employers will hold their people to those dates more stringently than others. In my experience, people will get these projects done as long as you give them some target dates and the resources necessary for success. I don't even give *them* target dates. I have the teams give *me* target dates (this helps with buy-in), and then I review those dates as the project progresses.

So now you have the Recommended Actions column completed. Notice in the example that I have a recommended action for everything, but that's not usually the case. Usually you just have recommended actions for the higher RPNs. You can also keep track of actions taken as this project reaches its end objectives. You would document those under Actions Taken. And then once the project is completed, you would go back and rerate severity, occurrence, and detection and get your new RPNs. These new RPNs should be lower than your old RPNs, which verifies that the project was successful. In the end you have to remember that the nature of these numbers is subjective.

At this point, you replace the old RPN with a new RPN, and then you move to the next higher RPN and start another project. Remember that this was designed to be a living document. Of course, on the FMEA you should also include revisions so you can keep track and document all those; that's extremely important. In all organizations, but especially in those organizations that are regulated with such agencies as OSHA or FDA or FAA, documentation proves that it was done. If it isn't properly documented, then it did not happen as far as the regulators and auditors are concerned. So get good at your documentation skill set.

FMEA used in CPI

•**The FMEA team should concentrate on preventing defects and not on improving detection methods**

Figure 186

Let's move on to the next figure. Another important point to keep in mind is that you're better off solving problems as far upstream as possible. Since as far upstream as possible is in design engineering, you really should start out with a design FMEA and then your process FMEA. But remember that the FMEA team should concentrate on preventing defects and not on improving detection methods. Solution #3 tends to be a better alternative than Solution #5 in most cases. Many studies suggest that detection methods are ultimately 85 percent effective, so you're better off improving the process and reducing the probability of defects until they're so remote that it no longer makes sense to measure and inspect for the defect under consideration. You want to get rid of inspection as much as possible, but you can only get rid of inspection when the probability of something bad taking place is extremely minimal. If you get occurrence down low enough, then eventually it wouldn't make sense to do 100 percent inspections. In very critical areas such as the aircraft industry, that may not be the case, but in many industries you want to reduce occurrence to the point where it no longer makes sense to perform inspections. This is usually true, but not always true, again, depending on the criticality of what you're creating.

The FMEA Methodology

1. **Formulate Team**

2. **Define Process** (Process Visualization)

3. **List Potential Failure Modes** (What could possibly go wrong?)

4. **Define Effects of Failure** (How will it impact the customer or process?)

5. **Describe Causes** (What could be the cause of failure?)

6. **List Current Controls**

7. **Calculate Risk Priority** (Severity X Occurrence X Detection)

8. **Improvement Action**

Figure 187

Let's summarize the FMEA methodology. In this case, we use the FMEA methodology to perform risk mitigation, which was a step in our original flowchart. However, as you will see later this is not the only element to risk mitigation. These are the steps for the FMEA methodology: First, formulate a team. Make sure it's a cross-functional team so that you get buy-in from the stakeholders and so that you can see potential problems from different perspectives. You want a good solid team. Now remember also that when you form new teams there tends to be this natural cycle: first you form the team, then they storm, then they norm, and then they perform. So when you formulate the team and there's a little friction right up front, don't worry about it too much; don't overreact. It's going to happen almost every time, so just move on with life and eventually things tend to work their way out. In all my experiences I can only remember one team that had to have independent counseling, from me, to overcome the storming stage. In that situation we did not vet the team members like we should have. As a facilitator, you may need to help, but again, don't overreact; let the team try to work things out on their own whenever possible. You should also give training to the team on how to be productive team members before getting started. Published rules for teams are also a good idea. Remember that your team will tend to react to situations to the same extent that you do, and if they storm a little bit, you just think, *No big deal; it always happens,* and they'll tend to react the same way, and they usually get over it fairly quickly. The important thing here is to formulate a team that has been properly vetted and prepared for the task at hand and make sure it's cross-functional.

Then you define the process. Make sure the process is defined very specifically—specifically enough to meet the objective of the project or the process. The most common tool that we use is the flowchart. Now there are very many different kinds of flowcharts. There are process swim lanes that not only identify the process steps but indicate who is responsible for those steps. You can look swim lanes up in most any quality statistics book if you want to use them, but they're all derivations from the typical process flowchart including value stream maps. Value stream maps are optimal if your objective is to minimize or eliminate waste in the process. Now you don't even have to use a process flowchart. Some people like writing it all out, but for the most part, people would rather look at a flowchart than read a large document concerning process definition. I personally find it very boring to read about processes.

The third step is to list potential failure modes. The question you ask to get the potential failure modes to the cross-functional teams: "What could possibly go wrong with this step in the process or this part of the machine?" In the process flowchart we usually refer back to a step in the process. If it's a machine or a design FMEA, we refer back to a schematic that shows parts instead of process steps.

Number four is to define the effects of the failure. How will it impact the customer or process? You answer this and other questions and document them on the FMEA form.

Fifth, describe the causes. What caused this? What could be the causes that made this failure mode take place when we realized the failure mode? What could be the cause of the failure? Just a voice from experience, but don't try to find the root cause of all failure modes or you will never finish the FMEA. In my opinion it is okay to list the symptoms of the problem at this time and perform a more thorough root-cause analysis should it have a high-enough RPN value to warrant a project.

Sixth, list current controls. Do you have current controls? Be sure to list those.

Seventh, calculate the risk priority number, often referred to as the RPN, which is severity times occurrence times detection. From here you form teams to work to reduce risk on the higher RPN failure modes.

A functional FMEA should be a living document where you are always working on the constraint or the high RPN. It is indeed meant to be a continuous process-improvement tool, with an emphasis on continuous.

Now we have discussed objectives and scope, process visualization, and risk mitigation in our standard methodology for controlling special causes, also referred to as assignable causes.

Control Mechanisms

- **Control mechanisms are used to control the high risk elements of the process (high RPN's)**

Figure 188

The next step in the flowchart is Control Mechanisms, which are used to control the high-risk elements of the process. In other words, we take the high RPNs, which represent high-risk elements of the process, and we come up with a plan showing how we're going to control these critical variables.

Control Mechanisms

- **Typical methodologies used as Control Mechanism tools include**
    - Training
    - Balanced Score Card
    - Auditing
    - Control Plans

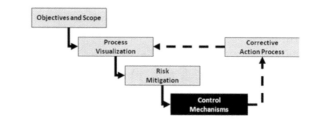

Figure 189

Typical methodologies or mechanisms used as control mechanism tools include training, balanced scorecard, auditing, control plans, SPC, and inspection. Inspection, of course, could be manual or automated, but these are typical mechanisms used to control high-risk elements of a process. This isn't an exhaustive list—these mechanisms are just the most common—so you may have other things that you put in a control plan. But again, these are the typical mechanisms for controlling a process. Just a reminder that this whole exercise is for controlling Special-Cause Variability and not normal-cause variability.

I attempted to put an example of a control plan in this book, but the form is rather large and the page of this book is rather small and in the end it was not readable. So what we will do instead is describe some of the headings on the control plan and leave it at that. If you desire to see a copy, I'm sure you can find many renditions by going online. The quality plan we will discuss here comes from the automotive industry and may be a little too specific for many organizations.

Commonly the first column in the control plan is Process or Part Number. This is where you take the higher RPNs from the FMEA and list them on the control plan. One question always comes up: "How many high RPN steps do you put on there?" Everyone is going to have a different methodology for selecting those. I usually respond with, "How many resources do you have or can you afford to control these high-risk elements?" That will determine how many high-risk steps I put on there. Of course you also want to take into account your liabilities. Obviously, you don't want to put the whole FMEA on there—only the higher RPNs. So come up with a procedure that meets the needs of your organization and effectively implement it.

Next is the Process Step or Name, the machine, device, jig, or tools for manufacturing, and then the characteristics that you're trying to control. In the next column you have special characteristics of the high-RPN part or process, and then the next column shows the process specifications. Move over an additional column and you will find evaluation method, or whatever you're measuring it with—a micrometer, a caliper, those types of things that identify the instrument that you're going to use for inspection, assuming this is applicable.

Then in the next column is Sample. How frequently do you take a sample? What is the sample size? The next column is the Control Method; after that the next column is the Reaction Plan. In other words, if this failure mode is realized, how are you going to react? When something goes wrong, you don't want to sit around and think, "What do I do now?" You're better off thinking, "What do I do when this happens? Before it happens?" That's the last column, which I consider to be very important.

You should have a reaction plan so that when this high-risk element is realized, you and your operators know exactly how they are going to respond to that situation. These are also referred to, in many circles, as "contingency plans." An example of this is "I'm going to contact the process owner or the manufacturing engineer"; then there will be a procedure for how the manufacturing engineer is to respond. The procedure number and revision should be put on the control plan.

You may come up with another control plan that works better for your organization. But this should point you in the right direction.

Training

- **The types of training needs to be identified for the various responsibilities through out the organization**

- **The types of training and who should receive that training should defined by a cross functional team**

Figure 190

As mentioned earlier, there are many types of mechanisms used for control. One of those mechanisms is training. Most any high RPN should have some training associated with it, and the types of training need to be identified for the various responsibilities throughout the organization. The types of training and who should receive that training should be defined by a cross-functional team.

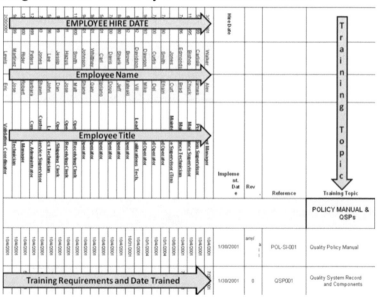

Figure 191

This figure shows an example of the training matrix. Notice that there is a hire date across the top row showing the name of the person the date belongs to and what his or her responsibilities are as far as titles within the organization. Notice also that there are lead operators and regular operators, plant managers, and so on. And then, in that last column, titled "Training Topic," it shows all the training the organization has; obviously I didn't put it all on here, because that would be a very long matrix with all the manuals and procedures that people need to be trained on. Then across the rows from the training topic it shows if the training is a requirement for a given individual, and if that person took the training, you will put the date training was completed and perhaps the test score to show evidence of training effectiveness. The point is that the training matrix is a very important part of documenting training needs and training completion, and every process on the control plan should have some related training.

It is extremely important that organizations show evidence of training effectiveness. This can be shown in various ways, but the most common way is by individuals listening to the training and then taking a test and passing it. In most cases this is sufficient in showing training effectiveness, and it's also important to document that.

Training

- **Training effectiveness must be verified**
- **Training effectiveness may be verified through**
  - Testing
  - Observation
  - Formal Audits

Figure 192

Balanced Score Card

- **The Balanced Score Card is used to communicate responsibilities and expectations to the members of an organization**

- **The Balanced Score Card holds employees responsible to the Strategic Plan of an organization**

Figure 193

The balanced scorecard is used to communicate responsibilities and expectations to members of an organization and is another one of those mechanisms that can be used for control. The balanced scorecard holds employees responsible to the strategic plan of an organization. There are many different types of balanced scorecards, and the one on the page before you is a rather simplified one, but what you do is take the strategy and break it up into key areas. In this case, we called it key result areas.

Balanced Score Card

ALPHA QUALITY
CONSULTING

Performance Management Guide FY04

BRADY, UT
84053

WWW.alph
aqc.com

Name: Jon Doe
Position: Process Supervisor

Date: 12/9/20
07

Key Result Area 1 - Quality & Regulatory

Performance Indicators	Weight	Rating	Score
Documentation errors related to operator error 1 = no improvement in documentation error rate 2 = 0-20% improvement 3 = 20-30% improvement 4 = 30-40% improvement 5 = 40% improvement	20	5	100
Audit observations related to Regulations. 1 = Repeats 3 = No repeats 5 = None	10	3	30
Safety Manual implementation (per schedule to be developed) 1 = Not implemented per schedule 3 = Implemented, but not being used routinely per audits 5 = Implemented and in use as measured by audit	15		
Process Conformance Rate 1 = seven months above prior year average. 2 = eight months above prior year average. 3 = nine months above prior year average. 4 = ten months above prior year average. 5 = eleven or more months above prior year average.	25		
Service Conformance Rate 1 = seven months above prior year average. 2 = eight months above prior year average. 3 = nine months above prior year average. 4 = ten months above prior year average. 5 = eleven or more months above prior year average.	15		

Figure 194

All the key result areas should be taken right from the strategic plan. Notice that Key Result Area 1 is Quality & Regulatory (and of course you have the name of the person there whose balanced scorecard it is). In this example, Quality & Regulatory is only one key result area. I didn't put the whole thing on the figure before you. Another one could be operations, another one could be customer service, and another one could be education. Whatever it is it must be connected to the strategy of the organization. From here you define expected performance so the employees know how their efforts are tied to the success of the organizational strategy. The point is that the Quality & Regulatory section of this document could be tied to performance on the high RPN factors from the control plan. Ultimately this form gives high visibility to important high-risk elements. Also notice that Key Result Area 1 is Quality & Regulatory, and one of the performance indicators is documentation errors related to operator error. Individuals receive 1 point if they have no improvement; 1 percent—27 percent improvement equals 2 points; and if you get 5 points, it means you have a 40 percent improvement in documentation errors. And then there's a weighting for the rating and ultimately a score where you multiply the weight and the rating together. The plant manager, or a supervisor, goes to these balanced scorecards usually once per quarter so he would know how well everyone is doing and if they are on track to meet the organizational goals. The manager would then tie this balanced scorecard directly to your pay raise. So the balanced scorecard is another way of creating control within an organization, and in this case, control to the strategy. I realize that I may be using the term balanced scorecard loosely and would encourage you to learn more about it should the opportunity avail itself.

Auditing

Audit Defined

- **"An Audit is a planned, independent, and documented assessment to determine whether agreed upon requirements are met in an objective manner"**

Figure 195

An audit can also be used as a control mechanism. An audit is a planned, independent, and documented assessment to determine whether agreed-upon requirements are met in an objective manner. You will not achieve discipline in organizational requirements without a functional auditing program. Audit results need to be tied into the balanced scorecard metrics. Also be aware that Deming did not like these kinds of tools, which rate employee performance. The way I see it is that he saw them as an attempted substitute for ineffective leadership. I agree with Deming in that if you have a Phase III organization this employee rating system is a destructive force. However, in Phase I and Phase II organizations it can be an effective tool. You may say to yourself, *There is no such thing as a Phase III organization.* This is not true—I have seen them. Although they are rare, they do exist and are always top performers in the industries they serve. Phase III organizations are as rare as Phase III leaders.

Auditing

- **You will not achieve discipline to organizational requirements without a functional auditing program**

- **Audit results need to be tied into the Balanced Score Card metrics**

Figure 196

Control plans should be the most audited document of all documents because a lot of the work has already been performed for the auditor in that the highest-risk elements have been identified and a procedure has been developed regarding how to control them, along with the accompanying contingency plans. When I go into an organization to audit, one of the first documents I want to look at is the control plan. The reason auditors audit the control plan so heavily is because they know that if the company is not disciplined in the most important elements of a process, then it is probably not disciplined in the less critical elements of the process. This is usually a pretty good assumption!

Control Plans

- Control Plans are simply a formal plan on how you are going to control the high risk elements of your process (identified through the FMEA)

- Control Plans are fortunately the most likely document to be audited

Figure 197

Control Plans

- The reason auditors audit the Control Plan so heavily is because he/she knows that if they are not disciplined to the most important elements in a process then they are probably not disciplined in the less critical elements of a process

- This is usually a good assumption!

Figure 198

Now, even with your best efforts, the control plan is still going to fail once in a while. As a result, you need a corrective-action process. This is just a method or a process where, when the control mechanisms fail, you document the failures and come up with some solutions to any problems that may arise.

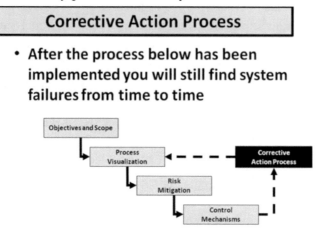

Figure 199

Now let's read that bullet point before we move onto the next figure. "After the process below has been implemented, you will still find system failures from time to time." As mentioned earlier, the corrective-action process is used to document these problems. This process is ultimately designed to eliminate the recurrence of these types of problems.

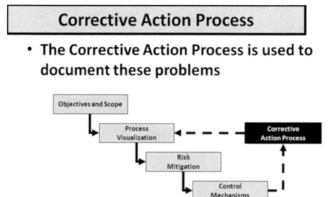

Figure 200

Corrective Action Process

- **The Corrective Action Process is ultimately designed to eliminate the re-occurrence of these problems**

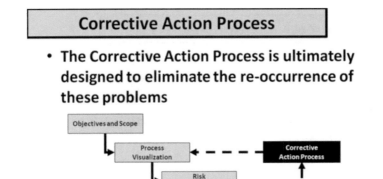

Figure 201

All corrective actions must have a robust root-cause analysis performed if continuous process-improvement is to be realized. In other words, the corrective-action system is really not very functional unless you do a good, solid, root-cause analysis. There are many models out there for effective root-cause analysis, such as the "Five Whys," which is the one I like. (I appreciate simple things.) Many times people like to perform corrective actions, but they're always just treating the symptoms, and when you just treat the symptoms, you end up with this recurrence problem that most organizations have. So remember to do a complete root-cause analysis on these corrective actions and implement procedures that will take care of that problem so you don't have recurrence. The key idea is to fix the system. The biggest indication that you're not having effective root-cause analysis is the return of the problem. And usually one of the biggest problems for that recurrence is that you treat it as a personal problem, so you're constantly retraining or punishing the operator. I'm not saying that retraining doesn't have its place, but usually it's not the root cause of the problem; usually it's a system problem. So you have to fix the system so that people can't fail while using it.

Corrective Action Process

- **After the Corrective Action on non-conformances are completed the Process Visualization is updated, Risk Mitigation is performed, and Control Mechanisms are updated accordingly**

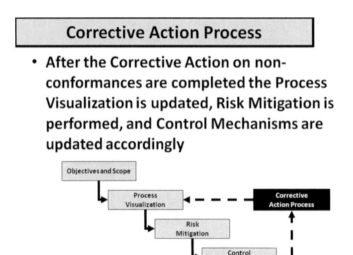

Figure 202

Let's read that bullet on the above figure: "After the corrective actions on nonconformances are completed, the process visualization must be updated, risk mitigation is performed on the new process or the new element of the process, and control mechanisms are updated accordingly." So ultimately this is the goal. Following the methodology that we just taught you should allow your organization to implement continuous process-improvement for Special-Cause Variability into the organizational culture and become "best in class"!

Continuous Process Improvement

- **Following this methodology will allow your organization to implement CPI for special cause variability into the organizational culture and become**

Figure 203

Six benefits have been identified as a result of the implementation of this process into organizations:

1. Quality monitoring of critical control points decreases the likelihood of process and product problems.

2. Quality consciousness of employees increases.

3. Quality items needing correction are readily observed.

4. The amount of time spent on inspections decreases.

5. The efficiency of inspections increase since they focus on important areas—in other words, areas with high RPNs.

6. The consistency of control mechanisms also increases.

Future

-   **This process will ultimately make our processes more predictable**

-   **Predictable processes are said to be "under control"**

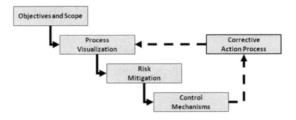

Figure 204

So what will this accomplish in the future? This process will ultimately make our processes more predictable. Remember that when we can control special causes, our processes become more predictable. Predictable processes are said to be "under control." So the ultimate objective of this process is to create processes that are under control—in other words, they are predictable.

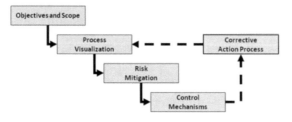

Figure 205

After your organization gets their processes under control, they can continue their process-improvement efforts by using methodologies such as Six Sigma, Lean, or Theory of Constraints. These tools are generally designed to reduce normal-cause variability. This isn't completely true, especially for Six Sigma. What I just went over—this HACCP system—is part of the Six Sigma body of knowledge. However, by far, Six Sigma spends most of its time teaching how to reduce normal-cause variability. As mentioned earlier, Lean reduces variability in time.

Most organizations consider Special-Cause Variability to be their biggest problem and usually invest about 90 percent of their process-improvement efforts trying to correct it. In reality, what I have found, and other experts in the industry both past and present have found, is that the vast majority of problems—Deming designated 85 percent—come from inherent variability or what we have referred to as normal-cause variability.

Most companies spend 90 percent of their resources working on 15 percent of the problem sources. I hope you can see the insanity of such a practice.

CHAPTER TEN

CLOSING THOUGHTS

Congratulations—you have made it to the final chapter! I hope you have found the journey both educational and inspirational. The objective of this chapter is to summarize the lessons learned and to add some final information that did not comfortably fit into other areas of the book. I am constantly pondering and expanding my thoughts concerning organizational transformation, and in this chapter I will publish my latest thoughts. These thoughts have not been tested over time like much of the information published in earlier chapters, which has been tested during endless hours of lecturing and response to mountains of student input in the form of end-of-lecture surveys. So welcome to the cutting edge of my current thoughts.

This work started out with a definition of organizational transformation. The definition of transformation is "evolving to a higher level of sustained performance." A mathematical argument was created to help the reader understand the need for organizational transformation. The argument had to be as objective as possible if this book was to have a potential meaningful impact on the society in which we both live. If the argument for organizational transformation was not objective, then it would by default be subjective, leading to all of society's energy being dedicated to needless argument. The argument explained the need for organizational transformation and suggested that two elements exist that require organizations to transform. These two elements are increasing "and" statements and increasing customer expectations. We learned that as "and" statements increase, the overall probability of success goes down. We also learned that "and" statements have been increasing ever since the European Renaissance. Not only have "and" statements been increasing over time, but they have been increasing at an exponential rate. To complicate the situation even more we found that the skill set needed to go from a 2 percent success rate to a 95 percent success rate was different than the skill set needed to go from 95 percent to 99.9996 percent (six sigma) and beyond. We also learned that the most often used skill set to get organizations from the 2 percent to the 95 percent success rate was personify, blame, and punish (PBP). At approximately a 95 percent success rate PBP becomes dysfunctional at sustaining process-improvement. We referred to this phenomenon as "hitting the wall." We learned that the natural response of organizations "hitting the wall" was to amplify the dysfunctional methodology. We referred to this portion of organizational existence as the "living hell." The "living hell" becomes an important part of the organizational transformation process as it is a point where the organization no longer feels great. In organizational transformation we understand that organizations "stop becoming greater the instant they think they are great." It may surprise you to read that I have never witnessed organizational transformation taking place before the "living hell" phenomena. The "living hell" phenomena is the event that allows the "I am great" cloud to release its moisture so you can once again get a better view of true potential. This is one of the reasons I wrote that "the main ingredient in perfection is imperfection." Remember that everyone needs a rainy day once in a while if they are to rise above the dark ages of human behavior. The "I am great" cloud phenomena is the number-one cause for organizational destruction, which is the opposite of organizational transformation. For the most part everything I taught you about the nature of organizations is also applicable to individuals. This is logical, since organizations are made up of individuals.

We then discovered that when an organization hits the wall it has two choices. The two choices consist of organizational transformation and organizational extinction. Most companies choose extinction, because they incorrectly believe that the methodology that will take them from 2 percent to 95 percent (PBP) is also capable of taking them from 95 percent to 99.9996 percent and beyond. Commitment to this belief system will ultimately be fatal to your organization. The art of knocking down the wall is what was referred to as "organizational transformation." We learned that organizational transformation has three subtransformations referred to as personal transformation, cultural transformation, and tools transformation. These transformations must take place in the proper order as well as in an environment of order. The strength of the proverbial wall comes from the fear within the organization. We also learned that organizations "will never become greater than that which motivates them," and fear is not a powerful enough motivator to create the power needed to sustain organizational transformation. Fear is the primary motivator of Phase I behavior and is the natural by-product of PBP. Fear is one of the more destructive forces in organizational transformation. Its destructive force is second only to the "I am great" cloud. The most effective antidote for fear is education. Effective education will evaporate fear and create the natural by-product of appreciation. If your education does not breed appreciation, then in effect you are not educated at all but are only well read. Successful organizational transformations start with effective education. In effect education weakens the wall to the point that reasonably effective leadership and transformation methodologies can knock the wall down, allowing us to "rise above it all."

Concerning the three subtransformations, personal transformation is the first step taken to prepare the organization for a successful transformation. The objective of personal transformation is to educate the organization on the nature of transformation and inspire it to higher motives. The people must rise above standard motives if transformation is to be successful. The higher motive drives us to go to work in hopes of creating more widgets per person. The creation of wealth (more widgets per person) will ultimately create more opportunity for those who follow us. Personal transformation should create an appreciation for the past. You will be blind to a better future if you are unwilling to appreciate the past, and you cannot realize a better future without first visualizing it. Ultimately a successful personal transformation changes motives. A change in motives is necessary because of the law of transformation that states that "you will never become greater than that which motivates you." I have never witnessed a truly successful organizational transformation without a successful personal transformation to kick it off.

The second subtransformation, cultural transformation, is the most difficult element of organizational transformation. Culture is defined as an organization acting out on its value system. When you attempt to change a value system you had best be ready for an all-out fight. This is the fuel that creates wars. Most leaders throughout history who have successfully changed culture have also been assassinated. The corporate equivalent of assassination is termination. Because of this, the most appropriate people to create culture change are the people who are most difficult to terminate, which should be upper management. If organizational culture is to be improved it must also be owned by someone. This ownership appropriately lies within the realm of leadership. In the world of transformation, culture is dictated by leadership. Organizational culture is an extension of the personality of the leader. If you are at the top of your organization and you don't dictate culture, then by definition you are not the leader of the organization. If you are the leader of your organization and you don't like the culture of your organization, then the first place to evaluate the problem is in the mirror. Leadership must accept ownership of culture or culture cannot be improved and organizational transformations will not be within the realm of reality.

The mechanics behind cultural-change requirement comes from the fact that analytical tools, which are necessary to improve "and" statement probabilities, will not work if they do not have a culture that is capable of supporting them. PBP is incapable of creating a culture that can support modern-day analytical tools. There are many reasons for this, but one of them is that PBP creates fear and the fear motive is incapable of collecting good data. The fuel of objectivity is data, and objectivity is the only form of problem solving capable of creating enough power for successful organizational transformation. Subjectivity's job is to control the power that objectivity creates. If you allow subjectivity to take over your organization, then you will be incapable of consistently improving beyond the approximate 95 percent barrier. One of the reasons for this is that subjectivity will always gravitate toward PBP and PBP is not capable of fulfilling the needs of modern-day markets, with their accompanying high "and" statements and relatively high customer expectations. Effective objectivity will naturally see problems as system problems vs. personal problems. A telltale sign that your organization is too subjective is when who you know is more important than what you know.

A telltale sign that your organization has the right amount of objectivity is when your organization perceives that the system is there to support the people instead of the people being there to support the system. If your organization sees that the system is there to support the people, then the organization will naturally attempt to work on the system to improve organizational performance. If your organization perceives that the employee's purpose is to support the system, then the organization will attempt to improve the people to improve organizational performance. To the untrained eye it can be difficult to differentiate the two perspectives. Suffice it to say that I would estimate that 99 percent of all organizations perceive the people to be subordinate to the system, thus suggesting that the path to improvement is to invest all organizational resources in improving the people and not the system. Granted, you must have people to improve systems. Your training dollar should be invested in teaching people how to improve systems. At some level people are flawed, but that doesn't mean that they are incapable of creating near-perfect systems. You do not have to be perfect to do perfect things. It is less expensive to improve systems to the 99.9996 percent level, and above, than it is to improve people to the 99.9996 percent level. From a business perspective this is why you would prefer to see the system as subordinate to the people. Let's put it this way: imperfect people can create near-perfect systems, but imperfect systems cannot create near-perfect people.

Continuing on with our discussion concerning cultural transformation we went over Deming's fourteen points. I like to look at Deming's fourteen points as Deming's attempt to try to define what a functional culture looks like. Remember that Deming's analytical tools worked well in Japan, but when he brought them back to American manufacturing the tools did not work as well as was originally hoped. As a result, I feel that Deming compared Japanese business culture to American business culture. The Deming points that stick out to me the most are constancy of purpose, changing motives, removing fear from the workplace (abolish PBP), building quality into the product or service and not inspecting it in (Solution #3 vs. Solution #5), and of course seeing problems as system problems not personal problems.

After defining what a functional culture looks like we turned our attention to the mechanics of changing culture. To understand how to change culture you must understand how to change people, and you cannot understand how to change people unless you understand human nature. The human-nature model rested on two basic assumptions, the first being "The mother of all motivators is survival." People will do amazing things just to survive. The second assumption was that "every person must perceive they stand out in a crowd or they will die." Because people do not want to die they will figure out a way to stand out in a crowd. The starting point of human behavior is referred to as Phase I behavior. Phase I behavior tears people down to give them the perception of standing out in a crowd. Phase I behavior will naturally identify uniqueness, amplify the uniqueness, and then belittle uniqueness. Phase I behavior is referred to as the cheap drug of human behavior. Phase I behavior is motivated by fear and tends to solve problems using PBP. From the Phase I perspective, problems are solved effectively and efficiently using PBP. Outside the Phase I perspective you will see that Phase I behavior causes more problems than it solves. Phase I behavior is inherently destructive. Phase I behavior believes that winning battles is solving problems, even though after winning battles the organization's performance never improves. If you solve a problem in a Phase I organization without a battle, then from the Phase I perspective you never actually solved a problem. Phase I behavior demands contention, and if contention is not there, then the feeling of moving forward will also be absent. If you choose to live your life in Phase I behavior you will receive the fruits of Phase I behavior, which include being envious, jealous, hateful, and easily offended. Phase I behavior is the birthplace of racism, sexism, etc. Ultimately Phase I behavior will make you and people around you miserable. I would recommend that you rise above it all. In the act of rising above it all you will have many critics say that you are not capable of rising above it all. If you are to rise above it all you must teach yourself how to ignore negative criticism. Critics who offer up purely negative criticism do so for only one reason, and that is to gain control over people. However, they can only control you with criticism if you care what they think. In the end it is up to you if you will give Phase I behavior power to direct your life. Remember that you must learn to ignore negative criticism if you are to rise above it all. People usually need help from others to rise above Phase I behavior. To rise above Phase I behavior you need to learn skills and talents. You may need help from others to gain these newfound skills and talents. Don't be motivated by your fears or you will never rise above Phase I behavior, because you can never become greater than that which motivates you. You will feel fear from time to time, but that does not mean you have to be motivated by it. The definition of courage is not the elimination of fear but the refusal to use fear as a motive.

Phase II behavior takes place when people develop their skills and talents to such an extent that they can use those skills and talents to stand out in a crowd. Standing out in a crowd by exercising one's skills and talents does not have the bitter aftertaste of Phase I behavior. The primary force that evolves human nature to higher levels of behavior is the fact that higher levels of behavior feel better than lower levels of behavior. People will spend a lifetime developing their skills and talents simply because at the end of the day they feel better about themselves. Phase II behavior still has the stains of Phase I behavior in that Phase II behavior still desires to witness others failing. The difference is that Phase I behavior desires everyone to fail while Phase II behavior only desires those who are developing skills and talents similar to its own to fail. Phase II behavior has a high respect for skills and talents. People in a Phase II organization will not let you lead them unless they perceive you as more skilled and talented than they are. As soon as they perceive that they are more skilled and talented than their leader, the leader can no longer effectively lead the Phase II organization. When Phase II behavior does something of value it will seek the well-deserved glory. Remember that Phase II behavior uses skills and talents to stand out in a crowd and cannot stand out in a crowd if it does not receive credit for what it does. In short, Phase II behavior seeks after its own glory. I am not saying that Phase II is bad; I am just stating it is the nature of human evolution. Remember that people are just trying to survive. Some people survive by tearing people down; other people survive by exercising their skills and talents. Phase II behavior is more constructive than Phase I behavior. Neither of these forms of behavior generates enough power to facilitate cultural change.

Phase III behavior is the crowning achievement of human behavior. Phase III behavior, applied correctly, has the power to change organizational culture. Phase III behavior seeks not its own glory but only desires to lift others up. Phase III behavior has the purest of motives and will never fail you. When acting out in Phase III behavior you will never look back and regret your behavior. To lead a Phase III organization you simply teach them. Phase III behavior will recognize correct principles and will use them for effective self-government. In a Phase III organization you can teach the members of the organization methodologies that will move society forward and Phase III will simply implement it. Phase III behavior will not desire recognition programs, nor will it respond to attempts to motivate by fear. Phase III behavior is only motivated by the opportunity to make things better. There will be no poor in a Phase III organization. You cannot force Phase III behavior, and attempting to do so is a moral perversion. Sometimes lower levels of behavior will try to force Phase III behavior for their own glorification. This will never work, because you can never raise an organization above your predominant level of behavior; in other words Phase I and Phase II behavior is incapable of creating a Phase III organization. You know that you are ready to evolve to Phase III behavior when Phase II behavior becomes boring. When Phase II behavior becomes boring, then Phase III behavior will feel empowering and will help you reach new levels of happiness. You cannot reach Phase III behavior without first mastering Phase II behavior.

Phase III behavior demands sacrifice, and sacrifice demands character. Character is defined as the ability to follow through with a decision long after the emotions of making a decision are gone. When sacrifice meets emotion emotions evaporate. When you perform a Phase III event the emotions will leave and you must be able to follow through with the good deed even in the absence of emotion. If you cannot sacrifice, then you cannot perform Phase III behavior. Sometimes Phase III behavior has to sacrifice its own popularity to lift others up. Phase III behavior is capable of doing this because it does not desire to stand out in the crowd. Standing out in a crowd is no longer a necessity in life—you have risen above it all. And why did you rise from Phase II behavior to Phase III behavior? You rose above Phase II behavior into Phase III behavior because it felt better. It is really quite simple. When you rise from one phase of behavior to another phase of behavior it will most likely be lonely because what you once had in common with your peer group you will no longer have in common and they may not enjoy hanging out with you like they once did. Rising above it all can be a lonely endeavor, so you will ultimately have to decide what is more important to you. Many people do not evolve to higher levels of behavior because they don't want to leave their comfort zones. Rising above it all demands sacrifice, and sacrifice demands character.

Your ability to sustain higher levels of human behavior is only as capable as your character is strong. When the sacrifices of Phase III behavior exceed your level of character, you will slide down to lower levels of human behavior. If you will "leave scratch marks" all the way down the curve and after bottoming out you scratch all the way back to the top, then you will effectively increase your character. "You cannot experience the rise without experiencing the fall." Be aware that when you bottom out in lower levels of human behavior, Phase I behavior will come out of the woodwork and try to convince you that since you're not perfect you can no longer do perfect things. This is not true—imperfect people can do perfect things. Phase I behavior will try to gain control through the art of negative criticism. Many people believe this and never again try to regain the joys of Phase III behavior. Remember that you do not have to be perfect to do perfect things, so pull yourself up and rise above it all. Phase I behavior will try to convince you that your weaknesses are something to be ashamed of when in reality these supposed weaknesses are only potential strengths. A weakness should be seen as a blessing and not a curse. The only time a weakness becomes a curse is when you accept that it is a curse and make the mistake of believing that you cannot overcome the weakness. You will often hear "but I was born that way." We all start out at Phase I behavior, but we do not have to stay there, because human behavior is capable of evolution. If you spend all of your days trying to hide your weaknesses because of the "I am great" cloud, then you will never overcome them and you will never evolve human nature. If you hide your weaknesses because you're afraid that people will make fun of them, then you will not evolve to higher levels of human behavior. You should not let critics dictate your life. Your life is to be lived on your terms and not on others' terms. If you do not become the captain of your own ship, then you will never rise above it all. There are a lot of people out there who want to be the captain of your ship—don't let them. Everyone has the right to be the captain of their own ship—don't give the gift away. Phase III behavior is the by-product of a people who are free to choose for themselves. You can become so independent that it can become difficult for people to live with you, so always remember the rule "moderation in all things" and at the end of the day do what you know to be right.

One element of transformation that I have not discussed but needs to be discussed is the principle that I refer to as the "Mother Bear." Having grown up near the mountains in Idaho, my parents would teach me the importance of never getting between a mother bear and her cubs. We were specifically told that if we ever saw baby cubs to run back to camp, because getting between a mother bear and her cubs would most likely be fatal. I took the lesson to heart, and it was my mind's favorite story to play over and over again in the form of a nightmare.

The "Mother Bear" phenomenon, in organizational transformation, refers to the need for upper management to take total ownership of the transformation. This individual is the ultimate leader of the transformation. Everyone needs to know up front that if anyone gets between the leader, or the "Mother Bear," and the transformation then there will be some real consequences to deal with. Assuming that someone is bold enough to openly come out against the transformation, the organization needs to hear the growl of the bear and the sound of limbs breaking as the "Mother Bear" chases down its prey. Some organizations transform more smoothly than others. If an organization is capable of a smooth transformation, then the "Mother Bear" will never have to growl and go on the chase. However, most organizations need a "Mother Bear" or transformation will take longer than necessary and may never take place at all. Many readers may consider this Phase I behavior, but it is not Phase I behavior. It is the act of Phase III behavior that is willing to sacrifice a person's popularity, if necessary, to help an organization rise above it all. The "Mother Bear" creates an environment of safety for the transformation to take place.

If you would like to meet someone who can teach you the technique of being an effective "Mother Bear," then you should arrange a lunch with Mike Matthes, a great VP from Jabil Circuit. Jabil Circuit is a global corporation with approximately 110,000 worldwide employees. Mike Matthes played college football for the navy, and perhaps this is where he learned the art of letting people know who is in charge. Wherever it came from, he has it down like no one I have ever met. Everyone in Jabil knows that Mike Matthes owns the transformation, and everyone knows that they do not want to get between Mike and the transformation. Because of Mike Matthes, Jabil Circuit is experiencing a relatively smooth transformation. If you are lucky enough to get a lunch appointment with Mike Matthes you will also want to invite Walter Garvin. Walter Garvin is a senior director at Jabil and was instrumental in organizing a transformation that effectively implemented Lean and Six Sigma tools in the Jabil organization. The two of them started the Jabil transformation and will be able to give you some solid insight into the mechanics of starting a successful organizational transformation. It has been my honor to work with these great leaders.

I will now provide one last thought concerning the nature of human nature and the three forms of human behavior. I will use the figure below to help explain my thoughts.

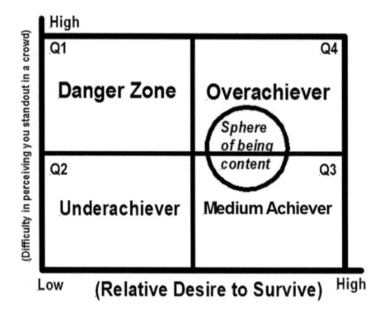

Figure 206

Notice that the figure above is drawn as two dimensional. In other words, there are two variables used to describe the phenomena. The horizontal axis shows the "relative desire to survive" and the vertical axis is the "difficulty in perceiving you stand out in a crowd." The figure suggests that not everyone is born with the same desire to survive. The figure also suggests that everyone has a different perception on what it takes for them to feel that they are standing out in a crowd. You must remember that standing out in a crowd is only a perception. Some people wake up in the morning and look in the mirror and that is all they need to feel that they stand out in a crowd. Other people have to "shake the world" to perceive that they stand out in a crowd.

Remember that these two variables were the two basic assumptions of the original model. You will notice that I took the space created by the two variables and broke them into four quadrants. Quadrant 1 is an individual who has a relatively low desire to survive, and it is very difficult for individuals in this quadrant to feel they stand out in a crowd. Quadrant 1 tends to act out in self-destructive behavior. Quadrant 1 is not healthy, nor is it a fun place to live.

Quadrant 2 is defined as a person who has a relatively low desire to survive but finds it relatively easy to perceive that he or she stands out in a crowd. This combination of attributes tends to make the individual an underachiever. The challenge with Quadrant 2 is that your perception of standing out in a crowd does not match society's perception of standing out in a crowd. You will feel you are something special, but society at large does not perceive it to be so. This can create a feeling of being picked on by society at large. Quadrant 4 tends to set the standard for what society defines as standing out in a crowd. Quadrant 2 behavior can potentially blame Quadrant 4 for being the reason others don't recognize their greatness. The traits that are most representative of Quadrant 2 are underachievement, the feeling of being picked on, and jealousy.

Quadrant 3 is defined as someone who has a strong desire to survive but perceives that he or she stands out in a crowd without a lot of sacrifice. I would suggest, with low confidence, that this is where the majority of mature people live their lives. For most people the "sphere of being content" partially lies in Quadrant 3.

The "sphere of being content" or the "sphere of contentment" is where we feel at peace with our self and what we spend most of our time trying to find. The sphere of contentment will be slightly different for different people, but I would argue that it will have an overlap between Quadrant 3 and Quadrant 4. Note that I call it the "sphere of being content" even though it is drawn as a circle. This observation suggests there is another dimension to this model. We will discuss this later.

Quadrant 4 is defined as someone who has a strong desire to survive but it is very difficult for him or her to perceive that he or she stands out in a crowd. This quadrant is what creates overachieving behavior. As mentioned earlier, Quadrant 4 is the behavior that defines, for society, what standing out in a crowd looks like. Quadrant 4 demands large levels of sacrifice and will ultimately demand the creation of character, more so than do the other quadrants.

The natural question then becomes how do we move between quadrants? Obviously we are born with certain characteristics that put us at a given location within the quadrants. I would argue that inherently we may start out at a given location, but that does not mean we have to spend our entire life there. I feel that environmental factors can also impact the quadrant. For example, you may find yourself in Quadrant 2 and feel like you are standing out in a crowd but society doesn't see it. So you feel a little jealous and ultimately realize that your perception of standing out in a crowd needs to be recalibrated. The recalibration puts you into Quadrant 1, the "danger zone." The danger zone is not a fun place to live, so you desire to find your "sphere of contentment." This desire will ultimately drive you to Quadrants 3 and 4. Most individuals, but not all, tend to generate a greater desire to survive as they approach Quadrants 3 and 4 because it is easier to want to survive as life becomes more rewarding. (You have more to fight for.) People who fight the hardest tend to be the people who feel that they have the most to lose. This suggests that society at large will evolve toward higher levels of contentment. One of the reasons I gave the earlier assignment to perform a Phase III event is because Phase III events tend to migrate people to more constructive quadrants.

The model shown in the figure above is two dimensional. In my opinion the reality is better modeled in four dimensions. The third dimension would be represented by a third axis that comes out of the page toward the reader (Z axis). The third dimension is the phase of behavior, or motives of behavior. The starting point of the three dimensions is the starting point of human nature, or what we called Phase I behavior. As one travels up the Z axis from Phase I to Phase II and ultimately into Phase III the nature of the two-dimensional relationship shown in the figure will change.

In the current figure, the "sphere of being content" is a cross-section of a sphere. As people reach the "sphere of being content" they will get a vision of greater contentment than what they currently have. If they continue to search for greater contentment they will work their way up the third dimension. As they work their way up the third dimension the circle on our current figure will grow progressively smaller until it no longer exists on the figure shown. This would suggest that the rules change as you evolve along the third dimension. Phase I and Phase II are limited in scope; you will rise above them as you progress, assuming you desire to do so. Phase III does not end. It is infinite in nature, and ultimately your desire to find greater contentment will lead you to greater spheres of contentment and you will never come to a point where greater contentment cannot be discovered. This infinite journey is the ultimate goal in the evolution of human nature. This is why I wrote "perfection is a journey, not a destiny."

There is another element of human behavior that I do not completely understand but do recognize its destructive nature. This is the destructive nature to believe negative lies more readily than believing positive truths. Let me tell you a story to help you understand this better. There was once a little boy who got abducted, and the little boy said to his abductor, "Why are you taking me away from my home?"

And the abductor said to the little boy, "I am taking you away from your home because you left the gate open and the dog ran away and as a result your parents no longer love you and have asked me to take you away."

The little boy believed his abductor and felt very bad. The years went by and eventually the cops found the abductor and returned the little boy to the police station where his parents were anxiously awaiting his arrival. When the little boy arrived at the police station the parents fell to their knees and hugged the little boy. As you may imagine the tears flowed freely. Then the little boy said to his parents, "I'm sorry I left the gate open and the dog got away, and I am really sorry that you don't love me anymore."

Hearing this from the little boy made the mother fall on the floor and cry out in pain. The father said to his little boy, "How can you believe such an ugly perverted lie? Don't you know that we love you more than anything in the whole universe? How could we possibly hate something that we have created?"

After the father spoke to the little boy he embraced the little boy and the mother in hopes that their love would heal the little boy. It is up to you to write the end of the story on whether the child ultimately believes his father or the abductor.

My experience suggests that people will believe the abductor before they will believe the father. I don't know why people will readily embrace a negative lie before they will embrace a positive truth. But that's human nature, and I suspect that we have to learn to work within the reality of the situation we find ourselves in. I call this "believing the big lie." Believing the big lie is the most destructive element of human nature, even more destructive than the "I am great" cloud. You can only see the brutality of the "big lie" from the Phase III perspective (the perspective of the parents). From the Phase I and Phase II perspective, the "big lie" seems completely logical. I do not know why this is so; maybe I will someday, but that thought has not yet matured. I feel that it has something to do with the harshness of judgments that come from Phase I and Phase II behavior, and in the harshness of these judgments is the only judgments with which we know how to judge ourselves. The discouragement that comes from Phase I and Phase II behavior is largely self-inflicted. Suffice it to say that I find people believing in the "big lie" to be very discouraging. If I had a magic wand and I had but one wish I would use the wish to destroy the "big lie."

Perhaps you have already come to the realization that I tried to make this book the magic wand. I fear it has fallen terribly short. Please know that I tried to make it as perfect as I know how. If it will but inspire one person to live a more fulfilling life and create more effective organizations, then my sacrifice will be but a grain of sand on the large beautiful beach of sacrifices that we call life.

Remember that "life is like a book, and you only get to write one of them; you are the only one authorized to write your book, so make it a great one!" This is my only hope.

"This is not the end but only a new beginning"

"Blue skies"

Thank you:

iUniverse Team

Fred Pingel

John Foote

INDEX

A

abolitionists, European 14

administrative lead time 234, 235, 236, 237, 239, 241, 242, 244, 250

allowable limits 72

alpha risk. *See* standard risk

American Loss Function 72

analytical tools x, 30, 79, 88, 91, 111, 202, 206, 224, 348, 349

"and" statement probabilities 19, 35, 44, 56, 58, 88, 107, 214, 221, 258, 281, 282, 284, 348

and people-constrained organizations 69

and reducing variability 64, 72, 73, 81, 82, 89, 96, 221, 223, 243

Japanese cars and 73

mechanics of increasing 56

PBP methodology and 135

probability statistics and 1, 2, 287, 288, 290, 291, 296, 299, 300, 304

reduce with new technology 60

statistics and 50

appreciation for the past 122, 189, 347

assignable-cause variability. *See* special-cause variability

auditing ix, 248, 283, 284, 332, 338

authority figures 44, 204

automotive industry 7, 23, 26, 67, 70, 71, 73, 82, 89, 90, 317, 333

95 percent standard and 23

cost model for quality and 71, 72

Deming and 80, 88

reducing variability and 64, 72, 73, 81, 82, 89, 96, 221, 223, 243

system problems and 26, 93, 102, 111

averages 250, 276

B

balanced score cards 336, 337

banners 100

behavior, human x, 129, 131, 134, 136, 137, 138, 143, 157, 165, 176, 191, 346, 350, 352, 353, 354, 355, 359

model for 9, 71, 72, 103, 105, 254, 260

Phase I behavior 129, 130, 131, 132, 133, 134, 135, 136, 137, 138, 140, 141, 142, 143, 148, 153, 154, 157, 164, 165, 167, 175, 253, 347, 350, 351, 352, 353, 355, 358

Phase II behavior 129, 130, 137, 138, 140, 141, 142, 143, 144, 153, 155, 175, 176, 351, 352, 353, 360

Phase III behavior 129, 143, 144, 146, 147, 148, 153, 155,

363

156, 157, 164, 165, 166, 167,
175, 176, 177, 191, 255, 267,
352, 353, 354, 355

belief
  in greatness 177, 181, 182, 191,
    192, 193, 194, 197, 201, 357
  in the big lie 360
belief 76, 127, 128, 137, 177, 192,
  346
bell curve 47, 242
Bell Laboratories 208
big bang theory 207, 208, 209
black belts 265, 267, 268, 282,
  285, 286
bottom-up transformation 84, 85,
  95
Boulton, Matthew 11, 12
brainstorming 267
bubonic plague 78

C

capability studies 258, 281, 284,
  304
centering the process 67
champions 208, 268, 284, 285
character 17, 67, 134, 146, 147,
  148, 155, 156, 157, 158, 164,
  182, 192, 197, 253, 311, 327,
  352, 353, 357
Charlemagne 40
Chicken Soup for the Soul 143
Churchill, Winston 201
coal mines 116, 118, 119
colliers 116, 117, 118, 119, 120,
  121
conditional probabilities 297
confidence intervals 226
constancy of purpose 91, 92, 93,
  104, 349
contingency plans 333, 339

continuous process-improvement
  19, 32, 97, 102, 105, 106,
  127, 252, 255, 283, 306, 307,
  331, 341, 342
and using different
  methodologies 249
model for 9, 71, 72, 103, 105,
  254, 260
projects 31, 32, 65, 110, 111,
  112, 124, 256, 257, 258, 259,
  260, 263, 267, 268, 272, 277,
  280, 285, 311, 324, 326, 327
transformation and x, 35, 38, 75,
  79, 95, 202, 210, 345, 346,
  347, 355
control mechanisms 283, 308, 332,
  340, 342, 343
auditing ix, 248, 283, 284, 332,
  338
balanced score cards 336, 337
contingency plans 333, 339
control plans 332, 339
corrective action process 341,
  342
described 68, 80, 88, 159, 278,
  280
root-cause analysis and 71, 282,
  284, 331, 341
training ix, 35, 97, 98, 104, 200,
  202, 259, 260, 264, 267, 285,
  286, 330, 332, 334, 335, 349
cosmic radiation 207, 208, 209
cosmology 76, 77, 78, 79, 207
cost model for quality 71, 72
cotton gin 18
courage 120, 134, 137, 158, 159,
  161, 162, 166, 179, 187, 188,
  191, 351
Cpk 67, 281, 300, 304
critical sigma 248
criticism 165, 350, 351, 353

cross-functional teams 313, 330
cultural transformation x, xi, 35,
74, 75, 76, 79, 81, 83, 87, 89,
115, 126, 127, 202, 206, 347,
348, 349
bottom-up transformation 84,
85, 95
Deming and 80, 88
difficulty of 110
Galileo and 39, 75, 76, 77
leadership and 347
Newton and 38, 39, 77, 78, 79,
122, 123, 189
revolutions 84, 85
tools and 31, 33, 79, 206, 249
top-down transformation 84, 85,
95
customer wants 246

D

Dark Ages x, 39, 40, 115, 177, 201,
209, 346
Darwin, Charles 15
data 36, 37, 43, 61, 63, 66, 98, 99,
203, 206, 207, 208, 219, 255,
257, 258, 267, 281, 282, 284,
289, 306, 321, 348
da Vinci, Leonardo 40
defects 100, 248, 308, 328
demand 18, 33, 93, 105, 116, 121,
134, 191, 224, 226, 227, 228,
231, 232, 233, 234, 236, 237,
241, 250, 251, 252, 253, 255,
265, 357
Deming, W. Edwards 79, 80, 88,
89, 90
about 1, 6, 7, 8, 9, 10, 11, 15, 19,
30, 33, 34, 35, 36, 37, 40, 41,
42, 43, 45, 46, 57, 63, 66, 70,
72, 73, 78, 81, 82, 83, 86, 89,
90, 91, 94, 97, 98, 99, 103,

108, 109, 110, 111, 113, 114,
115, 116, 117, 118, 119, 120,
121, 123, 127, 129, 138, 139,
143, 145, 146, 147, 148, 149,
150, 151, 153, 155, 162, 163,
165, 167, 176, 179, 181, 182,
183, 186, 187, 188, 189, 190,
191, 193, 195, 196, 197, 198,
199, 200, 203, 204, 206, 209,
213, 226, 227, 233, 239, 246,
247, 250, 251, 256, 258, 259,
261, 262, 267, 269, 280, 305,
316, 320, 326, 329, 330, 337,
344, 346, 351
and human nature 19, 25, 33, 41,
42, 129, 131, 136, 137, 142,
143, 200, 350, 351, 354, 355,
358, 359, 360
audits and 283, 285
comparing business cultures 82,
91, 349
cultural transformation and x,
75, 79
functional culture and x, 88, 99,
127, 349, 350
on transformation ix, x, xi, 1, 9,
10, 11, 19, 20, 21, 22, 24, 27,
30, 31, 32, 34, 35, 38, 39, 42,
49, 50, 56, 70, 74, 75, 76, 79,
80, 81, 82, 83, 84, 85, 86, 87,
89, 90, 91, 92, 94, 95, 97, 98,
99, 104, 108, 109, 110, 111,
112, 113, 114, 115, 122, 123,
124, 125, 126, 127, 128, 129,
132, 153, 165, 177, 178, 181,
197, 202, 203, 205, 206, 210,
219, 248, 253, 256, 345, 346,
347, 348, 349, 354, 355
red bead experiment 101, 102
Seven Deadly Diseases of
Management 104

See also Fourteen Points

dependent probabilities 2, 19, 35, 44, 56, 58, 72, 88, 107, 214, 221, 258, 281, 282, 284, 288, 289, 290, 292, 293, 295, 296, 297, 303, 304, 348

designing to standards 63

desire 41, 68, 72, 73, 85, 86, 92, 110, 112, 115, 117, 118, 124, 125, 132, 137, 141, 146, 148, 166, 167, 177, 178, 180, 181, 182, 191, 192, 193, 200, 224, 247, 286, 332, 352, 353, 356, 357, 358

Dickie, Bob 208

directional horn antenna 208

distance calculation 50

DMAIC model
  management support of 260, 270, 275, 284

DMAIC model 254, 255, 256, 257, 258, 280, 281, 282, 283, 284, 285
  analyze step 281, 282, 284
  auditing and ix, 248, 283, 332, 338
  baseline analysis 282, 284
  black belts 265, 267, 268, 282, 285, 286
  brainstorming 267
  champions 208, 268, 284, 285
  data collection 36, 267, 284
  gauge R & R studies 281
  green belts 264, 280, 281, 282, 283, 284, 285, 286
  improve stage 282, 283
  master black belts 285, 286
  mission statement for 275
  principal stakeholders 261, 269
  problem statement for 276, 278
  project scope 261, 277, 281, 309, 311
  project sponsor 261, 264, 268
  root-cause analysis 71, 282, 284, 331, 341
  sponsoring organization 261, 263
  team members 31, 267, 268, 313, 330
  uncertainty studies 281
  value stream charting 267
  yellow belts 267, 280, 281, 283, 284, 286

dysfunctionality 41, 205

E

education 40, 86, 98, 104, 112, 115, 116, 122, 124, 138, 182, 189, 337, 347

Einstein, Albert 209, 255

entropy 178

F

facilitators 111, 112, 319

failure, fear of 193

fear 17, 86, 98, 99, 103, 104, 112, 122, 135, 136, 154, 160, 161, 164, 166, 180, 191, 193, 206, 221, 347, 348, 349, 350, 351, 352, 360

Fife, Scotland 116

fire analogy 115

five solutions 59, 64, 71, 95
  centering the process 67
  change spec limits 7, 57, 58, 61, 62, 63, 64, 70, 71, 73, 300
  change the standard 59
  product inspections 88
  reduce variability 64, 65, 66, 71, 73, 74, 80, 82, 88, 91, 243, 244, 248, 249, 250, 252

five whys 341
flow charting 70
flow charts 70
Floyd (WW II veteran) 185, 186, 187
FMEA 314, 316, 318, 319, 320, 321, 322, 324, 325, 326, 327, 328, 329, 330, 331, 333
  described 68, 80, 88, 159, 278, 280
  detection criteria 322
  documentation and 271
  occurrence criteria 321
  preventing defects vs. improving detection 328
  process definition 330
  process vs. design 19, 26, 27, 32, 45, 58, 60, 61, 62, 63, 64, 65, 66, 67, 70, 72, 74, 88, 97, 99, 102, 105, 106, 110, 127, 204, 223, 226, 242, 244, 246, 247, 248, 249, 250, 252, 255, 256, 257, 260, 264, 267, 268, 279, 283, 284, 285, 286, 287, 298, 300, 302, 303, 304, 306, 307, 308, 309, 312, 313, 314, 315, 316, 317, 318, 320, 321, 324, 325, 326, 327, 328, 330, 331, 332, 333, 335, 339, 340, 341, 342, 343, 344, 346
  recommended actions 325, 326, 327
  RPNs 324, 325, 326, 327, 328, 332, 333, 343
  severity criteria 318
  target dates and 327
focus on the important 194
Ford, Henry 191
Ford Motor Company 79, 91
forecasts 233
form, storm, norm, perform model 267
Fourteen Points 79, 82, 88, 91, 92, 94, 99, 104, 105, 107, 126, 349
  constancy of purpose 91, 92, 93, 104, 349
  continuous process improvement 19, 32, 97, 102, 105, 106, 127, 252, 255, 283, 306, 307, 331, 341, 342
  leadership x, 35, 39, 83, 84, 85, 86, 92, 93, 94, 95, 98, 102, 104, 112, 125, 127, 128, 129, 132, 136, 144, 153, 154, 155, 176, 177, 180, 208, 270, 338, 347, 348
  loyalty and trust 96, 97
  merit ratings 103
  quality vs. inspection 68, 73, 88, 93, 95, 103, 155, 329, 332, 333
  quotas 102
  removing fear 349
  slogans and banners 100, 101
  training ix, 35, 97, 98, 104, 200, 202, 259, 260, 264, 267, 285, 286, 330, 332, 334, 335, 349
Franklin, Benjamin 14
freedom 121, 166, 178, 179, 180, 181, 185, 187, 188, 313
functional culture x, 88, 99, 127, 349, 350

G

Galileo 39, 75, 76, 77
Garvin, Walter 355
gauge R & R studies 281
Gaussian curve 47
General Electric 147
General Motors 71
Gourley, Gregson 188, 189

grandfather 158, 159
greatness, rules of 177, 182, 191,
    192, 193, 194, 197
green belts 264, 280, 281, 282,
    283, 284, 285, 286
gun industry 16, 17

H

heliocentric cosmology 76, 77, 78,
    79
hitting the wall 22, 109, 346
horn antenna 208
Hoyle, Fred 207, 208, 209
human nature. *See* behavior, human
Humanism 40

I

"I am great" cloud 346, 347, 354,
    360
Industrial Revolution 10, 11, 12,
    14, 80
influence x, 134, 135, 136, 140,
    154, 157, 164, 177
interchangeable parts 16, 17, 18,
    19
inventory 224, 228, 229, 231, 233,
    234, 236, 237, 240, 241, 242,
    243, 244, 246, 247, 248, 249,
    250, 251, 252, 253

J

Jabil Circuit 355
Jack: Straight from the Gut (Welch)
    147, 164
Japan 66, 67, 73, 81, 82, 89, 90,
    91, 92, 93, 96, 97, 99, 103,
    349
Jazz tickets 145
Jefferson, Thomas 14, 16, 17
Just in Time (JIT) 252

K

kaizen blitz 272
Keller, Helen 191, 192
King, Martin Luther, Jr. 128

L

leadership
    and ability to change culture x,
        83, 94, 98, 132, 153
leadership x, 35, 39, 83, 84, 85, 86,
    92, 93, 94, 95, 98, 102, 104,
    112, 125, 127, 128, 129, 132,
    136, 144, 153, 154, 155, 176,
    177, 180, 208, 270, 338, 347,
    348
    and Phase III behavior 155
    and successful transformation 9,
        30, 31, 35, 42, 74, 83, 97, 98,
        110, 112, 114, 129, 347
    and war 17, 18, 39, 41, 88, 89,
        91, 179, 186
    Deming on 79, 80, 81, 82, 87,
        88, 89, 90, 91, 92, 93, 94, 95,
        96, 97, 98, 99, 100, 101, 102,
        103, 104, 105, 106, 107, 111,
        124, 125, 126, 129, 338, 344,
        349
Lean methodology 244
LeBlanc, Honoré 15, 16
Lee, Craig 187
Levitston, Margaret 116
Lincoln, Abraham 82, 83, 128
living hell 27, 32, 34, 97, 346
Lombardi, Vince 181
lower control limits (LCL) 51, 52,
    53, 55, 56
Lunar Society 11, 12, 14
Luther, Martin 128

M

Mach 3 airplane 6
management by objective 102
Mary (nursing home resident) 138,
    139, 140
mass production 19, 20, 33, 108
master black belts 285, 286
Mathis, Mike 355
measurement 203, 206, 208, 209,
    212, 281, 284
merit rating 103
mistake-proofing 80
motion 196, 245, 246, 247
motivation 72, 164
    and Phase II behavior 352, 360
    fear 17, 86, 98, 99, 103, 104,
        112, 122, 135, 136, 154, 160,
        161, 164, 166, 180, 191, 193,
        206, 221, 347, 348, 349, 350,
        351, 352, 360
    higher motives 112, 114, 154,
        347
    personal transformation and 202
    pure motives 144, 155
    standard motives 112, 347
    survival x, 34, 81, 85, 94, 112,
        115, 129, 141, 151, 350
Mrs. Ransom 199, 201
mutually exclusive events 291,
    294, 295, 296

N

The Nature of Automotive
    Dynamics (Smith) 199
The Nature of Dynamic Weight
    Transfer (Lee) iii, iv, v, 187,
    200
NBA Jazz tickets 145
negative lies vs. positive truths 359
Newton, Isaac 38, 39, 77, 78, 79,
    122, 123, 189
normal-cause variation 305
normal distribution 44, 47, 48, 49,
    51, 52, 55, 56, 57, 58, 64, 65,
    210, 211, 212, 223, 225, 227,
    228, 233, 251, 305, 306
Normandy 183, 184, 185, 187
North, Simeon 20

O

objectivity 35, 38, 39, 40, 41, 42,
    98, 99, 177, 178, 205, 206,
    209, 348, 349
organizational transformation. *See*
    transformation
organizations ix, x, xi, 7, 26, 34,
    35, 36, 38, 40, 41, 44, 62, 65,
    66, 67, 68, 69, 82, 85, 89, 91,
    99, 109, 110, 111, 112, 113,
    115, 122, 127, 131, 136, 141,
    143, 154, 165, 175, 176, 177,
    197, 202, 203, 204, 205, 206,
    209, 219, 230, 248, 249, 256,
    265, 267, 282, 284, 286, 317,
    328, 333, 335, 338, 341, 343,
    344, 345, 346, 347, 349, 354,
    360
    and unique level of character
        197
    Phase III 112, 129, 130, 143,
        144, 146, 147, 148, 153, 154,
        155, 156, 157, 164, 165, 166,
        167, 175, 176, 177, 191, 255,
        267, 338, 352, 353, 354, 355,
        358, 360
overprocessing 246, 247
overproduction 247, 248

P

passion 125, 177, 192

patience xi, 193, 194
people-constrained organizations
    69
people problems vs. system
    problems 26, 33, 34, 41, 80,
    81, 93, 102, 111, 122, 349,
    350
perfection 180, 181, 346, 359
personal transformation x, xi, 35,
    74, 87, 108, 109, 110, 112,
    113, 123, 124, 125, 126, 181,
    202, 347
  as emotional event 110, 114, 124
  fire analogy 115
  motivation and 72, 164

personify, blame, and punish (PBP)
  people-constrained organizations
    and 69
personify, blame, and punish (PBP)
    19, 20, 21, 23, 24, 25, 26, 33,
    34, 41, 56, 63, 69, 90, 98, 99,
    101, 104, 108, 109, 122, 135,
    136, 154, 157, 197, 203, 206,
    208, 346, 347, 348, 349, 350
  as problem-solving methodology
    20, 136, 197
  automotive industry and 333
  Deming and 80, 88
  fear motive and 348
  people-constrained organizations
    and 69
  Phase I behavior and 143, 347
  subjectivity and 35, 41
  system problems and 26, 93,
    102, 111
Phase I behavior 129, 130, 131,
    132, 133, 134, 135, 136, 137,
    138, 140, 141, 142, 143, 148,
    153, 154, 157, 164, 165, 167,
    175, 253, 347, 350, 351, 352,

353, 355, 358
Phase II behavior 129, 130, 137,
    138, 140, 141, 142, 143, 144,
    153, 155, 175, 176, 351, 352,
    353, 360
Phase III behavior 129, 143, 144,
    146, 147, 148, 153, 155, 156,
    157, 164, 165, 166, 167, 175,
    176, 177, 191, 255, 267, 352,
    353, 354, 355
  See also greatness, rules of
Phase III organizations 175, 338
pioneer trek 189, 190
pity 191, 192
Plan-Do-Study-Act (PDSA) model
    105
poka-yoke system 80
popularity 147, 148, 191, 352, 355
pottery industry 14
power 12, 38, 40, 41, 86, 100, 110,
    111, 113, 117, 131, 140, 153,
    165, 166, 205, 209, 210, 347,
    348, 351, 352
principal stakeholders 261, 269
probability statistics 1, 2, 287, 288,
    290, 291, 296, 299, 300, 304
  "and" statements 3, 4, 5, 6, 7, 8,
    10, 11, 12, 21, 23, 24, 35, 44,
    57, 58, 59, 60, 65, 70, 71, 73,
    80, 81, 89, 90, 95, 108, 206,
    213, 223, 246, 290, 304, 345,
    348
  conditional probabilities 297
  described 68, 80, 88, 159, 278,
    280
  independence and 2, 289, 297,
    313
  mutually exclusive events 291,
    294, 295, 296
  "or" statements 2, 297
  scrap rates 217, 287, 300

See also "and" statement
   probabilities; statistics
problem solving 35, 36, 37, 41, 42,
   44, 66, 98, 203, 204, 205,
   206, 209, 254, 255, 256, 348
   brainstorming 267
   objectivity vs. subjectivity 35
   systematic 88, 203, 254, 255,
   256, 257
   value stream charting 267
   See also DMAIC model
process control 88, 105, 308
process improvement. *See*
   continuous process-
   improvement
process visualization 308, 312,
   331, 342
product inspections 88
production lead time 234, 235,
   236, 238, 239, 240, 241, 244,
   250
project charter. *See* DMAIC model
project scope 261, 277, 281, 309,
   311
Pyzdek, Thomas 260

Q

quality, cost model for 71, 72
quotas 102

R

random variability 102, 223
range of variability 63
red bead experiment 101, 102
reducing variability 64, 72, 73, 81,
   82, 89, 96, 221, 223, 243
relative work 194, 195
Renaissance 39, 40, 115, 345
revolutions 84, 85
risk mitigation 308, 314, 326, 329,
   331, 342
   See also FMEA
Rocky 146, 147, 194
Roman Empire 39, 40, 115
Roosevelt, Eleanor 193
root-cause analysis 71, 282, 284,
   331, 341
rules 30, 34, 35, 40, 43, 70, 71, 83,
   84, 136, 177, 182, 191, 192,
   193, 194, 197, 330, 358
   of greatness 177, 182, 191, 192,
   193, 194, 197, 201
   of influence 134, 177
   of transformation xi, 9, 27, 34,
   35, 39, 70, 83, 84, 85, 91,
   92, 94, 95, 97, 110, 112, 113,
   122, 132, 153, 165, 177, 202,
   203, 205, 206, 219, 345, 347,
   348, 354

S

sacrifice 144, 146, 147, 148, 155,
   156, 157, 158, 178, 179, 181,
   191, 192, 253, 352, 353, 355,
   357, 360
sampling error 219, 220, 221, 222,
   223
scope creep 309
Scottish coal mines 116, 118, 119
scrap rates 217, 287, 300
self-pity 191, 192
service industry 70, 71
Seven Deadly Diseases of
   Management 104
Shewhart, Walter 88, 105
Shingo, Shigeo 80
short-term profits 92, 93, 104, 112,
   113, 191
sigmas 54, 57, 58, 64, 213, 214,
   215, 216, 217, 218, 228, 229,
   230, 231, 237, 239, 242, 300

six sigma ix, 8, 49, 56, 57, 58, 59,
61, 62, 63, 64, 65, 66, 95,
197, 200, 213, 249, 254, 256,
257, 260, 263, 265, 266, 267,
270, 271, 272, 273, 274, 275,
281, 283, 284, 285, 286, 344,
346, 355
Six Sigma methodology 254
DMAIC model 254, 255, 256,
257, 258, 280, 281, 282, 283,
284, 285
Jabil Circuit 355
reducing variability 64, 72, 73,
81, 82, 89, 96, 221, 223, 243
with other methodologies 286
Six Sigma project charter. *See*
DMAIC model
skydiving 160, 166, 195
slogans 100, 101
Smith, Steve 199
Society of Automotive Engineers
317, 318
Solution #1 60, 63, 64, 66
Solution #2 61, 62, 63, 64, 65, 66,
67
Solution #3 63, 64, 65, 66, 67, 70,
71, 72, 73, 81, 82, 88, 89,
90, 91, 93, 96, 105, 111, 155,
233, 242, 244, 307, 328, 350
Solution #4 67, 68
Solution #5 68, 69, 70, 73, 88, 89,
95, 96, 328, 350
special-cause variability 306, 307,
320, 332, 342, 344
specialized labor 14
Special Olympics 143
specification limits 7, 57, 58, 61,
62, 63, 64, 70, 71, 73, 300
sphere of contentment 357, 358

SR71 Blackbird 6

stakeholders 74, 111, 255, 256,
261, 269, 283, 285, 329
standard deviation 48, 49, 51, 52,
53, 55, 56, 211, 212, 214,
224, 226, 228, 235, 237, 238,
248, 253
standard risk 229, 230, 236, 237,
241, 252, 253
statistical process control (SPC)
88, 105, 332
statistics 1, 2, 35, 42, 44, 47, 48,
49, 50, 56, 57, 91, 211, 214,
216, 219, 223, 228, 265, 268,
281, 282, 285, 287, 288, 290,
291, 296, 299, 300, 301, 304,
330
and tools transformation xi, 35,
74, 87, 126, 347
averages 250, 276
distance calculation 50
lower control limits (LCL) 51,
52, 53, 55, 56
normal distribution 44, 47, 48,
49, 51, 52, 55, 56, 57, 58, 64,
65, 210, 211, 212, 223, 225,
227, 228, 233, 251, 305, 306
sampling error 219, 220, 221,
222, 223
sigmas 54, 57, 58, 64, 213, 214,
215, 216, 217, 218, 228, 229,
230, 231, 237, 239, 242, 300
standard deviation 48, 49, 51,
52, 53, 55, 56, 211, 212, 214,
224, 226, 228, 235, 237, 238,
248, 253
subjective element of 42
symmetrical curve 55
upper control limits (UCL) 51
Z statistics 300, 301
Z table 57, 58, 216, 217, 218,
229, 230, 301

See also probability statistics
steady state theory 207, 209
steam engine 12, 13
Stokes, Henry 78
stress 41, 157, 158, 253
subjectivity 35, 38, 39, 40, 41, 42,
    44, 203, 205, 206, 207, 209,
    222, 348
support functions 70, 71
Survival Stories 129
swim lanes 330
symmetrical curve 55
system-constrained organizations
    69
system problems vs. people
    problems 26, 33, 34, 41, 80,
    81, 93, 102, 111, 122, 349,
    350

T

Taguchi Loss Function 72
Taguchi philosophies 66
target value 66, 70, 72, 73
teams, cross-functional 313, 330
Terry, Eli 20
Theory of Constraints (TOC) ix,
    248, 249, 286, 344
time, specification limits on 70, 71
Tommy (Phase III example) 148,
    149, 150, 151, 152, 153
tools x, xi, 20, 24, 29, 30, 31, 33,
    35, 42, 44, 65, 66, 70, 74, 77,
    79, 80, 81, 82, 87, 88, 91, 99,
    100, 103, 107, 111, 126, 202,
    203, 206, 219, 224, 246, 249,
    267, 314, 320, 321, 332, 333,
    338, 344, 347, 348, 349, 355
    supported by culture 77
tools transformation x, xi, 35, 74,
    80, 87, 126, 202, 203, 206,
    219, 347

top-down transformation 84, 85, 95
Toyota Motor Company 93, 97
Traditional Loss Function 72
traditional problem 58, 59, 61, 64,
    65, 66, 67, 68, 88, 95
    See also five solutions
transformation iii, iv, ix, x, xi, 1, 9,
    10, 11, 19, 20, 21, 22, 24, 27,
    30, 31, 32, 34, 35, 38, 39, 42,
    49, 50, 56, 70, 74, 75, 76, 79,
    80, 81, 82, 83, 84, 85, 86, 87,
    89, 90, 91, 92, 94, 95, 97, 98,
    99, 104, 108, 109, 110, 111,
    112, 113, 114, 115, 122, 123,
    124, 125, 126, 127, 128, 129,
    132, 153, 165, 177, 178, 181,
    197, 202, 203, 205, 206, 210,
    219, 248, 253, 256, 345, 346,
    347, 348, 349, 354, 355
    hitting the wall 22, 109, 346
    leadership and 347
    living hell 27, 32, 34, 97, 346
    model for 9, 71, 72, 103, 105,
    254, 260
    necessity of xi, 11, 353
    rules of 34, 35, 70, 83, 84, 177,
    182, 191, 192, 193, 194, 197
    subtransformations x, 35, 74, 87,
    107, 126, 347
    system problems vs. people
    problems 26, 33, 34, 41, 80,
    81, 93, 102, 111, 122, 349,
    350
    work becomes fun again 31
transistors 60
transportation 245, 246, 247
trek, pioneer 189, 190
tyranny 178, 180, 181, 185, 188,
    204, 205

U

uncertainty 226, 228, 231, 233,
234, 235, 236, 237, 239, 240,
241, 242, 243, 244, 245, 246,
247, 248, 250, 252, 253, 281
uncertainty studies 281
upper control limits (UCL) 51
US Synthetic 176
utopias 176

V

vacuum tubes 60
value stream charting 267
variability 63, 64, 65, 66, 71, 72,
73, 74, 80, 81, 82, 88, 89, 91,
95, 96, 102, 221, 223, 234,
235, 241, 242, 243, 244, 246,
247, 248, 249, 250, 251, 252,
301, 306, 307, 320, 332, 342,
344
  range of 63, 227, 239
  reducing 64, 72, 73, 81, 82, 86,
89, 96, 221, 222, 223, 228,
243, 246, 247, 248, 252, 253,
307, 328

W

waiting time 247, 248
war 17, 18, 39, 41, 82, 88, 89, 91,
179, 182, 185, 186, 187, 201
Washington, George 16, 17, 181
waste 41, 244, 246, 247, 248, 250,
253, 326, 330
Watt, James 12
weaknesses 164, 165, 166, 167,
353, 354
wealth 42, 47, 48, 73, 89, 113, 115,
121, 123, 146, 203, 247, 347
Wedgwood, Josiah 13, 14, 15
Wedgwood pottery 14, 15

Welch, Jack 147, 164
Whitney, Eli 17, 18, 19, 20, 26, 33,
108
widgets 113, 114, 121, 122, 124,
125, 253, 347
Wilkinson, David 208
Wilson, Robert Woodrow 208
The Wizard of Oz 159
work in process 247
Workmen's Compensation Fund of
Utah (WCF) 114
work standards 102
World War II 88, 91, 182, 185,
186, 187, 201
Wright Brothers 6

Y

yellow belts 267, 280, 281, 283,
284, 286

Z

Z statistics 300, 301
Z table 57, 58, 216, 217, 218, 229,
230, 301